SECOND SKIN

Second Skin

Inside the Worlds of Fetish,
Kink and Deviant Desire

Anastasiia Fedorova

GRANTA

Granta Publications, 12 Addison Avenue, London W11 4QR
First published in Great Britain by Granta Books, 2025

Copyright © Anastasiia Fedorova, 2025

Anastasiia Fedorova has asserted her moral right under the Copyright,
Designs and Patents Act, 1988, to be identified as the author of this work.

The copyright to the images in the plate section belongs to the artists
named in the captions. All images reproduced by kind permission.

All rights reserved. This book is copyright material and must not be copied,
reproduced, transferred, distributed, leased, licensed or publicly performed or
used in any way except as specifically permitted in writing by the publisher,
as allowed under the terms and conditions under which it was purchased or as
strictly permitted by applicable copyright law. Any unauthorised distribution
or use of this text may be a direct infringement of the author's and publisher's
rights, and those responsible may be liable in law accordingly.

A CIP catalogue record for this book is available from the British Library.

1 3 5 7 9 10 8 6 4 2

ISBN 978 1 80351 190 0 (hardback)
ISBN 978 1 80351 191 7 (ebook)

Typeset in Bembo by Iram Allam
Printed and bound by CPI Group (UK) Ltd, Croydon CR0 4YY

The manufacturer's authorised representative in the
EU for product safety is Authorised Rep Compliance Ltd,
71 Lower Baggot Street, Dublin D02 P593, Ireland.
www.arccompliance.com

www.granta.com

For Tim

CONTENTS

Introduction	1
Leather	21
Latex	49
The Dominatrix	70
The Gimp	92
The Chaser	110
Feet	123
Medical Gloves	143
Cars	155
Monsters	174
The Fetish Club	190
Epilogue	213
Acknowledgements	222
Notes	224
Further Reading	229

INTRODUCTION

It's a Saturday afternoon. I'm in a hotel room on the ninth floor, with pearl-grey carpet and curtains and pristine white sheets. Everything is soft and still. I stand in front of a round bathroom mirror enclosed in a ring light. Black latex gleams like an oil spill, or a freshly polished sports car. Before I zip myself into the catsuit, the material moves like wet flower petals, clinging to my skin. It is animated with its own life-like movement, as if the latex is breathing. I begin to pull the zip up – it runs up from my crotch, over my stomach, between my breasts. Underneath the layer of rubber, my skin is warm, porous and imperfect, my sweat slowly mixing with silicone dressing aid. The zip ends in the middle of the throat, and I glance at my reflection, my eyes gleaming with tiny bright light rings. The catsuit holds and elevates me.

A fetish garment is something which transforms how you view and inhabit your body. The moment you put it on, it creates a new, unknown erotic entity. In the mirror, I recognise my facial features, but I am not my usual self – I have stepped into uncharted territory, where I can temporarily embody something different. Rubber accentuates my curves, and yet I feel free of any gender. I am present yet expansive. This altered state is rooted in physical sensation: every inch of my encased skin is in contact with latex, and the sensory stimulation fuses into a slow and ambient, continuous high.

There are two of us in the room, and we're both in full latex. It is a date: we met in August, and now it's October. By the large hotel bed, my play partner waits on his knees, hands cuffed behind his back. The room smells of rubber now – a specific rich scent which is so hard to describe, evoking petrol and rainfall, earthy and chemical at once.

My fingers, gloved in latex, slide past his lips – an invasive touch, cold, not sensual, pushing against barriers and membranes. In rubber, there is no contact between the interior of his mouth and the organic surface of my body, apart from a faint feeling of warmth. Second by second, we enact a fantasy: him on a leash, me standing above him, wielding the control he's entrusted me with. Like most sexual scenarios, it has been lived out countless times before us. We slip it on like a second skin.

What brought us here? Desire, perversion, disposable income, love? Chasing an erotic high? We have, above all, an insatiable drive to know one another. Naked is not naked enough. Naked is too plain, too easy, too mundane. Instead, we choreograph our sexual encounter around latex skins: tailored, shiny rubberised cases bought from the same London manufacturer. Touch becomes another mode of yearning; an expression of desire which is more like a question than an answer. Two layers of latex stop our bodily fluids from mixing, yet the mental distance between us compresses until it dissolves into nothing.

We fuck in the intersection of sexuality, consumption, pop culture and senseless lust. I ask myself whether I would ever want to have sex naked again. I'd never thought that a wearable object thrown into the already heady mix of intimacy could take me places this high, this addictive.

Time drips slowly on the carpeted floor. The glimpse of the skyline becomes brighter, a slash of pink in the fading light of evening. Later, we peel the rubber off in the shower. Warm water gradually begins to stream inside the layers. The catsuits are piled in the corner of the bathroom – a crumpled, gleaming heap on light blue tiles. There is both relief and a slight sadness. This is the emotional drop – the shedding of skin – the return to human form.

Fetishes are a dirty secret. They exist simultaneously under public scrutiny and in the shadows, both hyper-visible and underground: they play out in clubs rammed with hundreds of bodies, on live streams for tens of thousands of subscribers, and in the pages of *Vogue*, yet there remains a sense of fetishes existing 'behind closed doors'. Normally, fetish is only allowed to exist as a self-referential system, locked away in the sex dungeon, never spilling out into other parts of your life – however complex, ecstatic and culturally rich this spillage could be.

I call myself a fetishist – sometimes. For me, fetish is a slippery darkness which has always resisted language. It stretches tight over my own skin and quietly accumulates heat, or wordlessly grows deep within me, or gazes back from a vintage porno magazine. In my shiny black latex catsuit and eight-inch heels, I tower tall like a creature on the poster of a fetish club night, or an exaggerated Eric Stanton drawing of a lady with a whip. I've recreated myself as a fetish item in traditional form, belonging in the underworld of gimps, human hounds in spiked collars, and other sexual deviants. I could escape into the familiar iconography of this terrain. But for the last three years, I have been out and open about kink. I'm trying to strip back these well-known shortcuts and gimmicks – trying to understand fetish, and what my sexual difference means in society today.

For there is more to fetish than just its countercultural visual signifiers. Fetish has cultural and emotional complexity, and at times even community-driven purpose. Moreover, the conversation around fetish always expands beyond its boundaries. It spills over into all the ways we relate to queerness and gender, our diversity of sexual expression, and the meanings of the obscene and the erotic in culture. Politically, governments still determine where sexual freedom starts and ends: as of 2024, sixty-four countries criminalise homosexuality; in the US, the overturn of *Roe* v. *Wade* ended the constitutional right to abortion; in Italy, lesbian mothers' names started disappearing from children's birth certificates in 2023. Our bodies and our sex are seemingly a private matter, and yet there also exists a ubiquitous network of control, from the policing of gender markers in our documents to restrictions around access to PrEP for HIV prevention and contraceptive pills. Fetishism is perceived as deviant and transgressive; it pushes against the limits of the appropriate. Fetishism redefines our relationships with inanimate objects and all the things we inadvertently objectify. It allows us to play with our identities in ways which go beyond the state-sanctioned imagination.

It is common to think of deviation, perversion and fetishism as something distinctly male, yet I have found that these categories are often used as a method of resistance by those who have been historically othered and repressed by the patriarchal vision of desire – women, LGBTQI+ folk, Black people, people of colour, and those subverting traditional notions of family and monogamy. When it comes to sexual conformity, it takes immense courage to step out of line. Yet nonconformity often makes people uncomfortable, at best. Have we amassed enough courage to look at these allegedly deviant desires directly? And what might we gain by expressing them openly and unapologetically?

When I talk about fetishism, I'm referring to a sexual practice which revolves around objects, commodities and concrete signifiers. To have a fetish means being drawn to a particular object for sexual pleasure or excitement – and to be turned on by the possibilities and scenarios this object provides. Today, the term 'fetish' is often used interchangeably with 'kink' – the latter a colloquial shortcut for any non-normative sexual preference or practice. Kink is a broad term; it's commonly used to unite practices which relate to BDSM, but it is also expansive enough to incorporate other fringe desires like voyeurism or love of bodily fluids. BDSM, in turn, stands for a range of erotic practices involving bondage, discipline, dominance and submission, power exchange and sadomasochism. The kink community can also be an extension of various fetish-specific ones, like the leather or rubber community: both groups mix at kink-positive raves and on kink-positive dating apps. Fetishes, in a way, fit under the broader umbrella of kink.

But these categories and definitions are often highly individual. BDSM, kink and fetish fit together like circles on a Venn diagram – and they can intersect or exist separately. For one person, their BDSM sexual preferences and their fetishes are closely intertwined. For a different person, their fetish has absolutely nothing to do with power exchange. One can be a fetishist and not partake or identify with the kink or BDSM community – everyone's free to keep their fetishes private, if they would so prefer. The terms 'kink' and 'fetish' are handy, but they also highlight language's insufficiency when it comes to describing sexuality and the limitations of our understanding of sexual difference. As with identifying as 'queer' or as part of the LGBTQI+ community, these labels are collecting together a vast array of sexual experiences, preferences and practices. Still, there's a strength to be drawn from naming yourself a 'fetishist': it so often serves as a means of connecting yourself to a certain group, culture or community, an act which can be especially valuable when faced with public disdain.

BDSM, kink and fetish are often grouped together under the umbrella of 'alternative sexuality' – another potentially fraught category which implies a degree of otherness. When I spoke to author and playwright Jordan Tannahill in my research for this book, he suggested a different term, which I hadn't encountered before: extended sexuality. I love how far-reaching this term sounds, with a promise of uncharted horizons, of pleasures not yet known. It also enables a more inclusive view on sexuality: it's not that you replace your 'regular' sexuality with a 'deviant' one – you simply look further, experience more, reach towards sensations which enrich your being.

'Kink' and 'fetish' are porous terms, but they're also emblematic of our urge to categorise and define sexualities, especially if there's even a slight deviation from the 'normal'. Here, I use both terms as tools to create a more open dialogue and a more creative, collaborative understanding of sexuality – as well as to uproot the narrow cultural judgement of what type of sex is normal. 'Normal', after all, is a moveable feast. As per the viral response to a tweet from *Playboy* magazine circa 2017 which read: 'Millennials aren't as interested in breasts as older generations. Why?' – 'It's 2017, Grandpa, we eat ass now!'

We are all born into a world of objects. And while seemingly inert and static, these objects are governed by a strict set of societal norms. According to the laws of this world, we are supposed to desire objects, acquire objects, and sometimes become objectified. In many ways, sexual fetishes are one iteration of a broader cultural phenomenon relating to object-oriented desire: our commercial impulses and the symbolic value we give to commodities. Getting in touch with your sexuality is scary because it introduces chaos into this system. Yet sexuality can also be a gateway drug for creativity and a sense of agency: it allows you to see, and therefore play with, the powerful, slow-moving undercurrents of culture, society and self. What if you savour things you're not supposed to? What if you find a safe space to play? What if you choose the erotic as a way of seeing?

When I was little, in Russia, certain commodities – clothes, cars, homeware – had a special, almost spiritual aura. The first fashion item I remember is my mum's Versace trousers. They were a simple black pair with the infamous Medusa head embroidered in gold on the back pocket. I only later realised that they were blatant knock-offs – so much so that the Medusa embroidery only vaguely followed the original Versace design. I might have been six or seven, and I didn't know what branding was – but I could feel that everyone around me was deeply excited by *things*. In that sense, I was a typical post-Soviet child of the 1990s, growing up amid the traces of the now-defunct communist era and the turbocharged consumer culture which followed in its wake. My fascination with the special powers we assign to objects originates right there, in the palpable reverb of consumer desire.

At that time, people craved all kinds of products: Dolce & Gabbana bags, Nike tracksuits, Italian leather shoes and jackets, fur coats, big boxy TVs, German toasters and mixers, VHS players, Adidas trainers, opulent jewellery and cars. The future was uncertain, the economy volatile and money scarce. Yet the shimmer in people's eyes when they laid hands on these new symbols of happiness, beauty and power was undeniable. Everything was a novelty. In the Soviet Union, there had been no advertising, no commonly accessible luxuries, no status-signalling and, most importantly, almost no choice of what to purchase. Suddenly, there was an avalanche of shiny goods, and one could use them to craft a new identity for this new era.

My parents were conflicted by consumerism. They were raised with political ideals of collectivism, placing the common good above frivolous pleasures. It's not that they didn't like *things* intrinsically, they simply found themselves overwhelmed. They hadn't had much choice for most of their lives: when the time came to shop for bed sheets, clothes, homeware and even books, they had to queue up for hours just to get the single option available in store that day. Their only shopping experience was of arduous queueing with a number written in ballpoint pen on their hand for their place in line, or of walking past lush stores for foreigners and party elites knowing that the goods inside weren't for them.

In the 1980s, they witnessed the sudden growth of a smugglers' market: sailors would bring in jeans, sportswear and Western music via Japan – but they did not participate. In the 1990s, with two kids, they were horrified by empty shelves in grocery stores, and at times relied on humanitarian aid from Germany. They sat on the sidelines, still hamstrung by the hangover of the communist regime, watching wannabe entrepreneurs rising to the moment. My parents, in their mid-forties then, strove to instil the importance of non-monetary values like kindness, intelligence and generosity in me and my brother. But it was obvious that they were grappling with the volatility of capitalism, the rampant choice it produced, the ubiquitous price tags which now had to be put on everything, the desires it unleashed, and the terrifying possibility of actual possession and ownership.

The 1990s were a time of scarcity, but as the regulations for selling and buying goods relaxed, a lot of people got involved in the resale market. My dad even tried his hand selling bootleg shoes – the remains of his stock still occasionally resurface in my mother's attic in the form of fake Reebok trainers of dubious origins. Knockoffs from Turkey and China were especially coveted: fake BOSS sweaters, Dolce & Gabbana jeans, Adidas tracksuits. Branding was ornamental: not a mark of authenticity but a way of augmenting something, making it better. A symbol added some extra value, even if it was placed askew or looked a bit off. Objects could be switched on, activated – rendered more attractive – by dint of the label they had. I have hazy memories of going to the market, curiously located in a sports stadium: a clever use of the cavernous space under the rows of seating. It was like a large, looping corridor cluttered with stalls selling bootleg branded goods, sunglasses, VHS tapes, leather and fur coats. There was something special about experiencing consumerism for the first time in a crowd of people, squashed among families, smugglers and entrepreneurial youths, all barely aware of this shared historical shift. I think about it sometimes when online fashion retailers offer a one-click checkout – a tiny dopamine hit compared to an ecstatic avalanche of history, but still: *shopping*.

In its own way, my childhood provided me with an intense crash course in capitalism and its power to elevate quotidian consumer objects into fetishes. In the word's original meaning, a 'fetish' was an entity – a talisman, a figurine – said to be worshipped for its magical properties. Over centuries, the use of this word in the West contributed to building a colonial worldview – separating canonical religions from other spiritual practices. But the contemporary theory of fetishism has strayed far from these roots and now constitutes an intricate dance between Karl Marx, Sigmund Freud, Thorstein Veblen and Jean Baudrillard, among other notable minds of the last few centuries.

The idea of commodity fetishism was first introduced in *Das Capital*, published in 1867, in which Marx suggested that when goods are produced for exchange in the market, they quickly surpass their use-value and are displaced from the labour which produced them. As the product of human labour becomes a commodity, it acquires 'mystical' qualities beyond its material origin. Writing not long after Marx, American economist and sociologist Thorstein Veblen then linked fetishised commodities with the aspirations and prestige which the consumer seeks. In *The Theory of the Leisure*

Class, he suggests that the consumer establishes a social, economic and cultural identity through the goods and services which they buy, own and use. This is why we choose a particular restaurant, decorate our homes a certain way and develop certain hobbies – those behaviours allow us to send the correct signals of our social stance and to feel a sense of belonging.

This landscape in which objects and commodities become a kind of language has evolved considerably with the arrival of mass-media-driven advertising and marketing. French philosopher and sociologist Jean Baudrillard viewed consumerism as a cycle of desire and dissatisfaction, driven by the pursuit of symbolic value rather than genuine needs. Upending Marx's concept of commodity fetishism, he argued that in contemporary society, commodities have transitioned beyond their use-value and exchange-value to acquire a symbolic value. The commodity becomes a fetish not because of its inherent qualities but because of its position within a cultural network of signs. And as the distinction between the real and the simulated collapses, signs and simulations become more real than the actual objects they represent.

Let's return to those Versace trousers and the embroidered Medusa head for a second. The label completely transforms the item's perception and price. Following Veblen, a pair of Versace trousers becomes desirable as an object which is able to signal one's taste and situate the individual in rapidly changing society. However, the bootleg industry reveals this power to be purely symbolic, malleable, not bound to authenticity, as Baudrillard suggests. The trousers are fake, but they still operate as a symbol of fashion, opulence, taste and the desirable lifestyle attached to these ideals.

Gradually, everything becomes a symbol: a diamond ring stands for eternal love, sports cars signify vitality and masculinity, a dry Martini is shorthand for metropolitan sophistication. An object always means more to us than the sum of its parts. As consumption became a source of deep gratification in the twenty-first century, it made fetishists of us all.

My first encounters with fashion might have been bootlegs, but they've inspired an enduring interest in consumer culture. In my twenties, I spent a few years working as a fashion critic. The fashion industry perfectly represents the Baudrillardian symbol-driven economy. I saw people perpetually chasing the high of the next cool purchase, be that limited-edition Salomon trainers, a Prada bag or a Supreme hoodie. I saw the transformative power which fashion facilitated as people were able to remake themselves: to put on a new persona bound up in their carefully curated choice of clothing. There was desire of many different kinds in the air as I sat in the audience at a catwalk show, my fellow fashion appreciators critically assessing the designs – while also dreaming, maybe just a little bit, of being as irresistibly beautiful and immaculately styled as the models. Once again, objects were shortcuts to a dream self and a dream life. In the fashion world, desire is often linked to a lack ('I need that bag . . .'), a feeling of being 'less than' ('because it will make me better . . .'), an unattainable aspiration ('and then I can get a coat to match.'). This tension between affirming one's identity through consumerism and being held in thrall by market forces undergirds so much of our day-to-day lives. With the rise of digitally driven demand, the cycle only accelerates, yet we seldom stop to consider it.

In my early thirties, I walked into a fetish club in East London for the very first time. The dress code was non-negotiable: leather, latex, PVC, nylon, lingerie, corsets and chains. Within the limits of these materials, you were free to play. I saw a very tall person dressed as a towering latex doll in six-inch heels. I saw someone devotedly kissing a pair of boots in the corner. Obsessed with rubber, leather, high heels or sports socks, this bunch of fetishists, queers and self-described perverts were out and proud about their unusual sexual desires. Yet of all the people I'd met before, they seemed to have the most grounded critical perspective on the objects they were devoted to. It was as if they had the key to unpacking the objects' power, to decoding what seemed cryptic and impenetrable. Instead of feeling small and insignificant against the magic of things, with a fetishist's perspective the opposite seemed possible – exploration, empowerment, freedom.

I have a complex heritage when it comes to objects, and this shows up in how I engage with them as a fetishist: I am a devotee, a stunned admirer; I am sensitive to textures, materials, smells; I acknowledge their power over me; I worship, sometimes desperately. But as a fetishist, I do not feel inferior to them. An object might be meaningful for my erotic life, but it does not determine my whole existence, my aspirations and my personhood. Fetishists are by no means excluded from the trappings of capitalism, they're simply upfront about the power these objects and materials hold. The realm of the erotic offers a new means of understanding how this longing shapes our lives, and what our relationships with objects say about how we live, desire and acquire.

Freud, the daddy of psychoanalysis, came up with his theory of fetishism in the 1920s. As with commodity fetishism, the Freudian interpretation deals with a lack – although of an entirely different kind. When a little boy realises his mother doesn't have a penis, whatever is in direct sight – be it a high-heeled shoe or a pair of lace panties – becomes a mental shortcut for that missing penis forever. Overcome with castration anxiety, the boy is then locked into the cycle of seeking fetishistic gratification in his adulthood, unable to engage in normative sexual relationships. I once relayed this to a friend over coffee. We concluded that a lot of people, especially from the younger generations, are not in the least bit ashamed of their desires: they have no problem mourning the loss of their mommy with a big dick by finding another mommy with a big dick.

Today, fetish has been coloured by Freud's definition and more commonly refers to a form of sexual gratification strongly linked to a particular object. One usually imagines a well-groomed middle-aged gentleman with a penchant for high heels or silk stockings, so engrossed with the object in question that the person wearing it becomes merely a carrier. Fetishism, defined by Freud as an exclusively male practice, has been frequently used to further belittle women – they're an inconvenient add-on to the desired high-heeled shoe. Yet Freud's theory crashes hard against how our understanding of sexuality has shifted – women's active expressions of sexual desire, gender fluidity, transness, homosexuality were all pathologised in Freud's era and have been emancipated since. Yet understanding of fetishism hasn't evolved to incorporate these changes.

After all, Freud never searched for rubber pornography on Discord forums. He never smelt leather on a sexy dyke in a sweaty club. He never had, let alone was, a hot girlfriend with a big strap-on. 'RIP Sigmund Freud, you would have loved *MILF Manor*', as the meme goes. *MILF Manor*, the 2023 reality TV show in which single women between forty and sixty seek love with single men in their twenties, is just one example of how pornified language has permeated the mainstream, for better or worse.

While the theory of commodity fetishism evolved to better reflect our current reality, sexual fetishism is still most often judged according to the framework from the early twentieth century. Theorists are usually dead set on neatly separating the two, but in this book I regard them holistically. With commodity fetishism permeating all the spheres of our life, it is inevitable that it would bleed into sexual culture. As we increasingly define and express ourselves through objects – branded garments, watches, lipsticks, homeware – these items come to define our gender presentation, our ideas of desire and beauty, and even the way we feel in our bodies in different situations. And just as sexuality is impossible to separate from personal history, sexual and aspirational desires are closely intertwined.

At the same time, the language of fetish has entered the mainstream. Our sexualities today – particularly for Gen Y and Z – are shaped by online culture, where referring to your partner as a mommy, baby, kitten or femboy has become completely normalised. Our relationships are technologically mediated through smartphones and webcams. We sext and send nudes. We are voyeurs, archivists and porn stars rolled into one. For the first time in history, our knowledge of desire is not limited to our own experiences or to those of our close confidants. As we watch the fantasies of others unfold in real time, it's suddenly much easier to grasp the diversity of human sexuality out there, the multiplicity of pleasure and fulfilment.

In 2015, London-based artist and dominatrix Reba Maybury released a series of zines through her independent publishing project Wet Satin Press. They explored fetishes which were slightly more removed from what we perceive as sexy, opening out into an uncharted dimension of the erotic. The fetishes depicted were pure in their very specific nature: one participant had a fetish for women wearing office-appropriate heels submerged in water; another one enjoyed wearing nylon on their face at home; and the third one was mesmerised by the air bubbles trapped inside women's dresses while they were swimming.

'The reason we wanted to publish these in print was because their imagery is so outstandingly original,' Maybury explained. 'Their creation and existence verge on folk art, rather than the sort of commercially sensational pornography that we are now so numbed to. All gendered and sexual stereotypes disappear, and we're left with a utopian vision of harmless but fascinating eroticism.' Each publication combined an interview with the fetishist with photo documentation found online, comprising truly unique erotic archives.

Fetishism, in this way, allows us to expand the understanding of sex beyond its normative framework, beyond the confines of our bodies seeking momentary gratification. Pleasure becomes cultural, creative, mindful, strange, unforeseen – with a unique blueprint for every person.

In her iconic 1978 essay 'Uses of the Erotic', Audre Lorde surveyed the horizon of possibilities which opens when one deploys the erotic not just in relation to sexual acts and desires, but in life in general, as a way of existing more fully. An understanding of your own extended capacity for joy brings with it a terrifying demand: that you live your life in accordance with the joy which you know to be possible; that you ask for more; that you provoke, unsettle and reach towards personal and political power.

A bunch of people at an orgy might have read 'Uses of the Erotic' – or they might not have. There are different ways to get there, after all.

I started writing this book because, while the world of kink and fetish was becoming increasingly visible in mainstream culture, there was still a lack of deeper understanding. We also seem to be on the brink of a shift, as people become more open to a nuanced and complex understanding of sexuality. And while we hear more authentic and outspoken voices debating the erotic, the conservative pushback is also on the rise. Sex – and especially allegedly deviant, perverted sex – is at the crux of heated debates, and it feels crucial to delve deep into its true complexity, its history and lived experiences.

One could argue that I was in the right place at the right time to feel the tide turning – post-pandemic London blossomed with kink-positive raves and fetish events, full of people hungry for discovery and connection. But there was another, much more deep-rooted reason: I grew up in a relatively conservative environment. Sex existed in pop culture – it was visible but it was never talked about. I received no sex education; my parents never gave me 'the talk'. Sex was a glaring void, something I struggled to talk about for the longest time. Writing about something is an excuse to spend time with it, to find the words, to tinker with ideas, to immerse yourself in the complexity. It is like learning a new language – terrifying at first, until it becomes second nature.

The more I taught myself how to write openly, politically and directly about sex, the more I realised that I was trying to write myself into existence. I wanted to reflect on certain embodied experiences which make me 'me': a queer person who likes to play with gender, a leatherdyke, a rubber pervert. These experiences do not define me fully, but they are integral to a certain part of me which exists in defiance of the conservative idea of how I should have been. My sexuality is integral to my ability to be free, to speak, to breathe.

My fetish, this second skin of mine, is another layer of difference atop that of my queerness. It feels natural to proclaim it with the same hard-won pride. But there is always a tension between privacy and openness, between sincerity and oversharing. There is respectability and assimilationism – and there is the closet, and being pushed into its shadows. There is exhibitionism, and there is being pigeonholed. There is the choice to trust your desire, and there is, of course, the fact that this kind of thing is not for everyone.

Second Skin is an invitation to think about fetish beyond the iconography – to think of it as a mindset, and a lens through which we might view the world. However, whichever way you cut it, fetish remains an object-oriented mode of desire. With fetishism, it always starts with an object – the actual physical object and the sensations it brings, or the idea of an object as a mental fixture – which sparks desire and reshapes our understanding of sex. Each chapter of this book therefore looks to a different material, object or power dynamic, capturing its allure while also celebrating the communities it inadvertently creates. We'll look at leather, rubber, trainers, medical gloves and more, as well as attraction to body parts and items which conjure an idea of the non-human, and consider how these personal desires become something culturally impactful which reaches outside the fetish community. Throughout, my focus is on the way in which fetish can be a tool for transformation, expanding the boundaries of the self, as well as the way fetish transgresses the boundaries of the erotic, spilling into day-to-day life.

Second Skin is not a comprehensive fetish history, but rather an attempt to capture a personal process of discovery, one which spans continents and moves between fetish clubs, hotel rooms, libraries and art galleries, as well as the interior spaces of one's mind. It does not cover an exhaustive list of sexual fetishes, and I don't seek to answer every question and resolve every complexity raised in the book. Rather, I hope to start a conversation, to ignite curiosity and to bring these usually hushed topics into the open.

Second Skin celebrates multiple points of view and perspectives, and while I tie the threads together, mine is not the only voice held in this book. I spent time in the archives, studying the stories of those who came before. I have also interviewed other fetishists, artists, writers, professional dominatrixes, sex workers, fetish club promoters, archivists and activists – a fraction of the burgeoning, vibrant community which I am proud to call my own. Some of these contributors appear under their own names and others are anonymised, depending on their preference. I am deeply grateful to every person who contributed their thoughts, their openness and their courage to this book.

There is no fetish without those of us who choose to play, both now and in times when playing was dangerous, and in places where it still is today: the rubberists, the leatherfolk, the perverted, who have risked everything to create visibility for their tribe. And while the stigma has lessened in some places, many people on the fetish scene still keep secrets, hide their faces and use fake names to avoid being outed at work or to friends and family. Yet people still make the choice to step into this world — they choose sex as self-creation and community engagement, a vehicle for remaking their body and reimagining themselves alone and with others, a method of reaching the deepest intimacy and accessing the fiercest queer joy.

The process of writing this book took me to unexpected places — and I don't mean my local BDSM dungeon or an obscure forum for car fetishists which hasn't been updated since 2008. In fact, the more time I spent putting words to paper to describe sensations, pleasures and histories, the more I appreciated the parts of it which elude language. I grew to love the obscure, the unnameable, the parts of the experience which could only be felt, not spoken. It is the nature of sex that it cannot be fully verbalised — its most thrilling, delicious and vulnerable parts fade when pinned down by words. This pushed me to try to find a new language, to evade set ways to speak, to try to feel into the dark corners of the experience.

So much of this book lies beyond glossy fetish photographs, beyond dirty words, beyond archival records. Electricity rushes through the body, and for a second silences everything else, leaving only throbbing, dribbling, wordless serenity. In my catsuit, there is a feeling of being poured into a vessel with thick rubbery sides. A compact space of ecstasy hidden away from our hyperconnected world. It is a return, and a departure. There is no time and no language. There is what you felt, and what I felt, and then it's over, with no trace but memory – and yet it has altered the chemistry of our bodies and, by extension, the world.

Pleasure is key to traversing that space between language and sensation, between identity and change. We often associate this word especially strongly with the erotic or the sensual, but it takes hold on our lives in many ways beyond that. While our preferred sexual gratification and erotic inclinations have to be analysed, dissected and explained, our non-sexual pleasures, from a pair of shoes to a corner-shop chocolate bar, are often treated as simply natural. Behind every single thing which we enjoy is a story we tell ourselves, shaped by context and narrative. Our pleasures are our world-building, and being aware of how they work, even the most forbidden ones, is a powerful bid for a deeper understanding of oneself.

I press my fingers into your white shirt. It's smooth to the touch, soft; but in the way the fabric moves there is something rigid, angular. In its folds, I can feel residual warmth from your body, which the shirt conceals, allowing you to blend in in the office. For eight hours of the workday, this shirt is in closest proximity to your skin. It makes you look respectable, formal. It breathes, sweats, moves with you. It's another surface of the cityscape: like office desks, like glass, like concrete and car parks, like the metal and rubber of the tube escalator, like the rare pockets of darkness down side streets.

The pressed cotton is ordinary, and yet it's meant to express a certain kind of power. I could sense it when walking through the City of London in my early twenties. I observed men in perfectly fitted suits: how their bodies moved differently – so confident, so calculated yet relaxed. I felt poor, out of place – scruffy in comparison. But I also felt a deep pull in the pit of my stomach towards their perfect outfits, towards respectability and power, the institutional, the masculine. I secretly fantasised about seeing their shirts crumpled, putting them on their knees, making them beg for it. It came out of nowhere. A yearning for sex as power.

Only fifteen minutes from the corporate offices of major banks, there is a dungeon unknown to most passers-by, tucked under a nondescript arch. It has all the usual furniture: a cage upholstered in leather, a couple of spanking benches, a St Andrew's cross. The light is soft and red. We walk in together. It's a conscious decision on our part to step into the dimly lit arena of a consensual fantasy, to put aside one version of ourselves and venture into the multiple, the polymorphous, the perverse. It's taking matters into our own hands. He wears a tailored white shirt. I'm wearing a rubber bodysuit under my clothes.

In the morning, I iron my partner's shirt before they go to work, as a little act of care. In that moment, there's the smell of coffee and the steam from the iron, and not much else – a dailiness, comfortable and enjoyable. I chose to inhabit the erotic space. Then I retract, and the object switches from 'more than' back to 'just'. The fetish – my relationship with their white shirt, with the male institutions it represents – falls flat and is inanimate once again.

LEATHER

An image on a scrap of white leather: a body reclining on bed sheets. The leather is slightly coarse. The body is an elongated curve, metal chains snaking from the neck, across the belly, in between the legs. A pierced nipple, an echo of metal. An elegant hairy armpit. The scrap of leather is a small square, and the image has been transferred onto it as a layer of fine film. There is nothing gentle or fragile about it; it looks temporary, expendable, but in a gritty, urgent way, echoing our expendable bodies.

The body belongs to the artist Jean Cleverley, who shot these self-portraits in 2023 while spending most of their time in bed trying to cope with a chronic illness. The images are created through the darkroom process of Polaroid lifts: 'It involves shooting a Polaroid and then putting it in warm water. The image floats off. And then you have to paint it with a tiny little brush onto the leather,' Cleverley explains. The process was slow, painstaking and fiddly, they tell me, with multiple images breaking – only five in the series survived. Using paper, rather than leather, would certainly have been easier, but it was not an option: 'I was experiencing a lot of pain and being in bed, and printing onto leather was a way to connect to the community I couldn't reach. It made me think of leatherdyke elders who I always looked at in photographs.'

The artist called the series *Coming to Power*, after the 1981 anthology subtitled *Writings and Graphics on Lesbian S/M*, edited by members of the lesbian feminist S/M organisation Samois. In Cleverley's self-portraits, the skin is caressed by the rough edge of a leather jacket, or a high-heeled red shoe. Some images reside on leather from cut-up leather trousers, some on intentionally purchased scraps. The history of scraps is sometimes personal and sometimes completely anonymous, or even random. Leather scraps themselves mean nothing – until they are infused with the history of radical gay fucking. Recontextualised by erotic touch, they become tokens which evade death and time.

Leather is a material defined by cultural memory, but also our ability to forget. We easily forget that it is skin previously belonging to an animal which has been treated, softened, tanned, dyed. But there remain little textural traces of a living being – in the folds and specs and follicles of the material. As we pull on thrifted biker jackets, we often choose to forget the item's past lives to make it a blank canvas for the new version of ourselves we hope to present. Though sometimes we remember the previous owners and wearers and the styles they emulated. For leather is an archive which extends much further than the individual garments; it is a conduit for collective memory, the renegade history which is stored within the skins.

Leatherfolk.
Leather daddy.
Leatherqueer.
Leatherdyke.
Leathersex.

The words roll slowly at first, but end with a harsh grip, an obscene full stop. It is comparable to wearing leather on your body: feeling held, protected, but also visible, 'out'. Since the 1950s, leather has been a gateway for queer communities – a rite of passage, a door through which to enter and recognise that you are surrounded by people like you. Over the years, the people have changed, the spaces have changed, the cultural priorities and laws have changed, but the waistcoats, the biker jackets and the leather trousers remain the same. And I don't mean as a visual or aesthetic; some of the original garments worn by gay bikers a half-century ago still float around, held in archives, passed on by lovers, collectors and eBay-savvy baby queers.

In queer sexual history, the figure of the leather daddy looms large. A tall, burly hunk in a biker jacket, tight leather pants, knee-high leather boots, leather gloves and a leather cap – that immaculate, slightly muted shine accentuating the tight muscles. He is a proxy for authority and masculinity: the daddy, the dom, the biker, the cop, the outlaw. Even if you have a limited interest in fetish culture, the archetype flashes through the mind immediately, while the murkier, dirtier, politically complex aspects of leather's heritage remain in the dark.

Leather is intimately linked with queer memory and theory. There are stories about the French philosopher Michel Foucault frequenting leather bars in the late 1970s – and some of his fans dislike knowing that he sought to be fisted. I came across a fragment of text once suggesting that fisting was a kind of knowledge exchange. While Foucault was a renowned philosopher, he was a novice at the leather bar. He and his fister exchanged wisdom in the hot, sweaty air of a dark room, particles of lube penetrating the skin, the barriers slowly giving in. His thinking was informed by practice; the sexual act was bound up in the theory.

The idea of this multidimensional knowledge exchange is constantly being renegotiated in the leather archives. They are both tools of radical political consciousness and an institutional end to more embodied, alive ways to remember: 'both a temple and a cemetery', as Andy Campbell once framed it. The Leather Archives and Museum in Chicago, the Tom of Finland Archives in LA and the UK Leather and Fetish Archive at Bishopsgate Institute in London, among others, preserve art and writing, personal belongings, diaries, clothing, furniture and S/M party flyers. Whenever I walk through the grand, green-tiled corridors of Bishopsgate Institute and leaf through a fetish magazine or read a horny letter from fifty years ago, I feel like I'm in on the joke, part of some crafty way to infiltrate an institution. Every time you touch something in the archive, not as a researcher, but as an idle, curious leather person, a special kind of ephemeral continuity is created. There is something about queer archives, and especially queer leather archives, which is not confined to libraries and files. They are keeping the memory alive through arousal, fucking among – with, for, in the name of – the dead. So many times, I looked through a smutty magazine and thought, 'These people are no longer alive.' And then, 'What a great way to be remembered.'

Leather goods are commonly sold across a varied price range. One can pick up a leather bag from a high-street brand for under £100 or opt for a Bottega Veneta compact clutch crafted from woven strips of lambskin for £2,870. In 2023, Volkan Yilmaz, better known as @tanner.leatherstein on TikTok, rose to popularity by mercilessly dismembering designer bags from Prada, Gucci and Louis Vuitton. As he cut through the seams, rubbed leather with acetone and burnt the shreds, he demystified the treatments and techniques of leatherwork. The viral appeal of his videos was due to their 'Eat the Rich' sentiment: the appeal of seeing something very expensive which evokes a particular social milieu being torn apart. They also speak to the enduring status of leather. Leather replacement materials have been on the rise for some time now: plastics which are incredibly cheap and increasingly good at imitating leather's texture, shine and weight, or more eco-minded alternatives like mushroom-derived fibres. Yet the attraction to the real thing remains – buttery soft and lustrous for expensive coats, a skin-like beige for luxury car seats, and creased and spit-shined for the perverts.

Leather's status as a luxury is tied to its history as a prized commodity dating back to ancient civilisations, as well as a rich heritage of artisanal craftsmanship which has flourished since the Middle Ages. Leather is adaptable, practical and linked to reliable supply chains, which has made it ubiquitous in the luxury world, a perfect canvas for its multiple iterations. Leather, unlike rubber, is durable and comfortable to wear, which allows it to exist in the fabric of the day-to-day while remaining an aspirational symbol. Leather belts and wallets are staples of subtle refinement, while shoes and handbags are easily elevated and fetishised by the fashion industry: think of the Hermès Birkin bag, a Louboutin high heel or the Louis Vuitton signature beige monogram pattern on dark brown.

At the same time, this air of luxury coexists with leather's countercultural appeal. As early as the 1930s, motorcycle clubs cemented the link between a black leather jacket and an image of rebellion. Marlon Brando's portrayal of the biker Johnny Strabler in the 1953 film *The Wild One* heralded a generation of post-war youth reaching for their own oil-black, sturdy Perfecto jackets. Political radicals from Leon Trotsky to the Black Panthers wore leather, and the material has since been adopted by punk, goth, and heavy metal subcultures, all of which means that leather now communicates a desire to disrupt the status quo. Leather retains connotations of dominant masculinity, and therefore, claiming it can be an act of defiance – Elvis, Michael Jackson, David Bowie and Sid Vicious all used it to subvert the masculine ideal. Leather exists within an enduring duality: finely tailored soft motorcycle-inspired jackets are hung up in upper-range high-street clothing stores, while, worn in a certain way, the material still projects the image of a renegade spirit seeking to disrupt the axes of power. Yet I write about leather here not to unpack its contradictions, but primarily because of its links with LGBTQI+ sexual radicalism, which echoes and sometimes subverts the canonical figure of the leather-clad biker.

Gay motorcycle clubs began appearing in the US in the 1950s, notably the LA-based Satyrs Motorcycle Club and Oedipus Motorcycle Club. Some early participants were war veterans, some simply felt rejected by homophobic society – the search for community and belonging was as crucial as the BDSM-centred sexual culture which was gradually emerging within and around the clubs. The first leather bars opened in the early 1950s: the Silver Dollar in New York, The Cinema in LA and Febe's and the Tool Box in San Francisco, as well as Hotel Tiemersma (later renamed Argos) in Amsterdam, which was the first in Europe according to oral histories. San Francisco's Tool Box occupies a special place in the history of leather bars and their visibility. In 1964, *Life* magazine published a story titled 'Homosexuality in America', which featured a large photograph of the bar. In it, leather-clad patrons are captured against the now iconic bar mural by Chuck Arnett, which depicted a similar gathering of stark silhouettes in black. It marked the mainstream catching up with the emergence of a new gay masculinity, which was moving away from what was perceived to be effeminate and towards the archetype of the hard leather daddy.

At the same time, leather bars operated in precarious conditions. Being gay was still illegal in most states, which meant that the bars were often subject to police raids. In 1976, the LA Police Department staged a raid on a leather community fundraiser at the Mark IV Baths. The fundraiser was a so-called slave auction, a popular format in which consenting BDSM-inclined patrons agreed to be auctioned for role-playing as slaves, with proceeds going to the LA Gay Community Services Center and other gay charities. Catching wind of the event, the LAPD stormed the venue, bringing along television news crews. They later released a statement that they had halted an actual slave auction. The incident exemplified the intense homophobia and paranoia towards the gay community and especially leatherfolk. The highly publicised 'slave auction' was condemned by the LGBTQI+ community itself, but for different reasons – some deemed the language and the practice to be racially insensitive, while others saw non-normative sex as a hindrance to the struggle for gay rights and the general respectability of the community. Leatherfolk were building their communities on shaky grounds, caught between the hostility of the establishment and the splintering opinions inside the LGBTQI+ community, as many viewed their practices as harmful, problematic and a threat to the possibility of general acceptance.

Despite the hostility, leather bars saw a brief golden age in the late 1970s and the beginning of the 1980s, when over twenty operated in the industrial area south of San Francisco's Market Street. Soon, leather transcended its origins as a niche subculture and was increasingly visible in mainstream culture and urban landscapes. The historically renowned fisting club The Catacombs in San Francisco opened at that time, as well as New York's Mineshaft and London's The Backstreet. In his book *Leatherfolk: Radical Sex, People, Politics, and Practice*, Mark Thompson estimates that by the 1990s, the number of motorcycle clubs, leather groups and S/M organisations in the US was close to 500.

More visible than ever before, the leather community was then hit by the AIDS epidemic – both the illness itself and the accompanying moral panic. The conservative establishment was eager to frame the epidemic as punishment for sexual excess, with fisting, cruising and having multiple casual partners deemed the signs of 'unnatural' sexual behaviours said to have caused the disease to spread. The existing reputation of the leatherfolk as 'bad gays', as well as their subversive aesthetic, meant that they became an easy scapegoat, condemned for their sexual practices both by the establishment and frequently by the broader LGBTQI+ community itself. For many, safety was to be found in respectability, monogamy and adopting normative sexual politics, away from the bathhouses and leather clubs. Leatherfolk, despite being heavily involved in fundraising and educational efforts to support those who fell victims to the disease, were increasingly seen as unclean, or even criminal.

'Intolerance takes many forms, sometimes crudely so,' writes Thompson in the introduction to *Leatherfolk*.

> In early 1991, for instance, police busted into a Boston home where members of the local leather community regularly met for private parties. No warrant was presented; words like 'faggots' and 'fucking AIDS carriers' were used by officers the night they brutally searched the house and the thirty men inside. Three organizers were arrested, and the names and addresses of others entered into public records. One man was so traumatized by the raid that he killed himself soon thereafter by jumping off a freeway ramp. Still, few in the Boston gay community expressed our rage over the trespass. 'What a colossally stupid waste of time,' stated the editor of a local gay newspaper. 'Let's hope our organizations spend as little time as possible on it.' Said another community leader, '[The raid] doesn't seem like a gay and lesbian issue.'

The marginal position of leatherfolk in AIDS-era queer culture left them vulnerable to persecution from the police. In the US, the 1990s saw numerous raids of leather bars, including Mineshaft, and private homes, targeting gay leathermen. In the UK, Operation Spanner, an investigation into same-sex male sadomasochism, saw 100 gay and bisexual men questioned by police and sixteen convicted for engaging in consensual leathersex, on the back of a private sex tape which ended up in the hands of the Met Police.

Greater Manchester Police first came in possession of the tapes in 1987. They were home videos of sadomasochistic sex which featured spanking, whipping, wax play and cutting. After the lead of the investigation was passed over to the Obscene Publications Squad of the Metropolitan Police and codenamed 'Operation Spanner', the raids and searches began both in private homes and at the offices of several gay magazines: *Sir*, *Gay Galaxy* and *Corporal Contacts*. Over the course of the investigation, police were unable to find any participants who had not consented to the activities which took place, nor any who sustained lasting injuries, yet in 1989, sixteen men were still charged with over 100 offences, including assault occasioning actual bodily harm and unlawful wounding. In 1990, the judge then handed down eight prison sentences of between twelve months and four and a half years. During the hearing and the subsequent appeals, the factor of consent to the activities was deemed 'immaterial'.

Operation Spanner was carried out in the social climate of pervasive homophobia – it was Thatcher's Britain and Section 28 was in effect, forbidding the 'promotion of homosexuality'. During the trial, the tabloids perpetuated broad anti-gay sentiments by describing the men involved as a 'perverted sex gang' and 'sadistic sex freaks'.

Imagine: you are taken from your home by the police; you are questioned, arrested, taken to court, fired from your job and dragged by the tabloids. You are thrown in prison, the course of your life completely altered, all because of the kind of sex you have in private with other consenting adults. Reading about Operation Spanner evokes a sense of grave injustice but also, for fellow kink and BDSM practitioners, a devastating feeling of exploited vulnerability. Because this is how you are in the moment, in play –

vulnerable, honest, true. To have that part of you exposed, shamed and condemned is unbelievably brutal.

The case had a broad resonance, sparking a debate about the limits of consent and the role of government in sexual encounters between consenting adults. In response, two activist organisations dedicated to promoting the rights of sadomasochists formed, Countdown on Spanner and The Sexual Freedom Coalition, and an annual S/M Pride March through central London began. Over three decades later, the case is largely forgotten, even though the questions it spurred about bodily autonomy and sexual difference are more relevant than ever. Society's approval remains a fragile matter, while its punishing rage towards the *other* never ceases.

Despite its severity, the shadow of persecution has faded with time. Now, certain fragments of this queer leather history are preserved in the cultural canon: artworks displayed to the public at major institutions such as MoMA or the Tate. The gravity and the political complexity of leather are not always remembered, yet these images loom large in art history. Robert Mapplethorpe famously documented the gay leather scene, with gimp leather hoods and penis piercing appearing in his works from the 1970s and 1980s, alongside more formal portraiture of community members. One of his most renowned photographs is the 1979 portrait of Brian Ridley and Lyle Heeter. The two men are head to toe in leather. Ridley is seated in a leather armchair, with chains attached to his ankles and wrists. Heeter stands to his left, resting his elbow on the armchair and holding in his right hand the chain attached to the collar around Ridley's neck. They are photographed in their living room, vases, soft curtains and other domestic details of the interior contrasting with their leather attire.

Catherine Opie's 1994 *Self-Portrait/Pervert* is another prominent example. In the photo, the artist is wearing a leather hood, her face obscured and hands resting on her lap, just beneath a chunky leather belt, both arms pierced by two dozen thick medical needles. On her chest is a faintly bleeding cutting of the word 'Pervert' in a curvy, decorative font. In her *O* portfolio, Opie documented members of San Francisco's queer leather scene, predominantly dykes. The politics of being a leatherdyke were especially thorny at the time, with the community often being ostracised by many non-kinky lesbians and feminists who subscribed to the idea that consensual sadomasochism is merely a reflection of the violence the patriarchal society enacts on women and should therefore be stopped. Opie portrays leather culture unapologetically, in a completely uncensored way, using her own body, turning what many discarded as a sick sexual preference into an act of self-creation and artistic freedom. *Self-Portrait/Cutting* takes this stance even further, musing on deviant sex and the possibility of social acceptance. A scene, as if drawn by a child's hand, is carved into the artist's back: a house and two stick figures with triangles for skirts holding hands. Pain and blood to stage what it means to build a queer family in the restrictively normative society – the queer body is always a source of trouble.

But while Mapplethorpe and Opie's images speak to radical erotic expression and the progressive politics of leather, even in the 1990s leather was not immune to commodification as an aesthetic. As authorities cracked down on leatherfolk on both sides of the Atlantic, Madonna's *Sex* book came out in 1992. A collaboration with fashion photographer Steven Meisel and art director Fabien Baron, it was one of the early examples of pop culture capitalising on the risqué potential of leather. It also set out the tension which still remains around the material, as well as the broader signifiers of kink, fetish and queerness: whether the aesthetics and politics ever actually converge. Frequently, where the aesthetic is permitted, the politics are far too threatening for the status quo.

At the time of its publication, *Sex* generated both a major media backlash and extremely high sales: in a matter of days, it sold more than 1.5 million copies worldwide and remains the fastest-selling coffee table book. Three decades on, *Sex* has retained a fair share of its shock value. One of the first portraits of Madonna captures her in a leather bikini with exposed nipples, leather bondage cuffs and a narrow leather mask. Legs spread, she sucks on her middle finger, with her other hand on her crotch. The opposite page simply proclaims: 'I'll teach you how to fuck.'

A quick flick through: Madonna burying her face in a jock-strapped ass. Madonna shaving pubic hair off an athletic man's body. Madonna sucking on someone's big toe. Madonna standing on a windowsill facing the street in a dykey white vest and boots, her ass exposed. Madonna being whipped by German actor Udo Kier. Madonna hailing a cab, naked.

The most fascinating spreads of the book, however, show the singer engaged in a threesome with two women: both have buzzcuts, piercings and tattoos. In one of the photos, Madonna is tied to a chair, sharing a kiss with one of the women, who is also holding a knife to her neck, while the other sucks on her nipple, which is exposed through a slashed black dress.

In the 1993 issue of the British fetish magazine *Skin Two*, Patrick Califia published an essay in response to Madonna's *Sex* book. While noting that it's wonderful to see real lesbians in mainstream erotica, he rightfully critiques the book for neglecting to note safety and consent practices. He also expressed feeling 'deeply ambivalent about somebody who has not paid her dues using my community as a series of bizarre backdrops for a photoshoot', worrying that *Sex* would only attract more tourists and moral crusaders to leather bars, clubs and dungeons. For leatherfolk in the 1990s, visibility was a double-edged sword. On the one hand, it created space for more representation and recognition. On the other, it attracted too much attention without necessarily uplifting their voices – and when the media frenzy was over and celebrities moved on to the next subversive horizon, they were left exposed and just as stigmatised as before.

For, while leather is a material, in the deepest erotic sense, leather is a community practice. As a result of political and social oppression, the 1990s leather scene produced some of the most incredible writing on the boundaries and lived experience of sex. Patrick Califia penned erotic fiction and theory, as well as editing the lesbian BDSM anthology *The Second Coming*, while the writing of Carol Queen (author of *The Leather Daddy and the Femme*) and John Preston straddled the line between erotica and porn. Susan Stryker's essays on San Francisco in the 1990s and its innovative S/M cultures paved the way for a multidimensional understanding of sex, transness and gender. Recent years have seen a new wave of interest in the community, with Siân A. Williams and Harri Shanahan's documentary *Rebel Dykes*, as well as *BloodSisters* by Michelle Handelman and Phyllis Christopher's photo book *Darkroom* all collecting together visual and artistic documentation of the scene. As these artistic perspectives find new audiences, a new generation of people are keen to play in leather and construct their identities and their sex based on the blueprint.

Yet the question remains: what does it mean to play in leather in the 2020s? Who has the right to invoke its aesthetics – and with what intentions? As the community spans a wide array of social classes and professions, does it still matter if you wear leather only occasionally, for a bit of fun after a day at an office job? As political views become more polarised and fractured, is leather capacious enough to hold all forms of nonconformity together? Has it ever been?

Leather history encompasses a broad spectrum of people and

radically different experiences, and not everyone is equally represented by the canon. The work of artist Ajamu X seeks to reimagine its boundaries and possibilities. Based in South London, he is best known for his photography focusing on Black masculinity and queerness, which he started exhibiting in the 1990s. In a self-portrait from 1998, he reclines on a chaise longue wearing a black leather mask, fishnet stockings and black heels. Not only does the image disrupt the racial preconception of the leather community as completely white, but it also subverts its rigid gender boundaries. Ajamu's work plays with signifiers of fetish – high heels, leather hoods, harnesses, whips – and it is full of sensuality, tenderness and introspection.

When we talked in his studio on a summer afternoon, Ajamu looked back at the reluctance he felt initially towards getting into kink because of 'the racial memory around what some of the objects represent'. Not only do some of the signifiers attached to the scene – whips, shackles, racialised language – present a problem, but there are also the stereotypes of Black masculinity which are perpetuated by the community, in the work of Robert Mapplethorpe and Tom of Finland, to contend with. 'That's why I generally work with thin, femme Black male bodies. For me, there is a long, 2,000-plus-year history of your typical male body and a particular kind of masculinity . . . I find these images restrictive, or rather, I just don't find them that sexy.'

One must resist idealising a homogenous vision of the leather community. To do so is to deny the way it has evolved as a result of debates around consent practices, dress codes, language, appropriation and gender. But we must also remember how leather has served as a tool for unity, cooperation and mutual care, and how leatherdyke spaces have served as a playground for gender experimentation and reinvention, inclusive of trans people and sex workers. The material consistently brings together people of diverse genders, sexualities and social stances.

Leather remains a thorn in the side of respectability politics to this day, as we can observe in the recurring discourse around kink at Pride: the debate over whether harnesses, leather suits, ball gags and human puppies have a space at Pride, which has become prominent in recent years. A number of young queer people and leftist commentators point out that the broader public does not consent to witnessing certain kink-related sexual acts and that this might also jeopardise Pride as a family-friendly day out. These conversations bring us back to the archives, back to the tension between sexual identity and mainstream acceptance, and the difference between acceptance and assimilation.

People assume that to enjoy supposedly deviant kinds of sex is to be free of shame. But the shame is deep set. To play in the dungeon in the company of others is to be witnessed, validated. At least, this is the role leathersex plays for me.

I left Russia at the age of twenty-two, before coming out. I had thoughts, feelings, doubts, questions but nothing solid enough to provide a stable sense of a queer identity. In the last decade, in the time since I relocated to the UK, LGBTQI+ rights in Russia have gone dramatically downhill. The so-called gay propaganda law of 2013 outlawed LGBTQI+ representation in the cultural mainstream – whether that's in the media, in public spaces or in education. The law focused on the argument of 'protecting the children', in a manner similar to Britain's Section 28, which was in effect from 1988 to 2003, or Florida's 2022 'Don't Say Gay' law. In the years since, hostility has grown steadily, in the form of both casual homophobia and outright violence. In spite of this, the community saw a brief renaissance in late 2010s, with a younger generation using online media – YouTube, TikTok – as well as art, bars and raves to create a largely underground yet bourgeoning queer culture. But it all came to an abrupt end as Russia descended into militarised conservatism, depicting anything which strayed from heteronormativity as a threat to national security. In February 2022, Russia invaded Ukraine, and in December a new anti-LGBTQI+ law was passed, banning 'propaganda of non-traditional sexual relations' to all age groups. If, previously, an 18+ marker could help you get away with running an LGBTQI+ website or social media account, now any depiction of same-sex relations in the media, advertising, books or on screen was forbidden. In 2023, Russia's Supreme Court ruled that the 'international LGBT movement' was an 'extremist organisation'. Transition was effectively outlawed shortly after. At the time of writing, any sight of a rainbow is now met with moral panic.

Any time I hear a remix of 'All the Things She Said', t.A.T.u.'s 2000 single, which is Russia's most well-known contribution to queer pop culture, playing at a queer rave, I feel incredibly lucky, but also lonely. As Russia's institutional homophobia reached its fever pitch in 2023, it felt like a point of no return, like some part of me will never be fully realised, at least in those remits of my native geography. But with that loss also emerged a possibility of being reborn as something new.

Within my own family, my queerness is sometimes treated as fiction. This always makes me angry and upset. But maybe I did invent myself as queer. Maybe I quietly nurtured something tantalising, monstrous, thirsty from a little seed beneath my soft guts. Blood is pumping in my ears as I remember putting my hands around a girl I've just met at a busy lesbian club night. I remember the grip of a strap-on harness on my hips, learning the mechanics of a movement which is new to my body. The flirtations at gay clubs which have now melted into a fog of longing. Being obsessed with my best friend's lips when I wasn't yet out. A couple arriving at a play party, one of them in a tiny white lace mini dress and the other in a boiler suit, the sole of her thick leather boot having just come off and tied back with a bow of black bondage tape. I remember looking at my friends playing with each other, both in leather chaps. I feel so lucky and so privileged to have been there, to have witnessed and smelt and tasted these moments. My personal leather archive. Leather as part of my erotic and political consciousness.

In her essay on the *BloodSisters* documentary, Daemonum X, NYC-based leatherdyke, rope top and educator, points out that 'What many outsiders don't know is that leather is more than just hot sex. Leather communities and organizations have a long history of activism, mutual aid, charity work, and dedication to education. [. . .] My absolute favourite part in the film gives me chills,' she recalls:

> The San Francisco leatherdykes rolled into Washington D.C. clad in leather and joined the march surrounded by the contingent from the National Organization for Women. They created a large enough gap in the march so that Tala Brandeis could wield her bullwhip that appears to be no shorter than twenty feet long (drools) on the back of a very willing bottom. This was public sex. This was sadomasochism. This was a political act of protest from a trans woman, leatherdyke sadist among a marching sea of feminists who had already decided that they weren't fighting for her rights because she didn't deserve rights. Her very existence was disrespectable.

To play in leather is to enter the shadow space. To hear the buckle of your leather jacket. To place the sole of your leather boot on someone's soft thigh – take it away, and blood rushes back to fill the print left on the skin. To feel a hard-on press against your leather pants. I have no biological penis and yet I revel in my figurative hard-on, my arousal which makes me feel bigger than myself. The unstoppable desire for gratification, my leather daddy touch. There is no way to disentangle leather, sex and politics.

In 2014, the Finnish postal service released a set of Tom of Finland stamps. They came as one postcard-sized sheet, the core image on which depicted two men: one is reclining on a chair wearing a uniform of some kind, a tight shirt and trousers, leather gloves, leather knee-high boots, a leather cap; while the other is sitting naked at his feet, between the widely spread legs. The naked man's right hand is resting lovingly on one leather boot, while the other is clutched between his thighs. Both men are looking at the viewer, but their connection is apparent. There is an unmistakable high shine on the leather items: almost hyperreal, they stand out more than everything else. The leather is essential to the chemistry, as is the viewer – or voyeur – they gaze at. The stamps, when peeled off, feature the face of each of the men, while a third stamp, hovering to the right of the tableau, features a ripe round ass, with a third face, with a chiselled chin and moustache, peeking through the gap between the muscular thighs.

By the time of their release, the stamps had been pre-ordered in 178 countries worldwide and the demand had broken the Finnish postal service's website. I remember this moment vividly because of a conversation with a couple of friends of mine in Russia. As the gay propaganda law came into effect, we joked about going to Finland and sending back postcards addressed to the government officials who had pushed the law, using the Tom of Finland stamps.

The hovering ass was an especially tantalising option – it was just so camp, so excessive, so absurd and full of life in a shamelessly homoerotic way.

Tom of Finland sold erotic drawings by post in the 1960s and 1970s. To protect his customers, he would burn the letters he got from them and wouldn't keep any information on them. The only thing he kept were the stamps from their correspondence. Over the years, this amounted to a huge bag of them, which are now stored at the Tom of Finland Foundation. The artist's relationship with postage stamps perfectly reflects the arc of his career: from the discarded letters of the early underground networks of distribution to avoid the crackdown of the authorities to the notoriety of being on actual government-endorsed postal stamps.

Tom of Finland is almost single-handedly responsible for the rise of the gay leather iconography which is now so ubiquitous. His leather daddies, muscly hunks, soldiers, builders, sailors and bikers are instantly recognisable for their humorous camp disposition and exaggerated physique. Their perfect torsos, chiselled jaws and big, hard cocks can be purchased not only in the form of monographs but as tea towels, mugs, coasters, water bottles, comfy sweaters, silk dresses, dildos, blankets and latex jockstraps. Fashion labels which have released Tom of Finland collections include Diesel and JW Anderson. In fact, Tom of Finland's work has not only contributed to the look of leather culture but has become a fetish in itself. His work is also a perfect reflection of how leather in gay culture went from a response to persecution to being packaged and sold.

Tom of Finland was born Touko Laaksonen, in 1920, in the Finnish town of Kaarina. Both his parents were schoolteachers, and Touko was raised surrounded by art, literature and music. By the time he was five, he was playing the piano and drawing comic strips. He later studied marketing and advertising, but when the Second World War broke out, he joined the military in the spring of 1940 and served in an anti-aircraft unit in Helsinki. His attraction to hyper-masculine types in uniform blossomed in the army: he was drawn to men in their 'irresistible jackboots' on city streets, which were dark due to the wartime blackouts.

After the war, he studied music at Sibelius Academy and started working on his first erotic drawings in secret. By day, he did freelance work in advertising and by night he played the piano at parties and cafes. From 1950, the demand for his erotic work grew quickly, and at the end of 1956, at the urging of a friend, Touko sent a few images to *Physique Pictorial*, a popular American muscle magazine. Being cautious at a time when homosexuality was still illegal, and thinking that Touko Laaksonen was too tough a name for American tongues, he signed them 'Tom'. The editor loved them. The cover of the spring 1957 issue features a laughing lumberjack drawn by 'Tom of Finland'. And so, Tom of Finland was born.

The initial images were somewhat restrained. However, the US Supreme Court ruled that nude male photographs were no longer obscene in 1962, which led to a relaxation in censorship codes restricting the depiction of homosexual acts. Added to this, homosexuality was decriminalised in the UK in 1967 (although it only applied to private sexual acts) and in Finland in 1971. As if it could ever have been contained by a legislative framework, the fantasy was no longer illegal, and by the 1970s, Tom of Finland was able to publish more overtly homoerotic work. His work then began to enter the mainstream art world, with exhibitions and a book of his work published by Taschen in the 1980s.

As Tom of Finland was fast becoming a household name, one of the characters he created, Kake, soon became synonymous with the archetype of the leatherman. Kake, who is the title character of an erotic comic book series published from 1968 to 1986, is muscly and moustachioed, wearing a leather jacket, leather breeches, knee-high leather riding boots and a leather peaked cap. Friendly and easy-going, he gets into various horny adventures with police officers, sailors, lumberjacks, businessmen, cowboys or fellow leathermen. Kake's muscles, leathers, enormous cock and playful grin, as well as his willingness to bottom as well as top, have become the epitome of Tom of Finland masculinity.

In the emergence of Tom of Finland as a pop cultural icon, the role of arousal as a creative tool remains a somewhat awkward part of the conversation. 'For him, drawing was a very private thing,' Durk Dehner, Laaksonen's ex-lover and co-founder of the Tom of Finland Foundation, has said. 'He would say, "If I didn't have a hard-on, it wouldn't end up as a very good drawing." And I thought, what is he doing? Here we are promoting him and building up his sense of mastery and he says something which is so guttural. I never brought it up with him, but I sat on it for a little bit and then it all made sense. Arousal accentuated all of the senses . . . His arousal was entirely interconnected with his mastery.'

And this arousal is quite obviously fetishistic: his gaze lingers over motorcyclists' and builders' gear, and, more disturbingly, policemen's aviator glasses and military uniforms; it distorts bodily proportions for a good jerk-off while retaining a camp humour. The Tom of Finland leatherman contributes to the excessive, sexual, playful yet reductive image of queer masculinity, at times loved by dykes and gender-nonconforming folks as much as by men. This legacy, however, is at times problematic. Eroticising masculine archetypes of authority is part of the Tom of Finland trademark, despite – or perhaps because of – their connotations of state oppression. When it comes to policemen, the artist usually explained that it was a way to reclaim his agency – turning a policeman into a camp pin-up helped to alleviate the fear of arrest or persecution. The fascination with military uniforms (inspired, no doubt, by those German soldiers of his youth) might be part of the reason why Nazi iconography and very similar-looking uniforms still linger in fetish discourse and certain fetish spaces. People's sexual fantasies can independently reach for the most taboo subjects and images, and the Tom of Finland iconography may have at times served to legitimise them.

'It's a really complicated beast to wrestle with. I indulge in it as much as I buck against it,' artist Steven Harwick says of the masculine leather archetype which originated in the Tom of Finland drawings. Based in New York, he has spent the last eight years creating a captivating group portrait of the queer leather community around him. He started self-publishing *Bound Leather* zine in 2017 and estimates he has photographed just over a hundred people for it, with seventy-five ending up on the pages of the 2022 monograph *By the Skin of My Teeth*. He tells me that he was initially inspired by vintage Americana and gay erotic magazines like *Physique Pictorial*.

Harwick has photographed plenty of leather men: cigar-smoking leather daddies, porn performers in tight leather shirts, sensual tattooed hunks in biker jackets and snow-white jockstraps. But he truly comes into his power as a community archivist when documenting how the leather community reaches beyond the confines of traditional masculinity: his leatherfolk are gender-fluid, trans, women, drag artists, sex workers, Black, Indigenous, femme of all ages and body types. The lens is unmistakably erotic, indulging in overt desire and voyeurism akin to Tom of Finland's work, while remaining empathetic and celebratory, highlighting his subjects' humanity, not just their empowered sex appeal. In part, this approach reflects how Harwick used the work to connect with a like-minded community: those born too late to witness the golden age of late-1970s to early-1980s leather bars, but also those who are sober and yearning for more spaces in which to connect, outside of bar culture.

Harwick had a hard time seeing himself in the leather imagery inspired by Tom of Finland's work when he was younger. 'It's through images that we are able to be seen and forge community. My holding up a mirror to you digs my own heels into place. I am carving out a space for myself by the skin of my teeth.'

Leather is a recognised staple of gay erotica, but for Harwick the attraction started before he was aware of its cultural cachet. In fact, he stole his first proper leather jacket from the lost-and-found bin at high school. 'I was immediately seduced by the smell and the soft, supple, lived-in creases and folds. Moreover, I became obsessed with imagining its life before I liberated it from its cardboard limbo,' he has said. 'I've been captivated by leather for as long as I can remember, but it wasn't until this moment with my salvaged motorcycle jacket that I came to understand what it meant to have a fetish.'

Of the many artists working with leather, Harwick comes closer than most to the multisensory appeal of leathersex, where leather meets tender, exposed skin. He wants the viewer to get the tactility of leather from his images by consciously focusing on the way it's folded, worn or lit, on the details which 'could evoke somebody licking someone's boots or burying their face into leather'. The feeling, the imagined scene which extends beyond the photograph, is essential to the vision. For him, it is the mental work of filling the voids which creates a fetish. Fantasy is a story we tell ourselves. History is a story we tell ourselves. Sometimes they converge.

'I definitely find that I'm much more interested in clothing items that have a history – I can imagine their story, or a previous owner and how they've interacted with these items that I'm now playing with or turned on by,' Harwick explains to me. 'This is the space where fetish operates for me or what the word means to me. This kind of alchemy elevates a pair of jeans that are lying on a bed into something that you can think about, imagining the legs that were in them once before, and what kind of action they saw in their day. That is much more exciting to me than walking into a leather shop and having rows upon rows of brand-new gear.'

Over the years, Harwick's work has attracted people who would happily donate their leathers to his collection. Most recently, he inherited a few items from someone who in his lifetime modelled for Robert Mapplethorpe and was active on the fetish scene. A friend who had cleared out the person's apartment passed on a pair of blue-collar-style work gloves and two pairs of leather trousers: classic leather jeans and high-waisted 1960s-style padded motorcycle pants. Harwick defines his creative work and general interactions with leather as a connective, community-based practice – receiving leather items from lovers, friends, people he only met briefly. Each relationship is unique – some want to find a new home for leathers they no longer wish to store, and some follow more nuanced motivations. 'I have this guy on Instagram who just sends me really expensive cowboy boots. He wants me to use them, to photograph people wearing them, but also he said I could fuck them and cum on them – and these are US$900 cowboy boots – and he's like: you'll send them back whenever you're done with them, but you have them for now. There is something remarkably anti-capitalist about just giving stuff to people and then not really expecting much other than some hot photographs come out of it.'

Leather, in Harwick's world, becomes an antidote to a society of newness, where we're constantly chasing upgrades, the dopamine hits of the latest 'new thing'. The desire-driven process of discovery is still part of it, but it mostly takes place on eBay. We talk about the unpredictability of reseller sites, this foray into someone else's sexual history, and how people with stunning collections of gear retire from time to time, listing their whole bounty up for sale.

'I feel like I've played with people that are just . . . I don't want to say tourists . . . but for whom putting on the gear allows access to a certain culture,' he says. 'It can be something that people put on and take off, and it's not in charge of their entire life or being as it is for me or other people. Which is neither a good nor bad thing. I feel like it brings new people into the scene all the time. It certainly makes for a lot of great eBay listings once they're ready to get out of the scene. I don't think you necessarily have to be one hundred per cent a fetishist to engage with fetish.'

Radical politics and mutual care are both essential to the leather community, and yet they remain porous. People come and go, but leather stays.

I head to the UK Leather and Fetish Archive on a Wednesday afternoon. It looks like a regular research area, with a dozen desks and shelves overflowing with books and files and a handful of computers of various ages. But the space also displays its difference with candour: a wide variety of Pride flags hang from the upper gallery; there's a huge promotional cut-out board for a Tom of Finland biopic; a black studded spanking bench; and a human cage which once belonged to The Backstreet, London's longest-running gay leather and fetish bar, which closed its doors in 2022. The cage is dark tarnished metal and looks a little like an Egyptian sarcophagus in shape. I know that in the bigger library room at the back, there is a painting which is a mock version of *The Last Supper*, but populated with leather daddies.

I am here to see a particular file. Last year, a couple moved into a house near Bolton, just north of Manchester. When they knocked down the wall, they found a stack of negatives. The photos depicted various men posing in leather, as well as private gatherings which could be identified as sex parties. Instead of chucking the findings away, the couple got hold of Stefan Dickers, the Special Collections and Archives Manager at Bishopsgate Institute, who has been responsible for the development of the institute's collections on the history of London, protest and activism, and LGBTQI+ Britain –

including the UK Leather and Fetish Archive. A few weeks later, the house revealed yet more findings: a stack of letters hidden in the chimney. After some quick research, they discovered that the person who had lived in the house at the time knew the men convicted as part of Operation Spanner. It was as if he couldn't bring himself to get rid of the letters completely, so he hid them instead, as if he was waiting for the knock on the door, terrified of being next. The letters and papers in the chimney were torn in half.

I sit down at one of the computers, and the contact sheets are displayed on the screen. Just like that, I get access to someone's private history. I zoom in on image after image, the contact sheets scanned so large that one can travel between them effortlessly, in pale yet full colour. Three men on a bench: the two on either end are donning full Tom of Finland-style outfits, with boots and leather caps; the one in the middle is sitting on the back of the bench, leather boots on the seat, jacket undone, with closely cropped hair. Behind them is a pale English park in early spring and a light blue Range Rover. A few more snaps of them in the park. One of the men in leather appears in a few more photos, indoors, on a mustard-coloured velvet chair, with a backdrop of red and beige boudoir-style wallpaper. A skinny young man, crouching in leather pants and tall, cherry-red Dr. Martens boots. The same man reclining on a bed in a leather jockstrap. An awkward behind-the-scenes: a young man in blue uniform and someone in leather chaps bending over, holding a bunch of impact implements. The dungeon looks like a home basement with very poor lighting. The analogue camera flash flattens the scene.

Most of the contact sheets are portraits of young men. Some appear in ordinary clothes: a young blond squinting at the camera in the afternoon light, in a grey top with cut-off sleeves, Casio watch on his wrist, holding a jacket over the shoulder. But, more often than not, they embody a fantasy. They wear guises from gay erotica and Tom of Finland books. There are many leather daddies in full gear, down to the boots. There's a wry skinhead, and a young man fishing topless in white jeans and high leather boots. There's a builder in a safety helmet, a tight T-shirt with 'Vogue' emblazoned on it and tight white briefs, with his penis hanging out. A sailor, a soldier, another soldier – a parade of uniforms. Timid-looking boys standing in the middle of the dungeon: one in a Rush poppers T-shirt, one in a leather harness and hood, one in a leather vest and white jockstrap. I look at a photo of a man in a leather harness exposing his penis. The penises, the pecs, the nipples are standard size; they're not the monumental hard-ons, bursting muscles and chiselled features of Tom of Finland's men. This creates a strange sense of intimacy, heightened by the fact that the photos are interspersed with holiday snaps and mundane details of home interiors: still lifes of a fish tank and a hi-fi.

'No one knows who these people are, not even the researchers,' says Stefan Dickers.

There are contact sheets of black-and-white photos from an older collection, which depict people in the army. Two more images stand out against the posed portraits which make up the bulk of the collection: a man tied up in full leather gear, his wrists tied behind his back with straining leather straps and chains. And a gentler scene: two young men embracing in dim light. The shadows almost envelop them, save for a golden glow where their embracing bodies, hips and arms meet.

'I've had people come into the archives who have cried because they couldn't believe this was their history being recorded. This is something that's been with them through emotional ups and downs – their own kink history and their sexuality – and now it's here, and it's being celebrated,' Dickers told me a few years back. 'This is important to me, as a kinky person who was ashamed of being kinky for a while. I don't ever want to be called normal or to normalise kink – but saying that the history of your sexuality is important is empowering for the kink community. I am very conscious of the power the archive has to make everyone feel proud about their own history.'

At the archive, I sit back for a second and trace the story of how I came to these negatives. From my gaze at the computer, I trace the images back to Stefan's hands, to the hands which held the camera, to the hot sex they yearned to document in a world where consensual S/M gay sex was persecuted. There is a tangential political link between me and the men in the photos – all of us perverts. Now you, too, are connected to us all in this orgy of an archive.

We could all be done in for leathersex in so many countries of the world. The hands which touch the leather, the hands which tear the letters – tomorrow could still be my hands.

LATEX

Latex requires dedication. It starts before it's even touched your body – in taking precise measurements of your chest, waist and hips to order a latex garment. The measurements have to be precise to ensure comfort. Then you wait, sometimes three or four weeks, for the latex maker to craft your order. Some say that even in the making, it's unforgiving – make a mistake gluing a seam and you have to start from scratch.

Latex forces you to slow down. There is no way of throwing it on quickly. It needs to be lubed and put on carefully – one careless pull, the tiniest puncture, and it splits. You must take your time, allow it to slowly envelop the curves of the body while you grow accustomed to its embrace.

Everything about it is a balance between a ritual and an inconvenience. It has to be washed by hand in warm water – soaked in the bathtub, or rinsed in the shower, with specks of water gathering on the surface like pearls. After it's hung to dry, it needs to be powdered and stored out of light. The material has its subtle vulnerabilities: sunlight will make it brittle; metal will stain it; oil will corrode it. The care permeates your life beyond the sexual aspect of fetish, becoming a habitual choreography.

Gradually, a relationship is formed between you and your latex. It's not only about looking and feeling powerful, other-worldly, and revelling in pleasure. Maybe sometimes you take it off and neglect it for a few days, leaving it in a heap in the corner. But then it is cleansed and laid to rest in the darkness – until it is revived again, alongside that part of you it allows to thrive. For some, those small moments are routine, but for some, they're a kind of devotion.

For me, latex will always be connected to silence. The silence of a muted video, of a deserted street. I discovered rubber and latex fetish online in 2020 at the height of the COVID-19 pandemic. Looking back at the years before, I remember that I wasn't happy. I was an assortment of unresolved identities hard to make sense of – queer, immigrant, gender-questioning – and felt chronically anxious. In that confusing time, my body had become the only place I felt safe. Then 2020 came, and there was nothing left *but* my body. It was strange, claustrophobic – but also quiet and peaceful. It was as if I'd been given a chance to get a little closer to that part of me which felt so comforting and so true, and which I sensed but didn't yet fully know.

My bedroom window looked out onto a fragment of gleaming sky and a green patch in the middle of an eerily quiet estate. My whole life fitted easily in this room. I walked to the corner shop to get some eggs and held intense eye contact with a person across the road. The yearning for touch was visceral, the tension between the desire for intimacy and personal protection hard to reconcile. Touch was everything, and touch was – suddenly – potentially lethal. After a couple of weeks of confinement, I wanted to unzip my skin and step out of it; having a personality and an intimate history within these four walls felt exhausting, and I wanted to shed myself for something, anything, different.

Perhaps it was that search for something different, for a clean slate, for play, for a different guise I could try on, which had led me to latex imagery online – as well as the fact that I was touch-starved and horny, of course. The bedroom latex experience: a common first time. Having once been a teenage goth and an avid sci-fi fan,

I was familiar with a classic latex look: a sleek, black, reflective material which elegantly envelops the body with the grace and flow of a liquid and the precision of armour. In 2003's *The Matrix Reloaded*, Monica Bellucci's character Persephone appears wearing a pearly translucent peplum dress – a latex creation so memorable that it has its own rich online discourse. The imagery which sparked my interest in the material in 2020, however, was a lot more DIY.

As the world turned into a range of lonely bedrooms dotted across the globe, latex flourished in online spaces. On my phone screen, I scrolled through images of people self-styled in rubber: video game streamers, amateur porn stars, nerds, gas mask collectors, burlesque models, latex makers and people like me, who had only just given in to their curiosity. The imagery, which I primarily saw on Instagram, was erotic but not explicit. At times, even the eroticism was incredibly subtle: someone posing demurely in their long latex gloves or a latex dress. Online sex work and homemade erotic content saw unprecedented growth during the pandemic, which contributed to the visibility of latex online. But it was also like tapping into a network: you followed one enthusiast, and through them discovered a handful of others, which then would lead you to a fetish photographer and a latex designer – the exposure grew exponentially. People of all genders, from all corners of the world, showed off limbs transformed by glossy rubber skins on their sofas and beds, on balconies overlooking locked-down cities, or in overgrown fields, far away from everything and everyone.

I was hooked on the shiny look and how it accentuated the body, but also on the element of performance in the photos. This self-expression was not confined to one's regular identity: the material was central to an alternative version of yourself. It facilitated emotion, seduction, disobedience, not giving a fuck, leaving behind whatever else was no longer relevant. I wanted some of that control, some of that agency. Before I ever wanted to wear latex, I wanted to be seen wearing it.

Latex doesn't really happen to you by accident. To stand in front of the mirror in a catsuit, you need to order that catsuit. And to order the catsuit, you need to arrive at a point where you're ready to spend £257 on something you can only (mostly) wear in private, just to have a particular experience. Latex demands a lot of care; it also commands a high price. Having a latex fetish is expensive, and this creates a barrier to entry. It also creates a hierarchy of sorts within the scene, limiting one's exploration with, or immersion in, the material. Some people amass impressive collections, with catsuits of different lustrous colours, bondage gear, ball gowns and immaculately tailored dresses and coats. Some save up and treat themselves occasionally, or shop on reseller sites. But before that first latex purchase, you don't even know for sure what the experience will be like. There is no way of knowing, until the moment comes for your body, the rubber and whoever else is in the room with you – until the chemistry takes hold.

The first item I bought was a pair of over-the-elbow gloves. 'Opera gloves', as they insist on calling them on all latex websites. They were black and matt, wrapped in tissue paper and lightly powdered with talcum, a little cool to the touch – they felt and looked very different from anything else I owned. I rubbed the silicone dressing aid on my arms. I pulled the gloves on, and their grip was a whisper. Once on, they transformed from a rubbery substance into a tight, shiny second skin which absorbed my body heat. I transformed too. I didn't yet fully know what I had transformed into – but I did know that nothing I had worn before had ever felt this way.

While the latex culture is very visually driven, there is a different dimension to the experience which opens up with actually wearing and handling the material. The sensation of wearing latex is shaped by its key property. It's a non-porous surface, and so it keeps all moisture and fluids on one side, and everything in the surrounding environment on the other. Your body temperature is rising under the thin barrier, causing a subtle sense of what I can only describe as a high. I remember that feeling being almost surprising. I questioned how the feeling of discomfort turned into pleasure.

Not every person who's ever worn latex feels the same way. I have friends who have latex catsuits but have to bargain with themselves whether the lengthy process of getting into one is worth the gratification. Some love the look but not the sensation. Even the sweat, which pools at one's feet after taking the catsuit off, or streams down your legs when wearing a latex dress on the dance floor, evokes polarised reactions. 'But I love it,' I always say. 'Of course,' they reply, 'you are a fetishist.'

After purchasing latex gloves, I kept browsing, deliberating what I could order next, how to nurture this new side of my personality. I ordered black stockings – my legs elongated and shiny in the mirror – and then a skirt. After trying them on, still in the privacy of my bedroom, I grew more and more curious about the sensations. But it was the idea of playing with others and meeting other fetishists that convinced me to order a catsuit. I loved listening to other people describing the sensation of full-coverage rubber, and curiosity took over. It was less about trying on the seductive feminine persona than about trying something entirely different – and sharing that intoxicating first time with someone else.

The first time I put on a catsuit, I was in a hotel room with diagonally slanted windows covered by white, semi-sheer curtains. The decor was neutral and inoffensive. Within the twenty-five square metres, we went slowly: two latex-clad cyborgian beings moving around one another in a careful choreography. I placed my spiked heel on his chest. He traced his tongue over my thigh. I stroke the back of his neck with gloved fingers. We have learnt this pleasure out of curiosity: searching out pornographic visuals to transmute into tactile experience. A closed circuit of erotics and memory. I thought of all the blood and electricity running through his body under the latex. I felt like I could reach out and touch something buried and viscerally honest – something beneath his conscious self.

Wearing a latex catsuit unlocks a new kind of sensory perception. Compressed by the pressure of its rubber shell, I travel to the most remote corners of my skin. I become a thick pulsing vortex. Time slows down, and I feel strangely peaceful. The sleek, smooth exterior clings close to my body, closer than any clothing or anybody ever has. I think of how we all chase this closeness. The catsuit draws the boundaries, and inside: so much electricity, oxygen and sweat; my heartbeat pounding, laughter rising; a tingling pleasure; the hum of my blood as it rushes towards the unknown.

Some people are guided by sensory satisfaction: the distinct smell, the cool smooth touch; some by the submissive or dominant states it helps them achieve in a carefully calibrated power play. I've been hooked by the potential for endless transformation and emotional catharsis. Rubber allows one to channel a creature devoid of gender or social attributes – it's a sweet spot where you can escape being perceived as your day-to-day human self. It allows you to delve into anonymity, embody the void and empty the mind. Latex holds you with steady pressure. It makes you acutely aware of the body – but also helps you to transcend the restlessness and sadness which comes with having flesh, blood and skin. Sometimes, after the pressure is released and the catsuit is at your feet in a sweaty pile, it feels like grief: for all the sensations which one's body can mediate, for all the future places one won't be able to enter without the particular high the catsuit facilitates.

Latex is about the push and pull between isolation and protection: the same poles embedded in the experience of a global health crisis. When you're in latex, you're safe, as nothing can penetrate its membrane. When you're in latex, you're alone, as the sum total of your sensory experience is confined to your body. I love the paradox of my first forays into a latex fetish – to be observing fetishism in private rooms all over the world, yet still yearning to connect and to broadcast my desires and discoveries digitally. There is a continuous interplay of closeness and distance. There is also the tension between individual experience and collective identity – there is fluidity and freedom in what a latex fetish means and what it looks like, and you're free to stretch and mould your own identity accordingly. At the same time, connection and culture play a crucial part in this seemingly solitary endeavour, through fragile, temporary connections people build through shared admiration of the rubbery touch. Latex has a recognisable iconography, an endearing surface, yet it is the deeper, sensory experience which nourishes a fetishist's life.

ASMR, a 2021 artwork by London-based Singaporean artist Bart Seng Wen Long, documents latex fetishism against the invisible backdrop of COVID-19. We see an anonymous latex-clad figure kneeling by a bed in a hotel room, their face buried in the soft surface, their ears covered with large white wired headphones. The room is bathed in dim yellow light. By the bed, there is a large painting in a golden frame with a small, red bird-like outline floating in blackness.

'Isolation is definitely a big theme. A lot of rubber fetishism hinges on non-contact. You're seemingly naked, but you're not naked. Seemingly exposed, but completely protected,' says Bart as we talk over Zoom, the background of his bedroom blurred around him. 'Someone in rubber likes to be touched, but there's always a membrane between the two of you. I wanted to take that unique mindset and externalise it in this photograph.'

In *ASMR*, our gaze is positioned looking in from an entryway, a view snuck between the door and the doorjamb, one which fails to grasp the entirety of the scene. At the same time, looking at the image evokes an almost participatory physical reaction – we're the voyeur who completes the scene, the peeping Tom who comes upon something private.

Bart grew up in Singapore, a society he describes as rich, safe and self-sufficient – all of which he considers factors which pushed his artistic interest towards perversity. Having relocated to London in 2018, his practice is now an elaborate and at times uncanny universe populated by rubber gimps, flirty catboys, AI-generated mommy dommes and anonymous pleasure seekers. His artistic interests span fetish objects, otherness, trauma, intimacy, mythology, and internet subcultures.

ASMR, he remembers, was created in Singapore during the pandemic, in one of the business suites of a renowned five-star hotel – seriously discounted due to the lack of visitors. Its eerie atmosphere is reflected in the photograph, as are the powers at play in Singaporean society, even if the viewer isn't able to fully decode them. The headphones, the painting, the slippers, the piece of cloth the figure clings to: these objects create a contextual web of erotic possibilities. We don't know what's playing via the headphones; we can't penetrate the person's mind. But for Bart, this isn't the point: 'I don't even think of the person as a person,' he says. 'I think of it as an object, one object in a room full of other objects.' They have surrendered their humanity in exchange for an obscure, object-driven, private pleasure. But, in this pleasure, they mirror the viewer's own sense of isolation – a dance between the orgasmic and the claustrophobic, between one's individuality and autonomy, and a longing for blankness, for oblivion.

The image also speaks to a much broader perspective on latex. In collaboration with Kaisa Saarinen, an author and climate researcher,

Bart is now exploring the material in the context of Southeast Asia's colonial history and environmental future. The lone rubber figure resting on the bed in a five-star hotel might be a perfect symbol of desire in hyper-capitalist modernity precisely because the story of rubber is embedded in the history of how this modernity came to be. 'Rubber is the lifeblood of the industrial world. Without rubber, the industrial revolution would not be possible; modern life would not be possible altogether,' Bart says.

Across Southeast Asia, rubber plantations have been the site of oppression, resistance and retribution – and remain the reason for growing deforestation. Garments for latex fetishists make up a tiny fraction of the rubber industry – most of the material goes towards tyres, mechanical parts and hoses. Still, Bart and Kaisa are especially interested in incorporating perspectives of fetishists from the region itself and how they feel about being drawn to something which continues to reshape their communities.

Despite its high-tech connotations, latex is an organic material produced by rubber plants which has been in use for centuries. It dates back to Mesoamerica in 1600 BCE and to the ancient Maya, Aztec and Olmec cultures: the Mesoamericans used the material to make sandals and rubber bands, as well as balls for ceremonial games. Its use then spread across the globe through colonialism. At the beginning of the nineteenth century, manufacturers then started experimenting with natural rubber as a waterproof solution to treat shoes and garments and to make gloves.

In a fetish context, the terms 'latex' and 'rubber' are often used interchangeably. Rubber is more frequently associated with the masculine gay scene, or in relation to heavy bondage, while latex has a more feminine or gender-expansive connotation. When it comes to the formal definition of the actual material, natural latex is a milky white substance which oozes from rubber trees and is then processed to become rubber. So, technically, it would be more accurate to speak of a rubber fetish, yet latex has stuck – perhaps for the viscosity of the word itself, with a big sexy 'X' at the end, to easily differentiate it from sturdy rubber boots.

Synthetic rubber, invented in 1909, comes from synthetic latex, which is derived from industrialised petrochemicals. Today, most practical, heavy-duty rubber products, like car tyres, are manufactured from a combination of natural and synthetic rubbers. And the material is inescapable – ubiquitous in our daily lives in all its many forms, as protective latex gloves, condoms, balloons, adhesives and paints, rubber pipes and fibre-optic cables, washing machine door seals, roofing membranes, wellington boots and waterproof coats. Rubber is a material born in the crucible of colonialism and global industrialisation. Rubber is quotidian and invisible. That is, until it becomes transformed under the touch and gaze of a fetishist.

With its high shine, latex is a visual shortcut for futurity. But, the organic origins of the material remain meaningful in the fetish context. Radical Rubber, one of the leading suppliers of latex sheets, emphasises that they are made from pure natural latex, free from silicone and other additives. Manufactured in Malaysia, these sheets are turned into garments by Libidex and other latex designers. The quality of the latex helps ensure that it's safe to wear, but it also means it's more perishable than other wearable materials. You won't find catsuits in fetish archives because they disintegrate much faster than leather, plastic or acrylic. For those investing hundreds or even thousands of pounds in custom rubber outfits which bring them the most exquisite, liberating pleasure, it is sad – but also, somehow, poetic. The material, much like the pleasure it enables, is ephemeral and precarious.

The emergence of rubber fetish was closely linked to the invention of the mackintosh raincoat, patented in 1823 by Scottish engineer Charles Macintosh. The mackintosh was crafted from cloth sandwiched between two layers of liquid latex, which were then glued together to ensure it was completely watertight. Mackintoshes quickly became part of the social fabric: they were adopted as the British Army coat for both world wars as well as used as overcoats by British Rail staff and the Metropolitan Police. By the 1920s, the coats had improved in quality and become widely available, and a new kind of rubber lover emerged.

The early rubber fetishist was inspired by the erotic thrill of donning the mackintosh – what, in fetish slang, was known as 'macking'. The burgeoning community mostly connected through the printed word, and not always in specialised fetish publications. Letters from and about mackintosh enthusiasts appeared in *London Life* in the 1920s, with thorough descriptions of pretty benign joys, such as parading rainwear at home. The Mackintosh Society was founded by Leon Chead in 1967 and became one of the world's first fetish organisations. It started with small gatherings of mackintosh lovers, who would come together in glamorous locations in West London, such as the Royal Lancaster and Hyde Park Hotel, to socialise, dine and watch fashion shows put on by various rainwear manufacturers. The society soon launched a newsletter for members – this was text only at first; photographs were introduced in 1975. Archival issues show that early rubber erotica was hardly erotic by today's standards: it mostly depicted women in raincoats or rubber capes, either in nature or in domestic settings, usually posing demurely, or at times flashing their legs in stockings, elegant heels or wellies. In some erotic stories, the weather itself is described with tender sensuality, enhancing the love for rainwear. However innocent the obsession though, soon enough rubberists were forced underground, with rainwear-related hobbies increasingly seen as pathologically perverse.

Enter: John Sutcliffe. In the 1977 documentary *Dressing for Pleasure*, the godfather of contemporary rubber culture reclines on a comfy armchair with a brownish flower pattern. A twin chair is in the shot, as well as an elegant table lamp. Sutcliffe looks like your usual bespectacled middle-aged man of the era, apart from the fact that he is dressed head to toe in a black shiny vinyl suit. Cigarette in hand, he talks about the sensations of different materials and the practicality of wearing a rubber suit under one's usual attire, while also musing on the fun one could have with various restricting designs – from padlocked rubber helmets to ankle and wrist straps – as well as the essential inbuilt crotch zip.

Sutcliffe trained as an aircraft engineer and served in the RAF, before setting up a company called Atomage in Hampstead in 1957 to make rubber and leather motorcycle gear. Legend has it he was courting a lady on his motorbike and decided to make her a custom waterproof – thus, Atomage was born as 'a manufacturer of weatherproofs for lady pillion riders'. Leather was a starting point, as it was easier to work with than rubber by using established manufacturing techniques. Sutcliffe's early designs were practical – for riding rather than bedroom play – but his passion for the materials was erotic and had already cost him his marriage and earned him a mental illness diagnosis. His early designs were undeniably visionary for the era – unlike the sturdy, thick masculine leathers, his silhouettes were feminine, emphasising the figure. Private orders started coming in – his operation was small, but he soon began to enjoy a bit of fame in London. He went on to design the leather catsuit worn by Marianne Faithfull in the 1968 film *The Girl on a Motorcycle*.

Constantly elevating his techniques, Sutcliffe spent the three subsequent decades designing clothes for leather, rubber and PVC fetishists, with an emphasis on catsuits, cloaks and gas masks. In 1972, with his friend Robert Henley, he published the first edition of *Atomage* magazine, which featured photographs of his latest designs and writing on leather and rubber. It was only available via mail order from the company, and the circulation was limited. Published from 1972 to 1980, the publication remains one of the most fascinating documentations of the fetish community.

Atomage started as an A5 pocket-sized edition which only featured one colour image on the cover and was mostly filled with erotic writing. But it soon grew to incorporate readers' letters and amateur photographs by rubber lovers from across the UK, alongside visionary editorials by Sutcliffe himself. Flick through a couple of issues, and you're immersed in a secluded world which existed in parallel to the conventional image of 1970s Britain. We see a woman lounging in a William Morris upholstered chair in a latex catsuit and spiked heels, a rubbered-up couple posing in their manicured garden, a figure in strict bondage by a cosy fireplace. In the analogue photographs of the time, latex hadn't yet acquired the sharp sterile shine of today, which somehow only intensifies the dissonance between homely interiors and hardcore fetish. The domesticity adds to the shock factor, even to the eyes of a seasoned kinkster: so, this is how it used to be? People would just hang out at home in gas masks?

The particularity of *Atomage* fetish imagery was perfectly summed up by American BDSM writer Patrick Califia. At the time, Califia was at the heart of the San Francisco leather underground and was clearly perplexed by fetish culture across the pond. 'The English are especially good at rationalising sexual deviation as if it were a logical extension of everyday life,' he wrote. 'I saw this tendency personified in an issue of the English fetish magazine *Atomage*. It featured a rare photo essay about a "happy couple" dressing up for an outing. Although they were posed so their faces didn't show, they seemed like a typical, rather pudgy pair of people getting dressed in a middle-class bedroom.' After putting on three layers of rubber clothing and heavy-duty waders, the well-protected couple embark on a walk in the rain – wading being a common theme in 1970s and 1980s rubber erotica, as if fetish was merely an extension of Britons' love of the great outdoors and general ability to withstand the damp.

Latex fetishism has a considerably different political history to leather, which was first and foremost the abode of LGBTQI+ leatherfolk – the fabric a gravitational point for pervy, loud, anti-assimilationist queers, daddies and dykes. A large number of rubber lovers were, in fact, like that 'pudgy pair' in a middle-class bedroom, practising fetish as a private pleasure rather than a political act. But rubber was still an expression of outrageous sexual and social non-conformity – and so, slowly but surely, it also became part of the countercultural fabric.

In the mid-1970s, the notorious SEX boutique on Kings Road, run by Vivienne Westwood and Malcolm McLaren, stocked a range of rubber clothes, which were popular among the emerging punk scene. The punk legend Jordan Mooney, with her peroxide blond hair and stark black eyeshadow, worked at the store at the time, often donning rubber outfits. The store's interior was covered with a spongy material sourced from the Pentonville Rubber Company, and the walls displayed chains, whips, and anarchic and phallic graffiti. After its soft launch at the store, rubber then made its way into Vivienne Westwood's collections before crossing over into the fashion world at large. The material did not have the same appeal across the Atlantic, though: in a different essay, Califia remembers purchasing a rubber outfit and swiftly being compared to a car tyre by a fellow leatherdyke. The politics of the UK rubber community could also be fraught at the time, mirroring the misogyny and regressive views on gender which existed in the broader culture.

Despite the material catching on within countercultural spheres, engaging with your rubber fetish still was a choice which required courage and out-of-the-box thinking.

The social complexity of being a fetishist is a looming spectre in *Dressing for Pleasure*, the short documentary directed by John Samson, which is a fascinating snapshot of the subculture at the time. The film is full of filthy pride. We see a full-scale fashion show with gimps, dommes wielding whips, and self-proclaimed rubber lovers wearing floor-length latex gowns or tailored dresses in pale blue, white, yellow and lilac. The fashions are starkly different to the latex offerings of today: the catsuits are sturdier and armour-like; the rubber helmets look like the heads of alien bugs. The floor-length gowns hint at a completely different cultural consciousness: slightly reminiscent of ladies' loungewear from a 1950s catalogue, they're impossibly nostalgic and a little absurd. Watching in 2024, I try to imagine the sensation of cool rubber petticoat on skin – to feel my way into the ideas of beauty, desire and sexual agency from half a century ago.

In the film, an array of rubber makers and appreciators give their perspective on the social constraints which accompany having rubber as a job, hobby or passion. Jordan Mooney tells a story of being harassed so much by members of the righteous public on a train that the railway staff were forced to intervene to protect her. The film also captures the more internalised burden of judgement, too. Latex fetishists, according to Glen Walker, who ran Kastley Latex Fashions alongside Irma Walker, are often lone figures. He admits that when customers eventually get married, most of them give rubber up. 'For some reason or another,' he adds, 'I've found that quite a number of rubber lovers are rather lonely people.'

Even though Sutcliffe was at the heart of the burgeoning fetish scene, the loneliness, shame and judgement of being classed as 'deviant' hindered him. In the mid-1980s, Sutcliffe was prosecuted for obscenity by the police, and the back stock and printing plates of *Atomage* magazines were destroyed. The business and the creator himself never fully recovered. In 1987, Sutcliffe died working at his desk. His legacy has remained mostly in the shadows.

Isolation, once again: a blissful bodily state sought through zipping oneself into a latex catsuit, and something punitive, imposed for explicit connections with fetish culture, for having a radical sexual imagination.

In light of this history, latex has long been mined for its subversive connotations. The material often acts as a visual shortcut to saying: *This is not just sex; this is dark, perverse and uncanny.* In a twenty-five-minute-long surrealist film for British designer Richard Quinn's Fall 2021 collection, hooded, genderless ballerinas twirl at a fantastic ball, fully clad in black rubber under flowery 1950s-style dresses. The scene is complete with cavorting latex kittens and puppies. Latex here is a portal to another dimension: the key to transforming into a doll, an animal or an other-worldly creature. Similarly, in 2022 make-up artist Isamaya Ffrench launched her debut beauty line with an eerie kink-inspired video. In it, she crawls through a gritty industrial space in a latex catsuit custom-made by Japanese rubber couturier Atsuko Kudo, her face covered by a latex hood criss-crossed by zips, her mouth provocatively framed by the material.

But while the amplified shine of latex in retouched editorial photographs is endlessly appealing, something remains lost in translation between fetish culture and this popularised aesthetic. On YouTube, there is a video of Kim Kardashian trying to squeeze into an ochre latex outfit for Paris Fashion Week in 2020. We watch her huffing and puffing while pulling on the thin rubber with no talcum powder or dressing aid – to the absolute horror of any practising latex fetishist. (This repeats three years later, in confused reviews of Kim's SKIMS latex range, which appear impossibly tight to get on). For a fetishist, putting on latex is a completely different process – frustrating at times but possessing its own ritualistic power. Watching Kim Kardashian struggling with the material makes one wonder why anyone would put themselves through suffering without a clear intention. Wouldn't another material, one more accommodating, be a better choice for a casual wearer?

There is a fine line separating fetish clothes and fashion as the two become increasingly intertwined in pop culture. But a fetish garment is something which transforms the way you exist as a body: first and foremost, it is the source of an erotic experience. It is external to you until it blends with you in the moment you put it on – and then you become one, creating a new sexual identity. Wearable fetish items are practical: a source of tactile pleasure, a tool, a piece of equipment. A fetish garment is loaded with sexual and transformative potential. It exists on many temporal planes at once, ruled by erotic possibilities. And just as beauty is in the eye of the beholder, the fetish is, to a degree, in the mind of the wearer. After all, you need a fetishist for a fetish to exist. The same dress arguably could be a deeply desired fetish garment or little more than a mildly uncomfortable fashion statement, depending on who decides to put it on.

The line becomes even more blurred when designers making latex are themselves part of the fetish community and have a vast amount of knowledge about its visual codes as well as an understanding of the material itself. Knowing how latex behaves both in the workshop and in the fetish club is the key to creating truly novel designs, as opposed to replicating existing designs in a different material. For example, London-based Edward Crutchley enlisted emerging designer Oliver Haus to craft a gown from lace-like panels of laser-cut latex for his Autumn–Winter 2024 collection. Floor-length and figure-hugging, it moved like flower petals or shimmering butterflies and took thirty-three hours to assemble. For the same season, Olly Shinder showed a radically different take on rubber in his menswear: interspersed with shirts and garments inspired by performance wear, there were tight bodysuits accentuating exposed chests and heavy rubber chaps. Even in the fashion context, there is a sense of erotic blueprint in these creations – if not made for sex, they are made with sex in mind.

When latex fetishists shop, they are unlikely to turn to mainstream fashion labels but choose specialist manufacturers instead. Libidex, founded in London in 1989 by designers Helen Saffery and Simon Rose, is a go-to for reliable quality and variety: from simple dresses to heavy rubber body bags, straitjackets and bondage gear. There is a 1993 photograph taken by the late, famously subversive fashion photographer Bob Carlos Clarke in which actress Rachel Weisz wears a black Libidex catsuit, her body impeccably shiny as she gives a side eye to the camera. Libidex pioneered the catsuit design constructed from separate panels, which has been in circulation for decades. (When I decide to buy my first catsuit, this is what I go for: the black front-zip Libidex; a model called 'Matrix'.)

A far cry from the secrecy which surrounded Sutcliffe and Atomage, today's latex manufacturers – Skin Two, Westward Bound, Atsuko Kudo, Soho's gay sex shop Regulation's brand, House of Harlot and Berlin's BLACKSTYLE, to name a few – cater to a range of fetishists, producing everything from jockstraps to latex gowns. But the new generation of small latex designers stand out for their attempt to bridge the divide between kink and style without compromising on quality or authenticity. Soft Skin Latex, for example, draws inspiration from sixteenth- and seventeenth-century menswear, corsetry, queer culture and clowns. Manchester-based MMLatex makes contemporary minimal pieces with heavy buckles and recently introduced a laser-cut latex fishnet. LA's

Busted Brand gives latex a mischievous and bold e-girl or undercover A-lister vibe (and also produced the latex cowboy outfit Beyoncé wore on the cover of her *Cowboy Carter* album: a red, white and blue ensemble with jacket and chaps). London's Aimless Gallery is a not-for-profit brand, raising funds for trans youth, which will make you anything from bright blue and pink arse-less chaps or a T-shirt which reads DON'T BULLY ME I'LL CUM :(to their signature twirly skirt and puff sleeve bolero in translucent rubber, which was worn by Chappell Roan in June 2024. This new crop of designers create for fetishists who might want to wear their latex out of the shadows: at raves and house parties, and maybe even incorporated into their day-to-day outfits, paired with a dress or jeans and T-shirt.

In more practical terms, although latex shopping is as addictive as aspirational shopping of other kinds, the process is quite different. While general online retail is moving towards the immediacy of one-click purchasing and one-day delivery, latex takes much more time and patience. Any order is usually made upon request, and the waiting times vary between two and six weeks. There is a tension between wait and gratification, a prolonged process of anticipation. Similar to fashion, fetish garments and latex specifically are desired commodities, but for those who take the material seriously, the desire is built on intentionality and commitment, embracing the ritual and care as part of its pleasure.

Throughout its history, latex not only evolved technologically, but its meaning and status shifted numerous times: from a colonialist commodity to the latest technological discovery to a token of sexual perversity to – finally – just another material to experiment with, albeit infused with a darker subcultural history. The new generation of latex designers create relatively free from stigma, in the spirit of searching, experimental sensuality. But, with its winding journey through history and its unique (and mildly uncomfortable) physical properties, it will always be a fetish. Cultural interest comes and goes, but fetishists stay, devoted.

In a darkened theatre, layers of white latex are spread on the floor, linked to a network of transparent tubes, which are not visible to the audience. The air flows, and the construction rises slowly. Its imposing swirl is like a meringue the size of a house, or an elegant bouncy castle. The audience waits until, finally, a person at the centre of the sculpture is revealed. Swiss singer Nemo is zipped in, and it is revealed that the construction is a sprawling dress crafted from inflated white latex. As they sing, their voice reaching otherworldly highs, a voluminous arc slowly rises above their head, connecting their shoulders.

The monumental latex dress was created by the artist and designer Harri. Born in India, he graduated from the London College of Fashion with an MA in Menswear. His graduate collection, titled 'Let's Put Him in a Vase', quickly went viral due to the success of his inflatable latex trousers – striped and colourful, they looked clownish, absurd and oddly elegant. His obsession with manipulating the form came from his bodybuilding experience. He tried a few tools for crafting outfits of extreme proportions before eventually coming across a book on inflatable architecture, *Bubbletecture* by Sharon Francis. Latex was the perfect material for his experiments.

The enormous white dress was shown at London Fashion Week in summer 2024. It took 100 metres of latex to craft it. The material was provided by Supatex, and the process was especially meticulous to ensure it remained inflated: all the latex had to be cut by hand and cleaned thoroughly so each section could be hand-glued together and rolled securely. As ever, latex demands dedication. It took 300 hours and 300 seams to construct the monumental dress.

Latex is ever evolving, both as a physical material and as a catalyst for inspiring cultures and subcultures. The contemporary aesthetic of latex fetishism is very different from that of the *Atomage* era. Today's fetishists and latex appreciators come from many different communities: from pro-dommes and sex workers to gamers, cosplayers, actors and influencers. There are latex photographers, latex celebrities and numerous fandoms. The technology of image production and consumption has had a direct impact on this world: digital photography, post-production and short video reels have created an aesthetic of seductive hyperreal shine. The shine is so beautifully amped up that it reflects everything: the camera, your gaze, the room, the whole world. Harri's inflatable trousers are available on his website and from a range of high fashion retailers. One pair looks like an elegant double-handled vase in shiny black, another like two bulky chunks of sculptured mint candy. There is something completely absurd about imagining these garments in daily life. Harri's poetic, humongous white dress was equally impractical – a visionary creation, expanding the boundaries of the material. But it was an item which was seeking to do what latex has always done – push the boundaries of the body and imagination.

THE DOMINATRIX

The contemporary idea of the dominatrix has strong visual codes. She's all jet-black hair and thick eyeliner, dressed head to toe in shiny vinyl or leather, paired with sharp stiletto heels. She stands tall, her slender legs wider than her hips. There is a sturdiness to her figure which is so different to the softness we associate with femininity. When she reclines, there is a relaxed playfulness: all elongated curves; pleased with herself, she doesn't quite care what (or who) is underneath her. Maybe she smiles a little, briefly, because she is entertained. She might lean back in a chair, like a director in a boardroom, her legs wide, unapologetically occupying space. The way she situates herself in space is a direct translation of her politics and her allure.

But depictions of a dominant female archetype long pre-date these stereotypes. In a popular medieval artistic trope, Phyllis, a beautiful young woman, is depicted riding the great Greek philosopher Aristotle like a pony. In numerous sculptures, paintings, tapestries and carved figurines, Phyllis sits on the bridled philosopher's back: sometimes she is clothed, sometimes not, sometimes she wields a whip, but she always appears very contented. The fictional story, dating back to the thirteenth century, belongs to the popular medieval and Renaissance narrative of fatal seduction: a prototype of the femme fatale who overpowers male intellect, virtue and self-control. The most striking visual representation of this trope can be seen in the huge number of paintings in the canon of beautiful women holding severed heads: Judith and the head of Holofernes, or Salome and the head of John the Baptist. Holding their gory offerings with much irreverence, they look self-possessed, sensual, proud, unconcerned. At the time, these images were a gateway into exploring power in the hands of women, as well as their sexual agency.

The emergence of the contemporary dominatrix, however, is linked to the history of sex work. Women who provided punishment for pay were known as 'governesses' and 'disciplinarians', delivering erotic flagellation to their clients as early as the sixteenth century. By the mid-nineteenth century, these practices had become more widespread in British society, with numerous 'houses of discipline' existing in London, catering to the aristocracy. It's around this time that the dominatrix acquires her fetishistic attributes. Take *Venus in Furs*, for instance. The 1870 novella by Leopold von Sacher-Masoch features a dominant character, Wanda von Dunajew, who appears dressed in furs, carrying a whip. The book's narrator, Severin, begs to become her slave, and Wanda becomes more and more excited about treating him in increasingly degrading ways, before abandoning him completely for a 'more masculine' suitor. Wanda is still fantasy (albeit partly based on the author's actual relationship with Fanny Pistor), but more tangible than the allegories of the ancient world.

The word 'dominatrix' entered common usage as late as the 1970s, on the back of pulp paperbacks, especially the 1968 Myron Kosloff title *Dominatrix* with art by Eric Stanton. Stanton, the American cartoonist, had a big influence on the dominatrix image, having produced a large volume of work between 1950s and 1970s which explored bondage, humiliation and gender play. His ladies often had a mid-century hourglass figure, their perfect faces reminiscent of Roy Lichtenstein pop art darlings as well as superheroines from comics. He even created a parody of *Wonder Woman*, called *Blunder Broad*, in which an inept superheroine is tortured by various super-villainesses. Around the same time, in Japan, Namio Harukawa was creating erotic artworks featuring large and voluptuous women dominating and humiliating smaller men, crushing and smothering them with their enormous buttocks and using them as human furniture. While gender roles were in flux and the global feminist movement on the rise, these fantasies of female supremacy inadvertently tapped into anxieties surrounding these shifts.

These same concerns ran until the turn of the twenty-first century, and are arguably still at play today. Hollywood films have often cast dominatrix-coded characters as anti-heroes: from the whip-wielding, PVC-clad Catwoman in *Batman Returns* to assassin Xenia Onatopp, who crushes enemies with her thighs in James Bond's *GoldenEye*. These depictions have firmly established the dominatrix as a stereotype: with a sly smile and dark personal history, she is elegant and seductive, she inflicts pain and humiliates, she is ruthless, and she more than likely hates men.

The dominatrix is always present but never in direct sight. She navigates grey areas, speaks of uncomfortable desires and unearths shadow selves. She hints at much which is feared by society: motherly rejection, sexual humiliation, a woman's mocking laugh. As a result, she's often held at arm's length, assigned a place in low culture and known only via a handful of reductive signifiers: thigh-high PVC boots, a corset, red lips, a tight leather catsuit, a skinny whip. She's on a phone booth sticker you see out of the corner of your eye – always in the field of vision, even if ignored. She promises the touch of the divine, the carnal and the underworld, a pleasure beyond acceptable social frameworks and gender hierarchies. Her image is desirable – and fetishised – but it conceals a presence which is feared.

The trouble with archetypes is that they are just that. They are symbols, shortcuts, unable to capture the complexity of an erotic exchange. However, to some degree the dominatrix *is* the archetype. There is a duality to her: both a well-known idea and a human experience; a fantasy and a lived reality; a performance and an authentic way of being. And to further complicate matters, those opposites are not neatly divided. They are easily confused, they merge along the edges and often inform one another. This is perhaps the ultimate power of the dominatrix: she is in control of the boundary between fantasy and reality.

The dominatrix offers a subversion of traditional social hierarchy – she is a fantasy, but also a trespasser of the gender boundaries, wandering beyond the woman's prescribed place in sexual expression. The fact that the dominatrix has a clear, intimidating iconography helps to isolate the notion of erotic power in women's hands – and to keep it within the boundaries of performance enabled by leather and whips. Within the patriarchal logic, women do not find pleasure in taking control, unless for a perverted motivation.

But erotic power exchange exists covertly in our surroundings. The fantasies of it lurk in mundane settings: in private and public spaces, on wipe-clean gym machines, in offices, when cleaning the house. Stories of sex, gender and power don't always have to rely on the fetish trope. The character of Yasmin in the banking drama *Industry*, for instance, steps into her power in the formal clothes she wears on the trading floor. She simply stands a little taller while sensing a weakness to exploit. Or take Gerri in *Succession*, verbally humiliating Roman through a bathroom door, almost surprising herself that she's going for it. In both instances, there is already a complex entanglement of power relations between the people involved, but also a sense of intimacy achieved through venturing into the riskier side of sexuality. There is no bondage, no whips – only the more subtle expressions of power achieved through a particular tone of voice, a promise or denial. This power exchange is ubiquitous – and no less intoxicating than the one in the dungeon. In fact, the stakes are higher – in the dungeon, consent and boundaries are always negotiated, while in the day-to-day the boundaries can blur.

To some degree, I think I've always known I was into power play. In my early twenties, I came across some writing by sex columnist Karley Sciortino, in which she recounted working as an assistant to a dominatrix. Rather than stories of hands-on sessions, what truly captivated me was that while experimenting with different dynamics, Sciortino got herself a 'book bitch', a person who bought her books in exchange for being humiliated over email. It seemed so strange and so multilayered that this story lived in my head rent-free until I got into BDSM a decade later.

I also remember that when having sex, before coming out as queer, before ever being out about kink, I was transfixed most often by looking at my partners when they came. I enjoyed the complete unravelling; I enjoyed being in control of their pleasure. I gradually learnt that pleasure could take many forms: I met a person who loved nothing more than to do your shopping and then have the door smashed in his face. He didn't want sex – he just wanted to be denied and sent away with a 'no, thank you'. The power exchange is endlessly diverse, from an email chain to an unglamorous act of service, even before we get to the more classic view of domination.

I finally decided to try on the archetype one afternoon, and so I put on long black latex gloves, a black mesh dress and high heels. Wearing high heels in my bedroom in the middle of the day was strange. But the gloves helped me get into the headspace. When the gloves are on, there's no need to be squeamish about dribbling mouths or any other aspects of physical touch, there's no need to be wary of someone else's strange and unfamiliar desires. However, in hindsight, the gloves and heels were not only for feeling in control but a form of protection. It was a casual encounter, and I was hoping that they would pull the attention away from me, so that I could play my part without revealing too much of myself. It was a comfortable way to dom – much in the same way as how one feels more powerful being fully dressed while someone else is stripped naked.

I have always admired people who can get into the headspace without any of the gear, who are happy to dom in their sweatpants. But really, the clothes are a small part of the picture. I've seen this in action, watching my friends working in the dungeon. They are usually dressed in leather, thigh-high pleaser boots or lingerie. A flawless flick of eyeliner, red lips, a leather skirt and a silky black blouse – I crush on all of them so badly. But the thing which is most memorable: each of them has *the voice*. Everyone has a different one. It could be velvety soft and mocking, with a slight ring of laughter. It could be strict, authoritative and unapologetic. When they're talking to a client who's lying on the floor, the power play has nothing to do with their proximity to one another, it's all to do with their tone and tenor. At times, it hardly matters what is being said. *The voice* has an intangible quality, it transforms the space, welding together a sense of intensity and safety. Watching the scene play out, I get a momentary pang of how the submissive might feel. I dread the moment when the allotted time will inevitably end, and I have to traverse the boundary of fantasy and return to reality – alone.

The expansive room at the Museum of Contemporary Art of Rome (MACRO) glows blue, like an empty dance floor, or a large meat fridge. It has a calm, institutional, eerie feel to it. Three rows of blue lights are hung close enough to the floor to expose the imprints. Hands, bellies, butt cheeks. The prints are smudgy, oily, organic on the reflective black floor. *Faster Than an Erection*, an exhibition by Reba Maybury, British artist and dominatrix, opened at MACRO in 2021, the culmination of almost a decade of the artist's exploration of power, gender, politics and domination under the alias Mistress Rebecca.

The sterile room in no way resembles a dungeon, it is completely free from the visual signifiers of kink which usually go hand in hand with the experience: no human cages or spanking benches, no boudoir-style wallpaper. The lamps evoke an office, a detention room and, somehow, MTV's 1990s dating show *Room Raiders*, in which the contestants' bedding would be scanned with a UV light. The show offered a similar revelation of conspicuous stains – embarrassment, shame, exposing the unspeakable and an otherwise invisible sexual past. *Faster Than an Erection* was created in part by Maybury's local submissive following her directions. The prints hint at how their body might have been positioned: face down on the floor, sitting, crawling, on all fours. The scene is both mapped and obscured, existing in a semi-opaque state in the viewer's imagination.

Maybury is less interested in the aesthetic of power exchange, which is expected to always be seductive and glamorous, and much more in how domination clashes with the existing social hierarchies. She has described herself as a political dominatrix, exploring how dominance and submission can at times be in dissonance with the participants' values and beliefs. Her book *Dining with Humpty Dumpty* chronicles the pro-domme narrator's relationship with a client who has a desire to be fed and fattened. Her encounters with the client kick off in an unglamorous American-style diner in a shopping centre in London's Islington. However, it slowly becomes apparent that his female supremacy fetish somehow goes hand in hand with his conservative values. In short, he lacks the desire to truly hand over control. Like many, he fetishises the idea of a 'strong woman' while holding on to outdated preconceptions of gender and refusing to acknowledge sex workers' rights.

In Mistress Rebecca's world, the paradoxes of being a dominatrix come to light. Men who yearn so hard to be shrunk, but can't help occupy space with an uninterrupted sense of entitlement. Men who yearn to fulfil every single desire of the dominatrix, but only as long as she performs a particular fantasy for them. Being a dominatrix only entails having momentary power over a man.

Maybury is clear about being a professional dominatrix who takes payment for her services, and her artistic practice unpacks the arising complexities of sex, power and labour. Historically, professional domination has occupied a precarious position in relation to broader sex work – with some arguing that if no nudity or penetration is involved, it can somehow acquire a higher, less marginalised status. For Maybury, however, professional domination is uncompromisingly sex work. As a political commentary on creating value, she has used her (consenting) submissives to produce parts of her artistic output for years, their drawings, writing and conversation becoming part of her books and installations. As a professional, she performs sexual labour, while her submissives produce art. Sex work is usually viewed with scorn and judgement, while art labour is perceived as refined – Maybury makes them converge and intertwine, demonstrating that both are, indeed, just work.

Introducing money into the power exchange transforms its meaning for many. We treat money as the ultimate source of power in society, and so we start to doubt who is in control. Though it is not the only instance when we exchange funds for care and intimacy, for a guilt-free space to examine ourselves. We pay our therapists and our physical trainers to a similar end – we pay for them to be in control, as they know what is best for us while, ultimately, we retain the power in the relationship, drawing our own boundaries. But adding sex into the equation muddies the waters.

The financial exchange is just the tip of the iceberg, however, when it comes to the power dynamic between a dominatrix and their client:

'A dominatrix's job is to understand the paradox of the dominant and submissive dynamic, which is that the bottom is often the one in control through their perceived vulnerability and it is the domme's job to tune into this and avoid allowing the submissive to feel like the boss at all costs,' Maybury writes in the publication which accompanied *Faster Than an Erection*. 'I must analyse their suffering, zoom into it, then play with it. The Dominatrix is considered radical because She weaponises empathy.' The artist has to work faster 'than the speed of their erection', where the intention is to control the other person's state of being and, as a result, reality itself. 'It is a practice which is both invigorating ... and pathetically hilarious in its predictability,' she writes.

The dominatrix is someone who is fetishised – for her long legs or perfect toes, her muscular arms, her eyes, her posture in sweatpants or elegant dress, her laughter, her strict voice, her hairy cunt, her manicured fingers holding a stack of cash – but also someone who is able to understand and command that fetishisation. Most importantly, she is the one who handles our ultimate fetish: power in the hands of those traditionally deprived of it by social order.

Once you've been looked up at from down below, it's hard to forget.

When I first got interested in BDSM, I was more into submission: the beautiful release of handing over control and finding ecstasy in pain and bondage. These experiences were equally exciting and affirming, and they inevitably fed my curiosity about what it might feel like to be on the other side. What would it feel like to wield this kind of control?

The first time I experienced it, the man who knelt at my feet looked like he'd been plucked from a religious painting: his eyes looked like those of a suffering saint: shame, frustration, devotion, ecstasy and an eagerness to be obliterated pulsing hot within the walls of my small bedroom, offsetting the dark, wet January afternoon. He looked so desperate for it. When I locked eyes with him, the erotic energy dragged us both into a parallel reality. It was a new kind of control – control as dominance, rather than the control as micromanagement which I felt I could usually access. I got high on this sense of being on top. I was in charge; he was open, horny, hopeless, spreading himself before me.

On some level, I was terrified. Not in the moment itself but in the hours and days leading up to the exchange. Being dominant was new to me, but there was a whole culture and language of femdom that was easily accessible online. I practised speaking in a slow, authoritative way. I tried to relax my body, so I could stand tall but not feel stiff. The more I practised, the more my excitement grew. Every time the soles of my high heels touched the ground, I knew the sound could echo through someone's body as an ache, a yearning, a need.

Learnt practices and behaviours are essential to BDSM and kink. There is nothing strange and inauthentic about learning skills, be it spanking or rope bondage, which by that point I had dutifully studied through online classes. But this was different. There was a degree of autoeroticism. In my mind, I was watching myself, anticipating a desiring gaze looking up at me from the floor. The behaviours and movements also illuminated a capacious lack which came with my gender. When was the last time I had stood this tall? Probably never. I couldn't remember ever having used this tone of voice: low, indifferent, with a stinging metallic edge of laughter. It promised not only a taste of the unfamiliar expression of power, but also fun, playfulness and freedom. And I absolutely, desperately, wanted to grow into this powerful new skin.

In the moment, I loved the intensity. I felt so present, standing tall against the gravity of someone else's want. I could tease, I could deny, I could end this at any moment. I could take away the pleasure. But I was also acutely aware that I'd become an object. I was a blank canvas on which he was projecting a fantasy: a dominant femme, a cold punisher, a steely seductress, everything that is described by the sticky, lewd-sounding word 'mistress'. I was being worshipped, and yet I was also wrestling to be seen; the subordinate's mind was clouded with fantasies of a perfect alpha female, leaving no space for me.

Being a domme, in that sense, can be both liberating and constricting. There is a lot of freedom to choose how you want to present and play. You can be tall, curvy, fat, hairy, gender-fluid, masculine, ultra-high-femme, tattooed, loud, quiet, rude, poised, shy – you can be present in pretty much any way and find your unique expression of power in it. There's no demand that you conform to feminine standards. But there is a flip side: knowing that any defining characteristics can be fetishised. You begin to ask yourself: does this person truly want me or just a particular type of mistress? In the world of professional domination, this creates a complicated conversation about difference, power and representation. Being a Black, trans or disabled dominatrix means claiming your difference as power and a source of income – but it also demands that you confront the prejudice and preconceptions of those who seek you out. And on a broader scale, anything – from your accent to body type to niche interest – can become a part of your marketable type.

'Fetish is an arena of the absurd because it is inherently about an infatuation with what is dead. When I am fetishized for My strength as a Woman, I must not allow the attraction of these men towards Me to be an attraction to someone without a heartbeat, but rather a desire rooted in action,' writes Reba Maybury. 'I am not an object, nor a plaything. My autonomy is palpable and much like an orgasm I am formlessly alive.'

Assuming a position of power is not straightforward. There is a lot to unpack in how and why it's handed over and what it means.

'A dominatrix is a full rainbow, but most people only see one colour, which is the fierce, menacing, vicious, dangerous leather- or vinyl-clad high-femme. I think there is a fixed archetype in most people's minds as to how she behaves, how she speaks, what she cares about . . . Or maybe they just have a fixed idea of what she does: she whips, chains and hurts you,' Domina Dia Dynasty tells me over a call from her flat in New York. 'It's a fascinating archetype because she's always very two-dimensional. Why does she do these things? There is not a lot of psychology behind it.'

Dynasty is a dominatrix with over fifteen years of experience and is well known in the international community. I first came across her work through *La Maison du Rouge*, a series of interviews and broadcasts which she ran on YouTube with her friend and dominatrix peer, Lucy Sweetkill. The series was named after their play space and platformed a wide variety of other pro-dommes speaking openly about their lives and work. Dynasty is also the owner of Femdom Farm, a lush thirty-two-hectare space in upstate New York dedicated to the exploration of nature, spirituality and kink.

Dynasty's career feels like an unlikely choice, given her upbringing. Hailing from deeply Christian Texas and being Chinese American, she had no access to any conversations about sex. Yet she says she always had a deep curiosity about it. At university, she studied photography and art, and later moved to New York. Upon arrival, she sat down and made a list of all the things she wanted from a future job: she wanted to make more money in less time; she wanted to wear costumes and sexy clothing, to be valued for her intelligence and skills. She then opened Craigslist. As a spiritual person, she thought of the website as a portal to manifesting the life she desired. In response, she found a listing: 'All-Asian Chinatown fetish play space will hire, no experience necessary, full wardrobe and paid training provided.' At that point, she was in her thirties and knew nothing about BDSM, kink or fetish, yet at the interview, she was hired on the spot. And so began her journey as a dominatrix.

Dynasty remembers that her first time experiencing 'top space' – the headspace one enters when assuming a dominant position in a BDSM scene – felt like being on drugs. She was instantly fascinated by the job. She was also mesmerised by the diversity and complexity of human sexualities. One day, a chef came in who wanted to be fisted, and he brought a tub of Crisco and yellow dishwasher gloves. She spent seven years at the dungeon and gradually discovered that the work was not only about catering to the needs of others, but also involved harnessing her own creativity: the ability to mix in her personal desires to access rich chemistry. 'I realised this is collaborative. This is a performance. This is a way of transforming somebody temporarily so that they get a break from having to be in control and having to be themselves, whoever they are out in the world,' she remembers. 'And the more I was realising these things, the more I skewed my interactions with people to be that little bit more real and caring. "I'm going provide a safe space for you to fall apart. And then maybe I will make you fall apart, but then I will put you back together again."'

While fostering her own style of domination, it took her a while to find an authentic way to express herself. 'I am an Asian woman, and Asian women are highly fetishised and objectified as

Lotus Princesses or whatever white guys like to call us. We are also an archetype in their minds, and they often equate us with sexual submissiveness, service, obedience and delicate beauty . . . I felt like neither: I wasn't a lotus flower, and I didn't fit the traditional dominatrix archetype because I was short and goofy. I tried to perform that every once in a while, and it just didn't really feel right.'

The more she worked, the more she started to realise that there weren't any rules about how to look and behave as a dominatrix. She started wearing softer clothing, lace, silky robes and extravagant dresses. Now in her late forties, she admits she doesn't want to wear heels anymore: 'I don't want to hurt myself trying to fulfil this idea of who I should be. I just want to be me.' Indeed, today, there's much greater diversity in what a dominatrix might look like. But she also points out that a person who appears to dress like a dominatrix might not be one at all. The definition is expanding, and people are becoming more playful with it. The aesthetic of power and control has shifted. It used to be leathers – now it could be a Von Dutch hoodie, a thong and a vape.

But while the look is malleable, the politics are steadfast. For Dynasty, it is an integral part of the job and the lifestyle. She feels strongly about maintaining solidarity with other sex workers, especially trans sex workers and people of colour in the profession, who are often subject to violence and abuse. She remembers the shootings at two spas and a massage parlour in Atlanta in 2021, in which six Asian women were killed. These acts of violence happen without consequence too often, and they run alongside more systemic pressures: banks who refuse their services to sex workers, and legislation like FOSTA-SESTA, a bill designed to limit sex trafficking but which has been punitive for sex workers, making it difficult to advertise online. In response, the dominatrix community has a very strong culture of mutual aid and care. Being a dominatrix in this volatile political climate is to defy expectations, to continuously redefine what power means.

'Sex work is inherently political because it's about power. We are straddling power and riding it around like a horse and telling it to kiss our feet because power has always belonged to the white man. The white man being the coloniser, the people who write the history, the people with the money. Most sex workers I know are women of colour, and we are taking a position of power within the service paradigm. The dominatrix in particular flips that power paradigm upside down, where you pay me to do work for me,' she smiles. 'How ridiculous: you pay me so that I can tell you to clean my house.'

When I find myself in the role of the dominatrix, I have the most intimate encounters with fetishism. Think of someone who is ecstatic to offer their services as a footstool while you're checking emails, willing for you to rest your feet on their back. Or someone with a fetish for heavy leather boots, who suddenly just lies there very quietly, giving them the gentlest of kisses. Or pressing a latex glove to someone's lips and seeing them completely transfixed. These experiences are special – they change you. There is an intimate sense of involvement which alters your erotic chemistry. It involves learning, exploring and feeling deeply. Despite that, a woman's role in fetish culture is rarely explored in depth and most frequently reduced to a conduit for the male gaze. A woman's foot in an elegant stiletto heel, a woman's body cinched into a corset, a woman's hand resplendent with a crimson manicure. You are allowed to be an object but not a subject.

In 1994, academics Lorraine Gamman and Merja Makinen published a book titled *Female Fetishism: A New Look*, in which they sought to readdress the twentieth-century Freudian interpretation of female sexuality, which they saw as passive, unimaginative and phallocentric. They were perplexed by the alleged rarity of fetishes in women, given that the actual historical clinical data suggested otherwise:

'Women made up a significant number of the case studies cited and yet the clinicians each claimed their own female patient was a "rarity". Why didn't they notice that female sexual fetishism, when conceptualised and analysed in the active sense, recurred again and again?' they ask.

Gamman and Makinen went through psychoanalytic literature from the early twentieth century, including the works of Havelock Ellis and Gaëtan Gatian de Clérambault and surveys from Gilbert Hamilton. They unearthed archival records of women with fetishes for silk, dolls, rubber, cars, jewellery and even books. The examples ranged from kleptomaniacs to a lady who masturbated with silk and another who liked to get off while holding a non-erotic book, as well as rubber and mackintosh fetishists. Yet the consensus at the time seemed to be that women lacked the imagination and intellectual ability to be true perverts.

There is an argument that women, as those who are themselves commonly fetishised, have a different, potentially deeper relationship with fetish. Gamman and Makinen point out that 'modern women often see themselves in fragments' – legs, eyes, lips, ultra-long varnished nails – which is in part a consequence of the prevalent objectification of women's appearance. (This doesn't even have to be overtly sexual in tone; take advertising, for instance – the eyes with perfect long lashes, the slender legs, the silky hair.) What is a woman if not the sum of her parts?

Stepping into the role of a dominatrix is to be hyper-aware of this fragmentation. It also has the potential to be a source of power we don't always possess in the day-to-day: to take the parts and make them into something we have agency over, to create ourselves, to be aware and in control of the desiring gaze, in a world which is going to fetishise us either way. And who said that auto-eroticism is not great fun in and of itself? Seeing yourself through the eyes of others is one thing, but seeing yourself embodying your own fantasy is quite another.

The best things about experimenting with erotic dominance are actually far beyond the look, the archetype, the fetish. You need these things to get there, but then they fall away. What stays is the deep sense of care and intimacy. You reach a greater level of emotional and physical intensity. You get to understand something vulnerable and rare about yourself and others – and walk away with a greater sense of empathy.

But the two things can be true at once – the artifice and the realness, the performance and finding greater authenticity through it.

I meet Mistress Eva Oh in her home. It's a beautiful clear afternoon, which fades more slowly than is customary for London in the winter. In the floor-to-ceiling windows, I can see a big, cream moon rising over the perfectly polished glass of the blocks of flats in close proximity to the City of London. Behind the glass, people go about their evenings, sit at their desks in an amber glow, prepare dinner, move from room to room – little figures with their private lives in a busy city.

The flat is warm, decorated in grey tones, with soft sheepskin rugs dotted here and there. Opposite the sofa, there is a framed portrait of Eva shot by LA-based photographer Alexandra Kacha: she is reclining by the side of the pool, dreamy azure water in contrast with the black shiny latex of her bodysuit. Her elegant heel rests on the head of a man submerged in the pool, anonymised by a latex hood. In one corner of the living room, there is a narrow cage, around six feet tall, in matt black metal. In the other, an imposing throne-like bondage chair. Both fit in with the minimalist grey (regular purpose) furniture. It might be intimidating for some, but for bondage enthusiasts, having something like this at home is aspirational.

Eva has been a dominatrix for over a decade. She first started working in a dungeon in Sydney in 2011, a decision spurred on by a joke from an ex-partner, who suggested that her personality might well be suited to this kind of work. She walked into the dungeon after quitting a job in a strategic consultancy and with very little prior knowledge about BDSM. At the start, she did session-based work: a person would come into the dungeon and request a session, and she would have a few minutes to plan an experience in her head before proceeding. This work allowed for a rapid refinement of a variety of skills, from wax play to flogging to water sports, as well as an understanding of the language and logistics involved in the profession. She knew from early on that her calling was the dungeon rather than the boardroom.

A few years down the line in her career, Eva started working independently and focused on building long-term relationships with a few high-net-worth clients. She also strategised, beginning to view her work as a business. She developed an online platform for submissives (youwillpleaseme.com), an OnlyFans page, a podcast (*#teakink with Eva Oh*) and consultancy calls with aspiring dommes. She starred in the 2023 erotic film *Grief Encounter*, which followed a woman who obsessively visited funerals to pick up men, seeking out the recently bereaved to feed on their raw, volatile emotions. In the film, the character described herself as 'an emotional extremist'. The script was inspired by interviews which Eva had conducted over two years.

Now based in London, Eva describes herself as a 'third-culture kid', having been born to a Malaysian family based in Australia. She also lived in Bali for a time and has travelled extensively, working in many countries. On social media, her lifestyle has an air of effortless glamour to it, with a slight edge – a softer, more sophisticated fetish aesthetic. She is also incredibly personable, often sharing details of her work and life in podcasts and videos. This has earned her a fanbase even outside the kink community. To spend a day with her, clients pay in the region of £10,000.

Eva admits that what she loves the most about the work is the ability to strip people of the artifice, of their own carefully constructed idea of themselves. It always starts with a series of conversations as she tries to gain a deeper understanding of their personality and what brought them to her. Underneath the layers, she finds a source of emotional intensity, which she's loved since her very first session. 'I like seeing them surprised,' she smiles. 'It looks different on each person, but they're just caught off guard. I like that. Because then they don't have space to pretend anymore, which I absolutely hate. I'm not very good at being around that, this facade that people create.' Though she admits that working with wealthy clients brings its own challenges on this front. 'The people who end up seeing me are mostly men, and a lot of the time very much invested in their own perspective as opposed to even beginning to understand how to look for a different one. I used to give that more space, I used to be more understanding . . . Of course, I'm still understanding of the fact that they have their experience, but a large majority don't actually have an interest in stepping outside of themselves.'

When I first met Eva a few years back, we connected over some writing I'd done and which I'd self-published, mostly for the BDSM community. I found myself incredibly nervous; it was like meeting a celebrity. I was struck by her generosity and candour. But there was something else which stayed with me: meeting Eva illuminated a radically different perspective on living an independent life as a woman. She was open about being a dominatrix, unapologetic about being out as a kinkster, a fetishist and a sex worker. She carried her desires – erotic or otherwise – proudly and joyfully. This way of being seemed very endearing even outside of the context of kink.

But while openness is Eva's preferred choice, there are external limitations placed on how authentic she can be. In today's online environment, anything remotely erotic or sexual puts one in a precarious position. Paradoxically, real people are often censored much more frequently than sexualised bots, and sex educators get deleted much faster than revenge porn. In sex work, people routinely lose a source of income through an Instagram deletion; some have even successfully taken Meta to small-claims court over it. With an audience of over 120,000, Eva admits that censorship has sadly been a determining factor of her narrative: 'I think about self-censorship all the time and what my career would look like without having to pander to social media. Because I can't even mention the word 'sex'. I can't even sit with my legs a bit open. I can't sit like that, I can't write this – you start to self-censor yourself, and my whole career is different because of it.'

The latest tension between sex work and tech is AI. An industry of AI companions is on the rise, with many companies, including Replika and Soulmate, offering companions capable of erotic role play. The likes of Foxy AI even allow users to chat with digital versions of real dommes. It's an area which Eva is trying to get ahead in: 'At this point in time, I can somewhat control the narrative,' she says. 'I can be the first to market myself as opposed to somebody else doing it . . . You put in a fair amount of information about how you want it to react, to behave, to come across. There's a lot of power in that directive. And I don't know if I've ever revealed those things about my process.'

The internet of tomorrow includes the terrifying possibility of one's likeness acquiring a life of its own. AI tools already allow us to generate images, video and audio of individuals which are almost indistinguishable from the source. Whether for identity theft, misogynistic online campaigns (such as the infamous sexually explicit AI-generated deepfake images of Taylor Swift which went viral on X) or personal gratification, there is no longer a guarantee that someone somewhere hasn't already created a simulacrum of you.

In this context, AI carries the risk of flattening the intricate power dynamics – not only between the dominatrix and her submissive, but between the dominatrix and her cultural perception. The dominatrix is a composite of symbols: the iconography of male desire, a symbol of the patriarchal worldview which can't fathom that a woman would ever truly revel in erotic power. In reality, however, the dominatrix reasserts control with creativity, wit, a skilful hand, her human touch, her empathy. At the hands of a pro-domme, AI will be a great tool to optimise and elevate their work. But in the hands of those who are interested in making a quick profit, the technology risks a loss of nuance and the dynamic reverting to stereotypes. After all, technology is always created by people and, as a result, often perpetuates existing biases and entrenches inequalities. But then, if there is more to the dominatrix than the visual attributes, the cookie-cutter fantasies and the high heels, is there really any need to worry?

When asked why the dominatrix remains a highly fetishised and much-disputed figure in society, Eva replies plainly, 'Because she's not given actual space to exist.' For her, the question is less about how tech might entrench or warp existing dynamics, and more about the wider politics. 'I wouldn't have a market if the patriarchy wasn't as strong as it is. The bigger question is: how do we make me irrelevant?'

The dominatrix emerges from a thorny history of gender inequality, from the social preconceptions of gender performance and the complex politics of sex work. Bearing the weight of this context, she is so much more than just a seductive image. To reduce her to the product of patriarchal fantasies would be too limiting. Instead, maybe we ought to take a more considered look at the reasons why we play with sex and power. Most often, it is not to replicate the social hierarchies which constrain us, but to loosen their grip, to imagine a world of different possibilities and different roles. When we ethically play with power, we can see beyond the stereotypes. The dominatrix engages in power play with honesty, commitment and empathy – perhaps this is what continues to make her truly intimidating.

THE GIMP

This chapter incorporates insights from real-life gimps: people who identify with the term and have generously and anonymously contributed their thoughts and recollections. I think of them as a Greek chorus of gimps: a collective speaking to a shared experience.

> *It's a special privilege to gimp, in that it's a temporary and secure exercise of one's right to anonymity, surrender and passivity.*
>
> GIMP 5

On the night of 4 February 2024, police forces stormed into Fabrika, a club in the city of Yekaterinburg, east of Russia's Ural Mountains. On that night, it was hosting an erotic party titled 'Blue Velvet', which the founder Stanislav Slovikovskiy had been running for ten years. In an interview with BBC News's Russian Service, Slovikovskiy remembers seeing around fifty people from various police departments and 'many masked civilians' entering the club. In the blurry photos from the raid, one can make out bulky silhouettes in the purple glow: policemen in heavy jackets, leather boots and, frequently, balaclavas. The masks not only obscured faces to protect identities, but also allowed the individuals to merge into a collective entity, an invasive and intimidating governmental force.

But on this occasion, the masked police forces were faced with a crowd of clubbers who were also wearing masks. For every event, Blue Velvet produced around 200 balaclavas for the guests to wear. 'The main idea of Blue Velvet is anonymity, and balaclavas are the main fetish of the party. It's not you who attends the event, but a character,' the founder commented.

Blue Velvet originally started out as a gathering based around screenings of erotic short films and gradually evolved to incorporate erotic performances. As the organiser insists, the party was never centred around sex, but rather creative and erotic experimentation: events were often themed, but welcomed leather, lace, latex, harnesses and other fetish clothing. It was intentionally difficult for those from outside the community to come across it: one needed an invitation which came directly from the party organisers. In an increasingly conservative Russia, Blue Velvet was a place for a diverse range of people to leave their day-to-day selves behind, alongside their names, jobs and inhibitions, and step into a space of erotic anonymity. On the evening of the raid, it quickly became clear that the right to be anonymous, faceless, is a prerogative of power: after shutting down the club night, the police forces collected personal information from those in attendance.

The raid on Blue Velvet was one of many which targeted sex-positive parties following Russian legislation which declared the 'LGBT movement' to be 'extremist' in November 2023. While fetish, kink and BDSM activities are not subject to the law, authorities see them as a potential 'cover-up' for LGBTQI+ gatherings. But more broadly, for the Russian establishment, queer and sex-positive parties are an easy target to seed moral panic, a frivolous symptom of societal failings which should be eradicated through preventative measures, of which obscurely motivated police raids are a popular go-to.

A crowd of masked policemen faced a crowd of masked club-goers. A faceless axis of power met the collective embodiment of sexual trespassing, bodily autonomy and anonymous pleasure-seeking, Sadly, in this case, obscuring one's face was not enough to provide protection against institutional scrutiny. Initially, there were no hard facts confirming that it was a queer and therefore outlawed space. The authorities carried a fear of 'no face, no case': without removing the masks, they had no individual to institutionalise – just a body, in a moment of pleasure, uncontrollable and fluid.

Gimping for me is the practice of enclosure, of letting go of myself, and of my day-to-day life, work and pressures. It is a freedom from life's challenges, going back to a simplistic state. There are lots of things I love, from the process of putting on my latex, the smell, the sensation of touching latex. For me, my biggest love is the ability to let go.

GIMP 2

I choose a quiet space. I pull the hood on in my bedroom and look in the mirror. At first, I laugh. It's out of surprise. I have never looked in the mirror and seen something else look back at me. It is not my face, which I have seen grow into its current shape over the years, so familiar that its subtle changes as I age go unnoticed day to day. It's a different me under the sleek surface of the mask. At first, I can't help thinking about a cartoon raccoon bandit in a little eye mask trying to conceal its identity, but the longer I look at myself, the more accustomed I get to it. I once read somewhere that we have a special facial expression reserved for looking at ourselves in the mirror, which means no one ever sees our face the same way we do. I wonder if this expression is still there, beneath the rubber. Or have the muscles which make me look like 'me' relaxed into something previously unknown?

Our relationships with our faces are, of course, deeply personal. But as we traverse the third decade of a highly digital twenty-first century, our faces have become increasingly laden with practical uses: I have my face scanned to unlock my iPhone and to log in to online banking; I have my face scanned a dozen times a day to use various apps; it's scanned when I enter or exit the country; I rely on it to get visas; it constantly appears on local CCTV.

I log in to a website which scrapes the internet for your likeness, going as far as deleted social media accounts and private photo galleries. I look through old selfies from Facebook, circa 2011, events I'd forgotten I'd attended; a few photos from fetish parties pulled from password-protected sites; street style photos in clothes I no longer own. Sprinkled in are a few photos of me in a wig from a now-defunct OnlyFans account. Both the OnlyFans account and the Twitter account associated with it have long been deleted, and at first glance the pictures don't look much like me – yet the algorithm picked them out due to the precise metric of my features. My face, just like everything about me, is data. Quantifiable, granular, precious. My face is a future deepfake. Maybe already an actual deepfake, catfishing someone for cash in a sweet AI-generated whisper. My likeness is a commodity, and I don't feel as in control of it as I should. I am worried, but there is also a degree of apathy: I want to stay connected, I want to reap the fruits of convenience, so over and over again I click 'consent' to my face and data being processed.

Anonymity is something most of us enjoy on a daily basis, without thinking much about how essential it is for co-existing with others. We have the ability to pass through spaces and other people's lives and remain unknown. In ordinary situations, revealing our identities requires consent – or at least, traditionally it did. With the leaps in both facial recognition technology and AI in recent years, the end of anonymity is not only the inevitable future, it is, in some situations, the present. The rising capabilities of AI open the door to easily matching one's face to one's name. A stranger is able to take a covert snap of you in a public place and use a website to match it to other photos of you. We're all just a few clicks away from having our anonymity removed like a thin veil.

In the twenty-first century, our erotic existence is also shaped by this hyper-visibility, as well as the digital nature of our communication. All kinds of sexual content are easily accessible online, allowing us access to a multiplicity of desires and identities while also threatening us with exposure under the all-seeing eye of the laptop camera. We dread our faces being connected to the desires we type into our browsers. We dread non-consensually becoming AI-generated porn stars. Where sex tapes were the lurid currency of media exposure in the twentieth century, deepfakes threaten to make everyone indecent and accessible.

In this context, pulling on a hood becomes a distinctly powerful, and disorienting, experience. When the hood is on, transgression happens; there are very few places in society where wearing a mask is acceptable. Hiding one's face is mostly perceived as a fringe or malicious practice (hence the continuous debate over religious dress codes), if not used in the tradition of carnival-style performance. Wearing a gimp mask is unsettling and electrifying, as you become someone (or something) who sees and feels but is completely disconnected from your previous social and digital history. You are strange, hollow – and free.

Each time I apply my hood, I have an enjoyable time, whether that time is spent being sexually deviant or washing dishes. Either way, I'm a happy boy.

GIMP 1

The Gimp

> *'Gimp' to me means someone who thrives in full rubberwear. It's a sense of community while remaining anonymous. For me, gimping is safe, as I am fully covered. For my identity, as a sub and as an ace lesbian, wearing full gimp means that no one can perceive me. I feel the best/safest/sexiest/queerest version of myself when I am covered fully. Gimping is also great for sensory deprivation (I'm AuDHD), and I like that it creates a barrier around skin-to-skin contact as well as a way to not mask as much (because I'm wearing a mask!). I know that in gimp, I can share as much or as little as I desire or want.*
>
> GIMP 6

A hood – a tight-fitting head covering with holes for the eyes and/or mouth – is a staple of the fetish culture, practical as much as symbolic. Hoods are commonly crafted from latex and leather, or almost any stretchy material, like elastic, lace, nylon, velvet and a nondescript black synthetic cloth used by mass online retailers and sex shops. In shape, they are similar to ski masks, or police and military head coverings, or a raver's colourful balaclava. Yet where these utilitarian garments tend to be baggy and one-size-fits-all, there is often a more acute design sensibility in the fetish items. Touch a latex hood, and it becomes apparent how complicated it is to craft an elegant, nicely fitted covering for one's face. A typical hood has an intricate design. The front is a heart-shaped panel with two almond-shaped cut-outs for the eyes and one for the mouth. This could be lip-shaped, to emphasise their plump contour, or small to modify the features and create a cartoonish bow mouth. Some hoods have no mouth hole at all, and some skip the eye openings – depending on which sense the wearer would rather forgo at that specific moment. There is a small, moulded hump with two holes for the nose. The sleek round shape, which covers the back of one's head, is crafted from three separate pieces of latex with discreet, barely traceable seams.

These elements are usually consistent across most designs of latex hoods, but their appearance and functionality have been tweaked, improved or elevated by numerous latex makers. The same goes for bondage leather hoods, which one can find in any well-equipped dungeon. Latex designer Gemma Pickerill explains that a hood is usually made from twenty separate pieces of material. Her creations, under the brand of Soft Skin Latex, often mimic the features of a clown: with a coquettish frill around the face, red lips and big contoured eyes with a harlequin tear. Designer Dayne Henderson, meanwhile, is well known for sculptural masks adorned with inflatable horns and spikes, which require pristine craftsmanship. The gimp mask, an item with a long-standing community practice, is constantly being reinvented.

When I put it on in the club, I'm struck by how much it alters my experience, aurally. The latex stretches tightly over my ears and it's immediately as though I'm underwater. Voices are muffled and the ambient club sounds – the reverberating, full-bodied beat, the hum of the crowd, the buzzing bar, the consumption of drinks, the fucking – are still there, but it feels like I'm using a different kind of hearing, one which registers through the vibration of my skin and the bone. It's not exactly like putting one's ear to a shell, but it's not far off. The tight layer of rubber is gently remoulding my features: my lips plump through the mouth hole; my eyes, separated from each other by black latex, are gleaming and water-like. With a sleek stroke of eyeliner, they could have been anyone's eyes.

I float in the ambient noise of the club. While my body is physically present, in close proximity to other bodies and their heat and movement, my head is elsewhere. It's like looking down at my own body in a video game. The connection between the cognitive input and the feeling is unstable – they converge and separate. And I am suddenly aware of my new status as a faceless entity.

The Gimp

I think immediately of the identifying features my body might possess: tattoos, a particular item I'm wearing. Erotic anonymity is enticing, especially when at the heart of a party crowd. Think of the sprawling orgy scene in *Eyes Wide Shut* or Shakespeare's identity mix-up in *A Midsummer Night's Dream*. Anonymity promises playfulness, transgression and the possibility to reimagine yourself. Nothing conceals one's identity quite like a hood – this is more than a subtle touch of a Venetian Carnival-style half-mask – the colour and texture of your hair are hidden, the blueprint of your face is altered, your age, and sometimes even your gender, is blurred. Moreover, a hood at a fetish party is a social contract. Even if you do recognise someone under the head covering, it is highly unlikely that you'd try to engage with them in a usual manner. They have established a boundary, a distance between you, through an anonymity which feels too delicate to disrupt. Put simply: there is no small talk with gimps.

For me, the term gimp represents a lifestyle and sexual choice to allow others the full range of control and custody over my entire being. Relinquishing my autonomy for the enjoyment of others. Being a gimp allows me to express my submissive nature. I like to have little to no decisions in my hands as a gimp. Not out of laziness, but out of a deep need to serve others.

GIMP 1

Strip everything away and let me do what you need me to do. Gimping gives me the ability to serve without any judgement in an age of looks. It allows me to be a tool and excel. I just perform the tasks asked of me.

GIMP 3

The word 'gimp' has long been separated from its original meaning. It was first used in the textile industry to describe a kind of reinforced trimming for dresses, curtains or furniture. Beginning in the 1920s, it then mutated into a derogatory term for a person 'who is perceived to be inept, deficient or peculiar', and frequently a disabled person. The route by which it traversed into the fetish culture is uncertain. The *Oxford English Dictionary* suggests that the etymology could be linked to the passive role assumed by a submissive partner in some contexts, or perhaps arising from the term being used as part of verbal humiliation. There are also theories suggesting that it was popularised by Tarantino's 1994 film *Pulp Fiction*, where it is used to denote a specific, otherwise unnamed, silent character wearing a bondage suit. Reclaimed slurs are often used to define one's sexuality and assert pride – queer, dyke and pervert are all timely examples – but 'gimp' is slightly different. As it's mostly used in the play context rather than as a political identity, it feels like the community absorbed the word and its offensive history without as much reflection. It's possible that the word hasn't been subject to enough criticism as it was assimilated into erotic play and grew to signify a person, typically a sexual submissive, who is dressed in a rubber or leather suit which covers the entire body, including the hands and head.

In April 2024, several UK tabloids published nearly identical articles proclaiming 'the worrying rise of gimp men'. It started in Somerset, where a figure in a black bodysuit and face covering had been regularly appearing after dark since 2016. 'As soon as I got over the first railway bridge, I noticed something on the ground which I thought was a badger,' an unnamed witness told *Somerset Live* in 2019: 'As I got closer I could see it wasn't, but in fact a man with a mask on, who was crawling and writhing on the ground.' In 2023, a local gardener was convicted of two offences under the Public Order Act of intentionally causing harassment, alarm or distress and was banned from wearing and possessing a gimp suit for five years, as well as 'crawling, wriggling or writhing on the ground' in it.

Other articles outlined similar incidents, with masked individuals appearing in various locations in England including Gloucester and Suffolk. The *Daily Mail* went as far as to create a UK map with boroughs in which there had been gimp sightings coloured in red, with small drawings of black masked figures on top. But there were two cases which differed slightly. One was the 'Gimp Man of Essex', which went viral during the COVID-19 pandemic when he went shopping at Tesco while dressed in full rubber gimp gear. In fact, he has been around since at least 2014, when he started donating £1 to the charity Colchester Mind each time someone took a photo next to him and uploaded it to his Facebook page, raising over £3,000 for charity. The second was a theatre-goer who wore a blue latex suit to a matinee performance of Shakespeare's *The Comedy of Errors* at The Globe in London. Despite complaints from other attendees, especially regarding the fact there were children in the theatre, The Globe stood by its decision to allow the patron to remain at the performance. 'As the outfit did not contain offensive or discriminatory slogans or wording, the decision was taken to permit the visitor to remain on site,' the theatre manager stated.

Terrifying innocent citizens by emerging from the foliage or wriggling on the ground is absolutely not OK. Anyone would be mortified by that, even if you are a regular at fetish clubs or a rubber lover yourself. The figure of the gimp, however, creates a moral dilemma. While engaging in the antisocial behaviour of ambushing and scaring bystanders is definitely wrong, is gimping more acceptable when performed calmly in broad daylight? Is going to the theatre or the shops in your rubber hood and catsuit simply exercising your personal freedoms? Where does freedom end and perversion begin, especially as those notions are so subjective?

Strictly speaking, not all of the gimps sighted and then documented on the *Daily Mail*'s map wore rubber outfits – the uniting factor was a mask used to ensure anonymity. Yet the figure of the shiny latex gimp lurking in the darkness behind peaceful suburban houses is distinct in the British collective imagination as a symbol of perversity and a hidden, sinister sexual agenda.

Against this backdrop of moral panic, it might seem unlikely to find anything relating to gimping at Tate Britain, one of the UK's leading art institutions. And yet there it was, at the 2024 *Women in Revolt!* exhibition dedicated to 'art, activism and the women's movement in the UK 1970–1990'. The rooms were packed tightly with artworks and archival materials documenting the women's liberation movement. A third of the way into the exhibition, however, there was a small cluster of framed photographs, five sleek black frames in total. A square Polaroid surrounded by the bright white of the mount: at first glance, the image appears almost completely black, but look closer, and it's a subtly shiny ink-black figure. The photograph was taken by artist Jill Westwood, who also created the rubber garment. She has been using liquid latex to make wearable art pieces since 1978 and became part of London's fetish scene after moving to the city in 1980 (with a couple of friends, with whom she also ran a boutique called Fetish or Death). Westwood was also a member of the industrial noise performance art group Fistfuck, which incorporated BDSM inspirations into its live shows. Her artworks using rubber are miles away from the tabloid images of gimping. They also differ substantially from contemporary latex imagery. The Polaroid, titled *Hermetic-Female*, is static and eerie, evoking the isolation and objectification which go hand in hand with femininity, while completely rejecting the sexualisation of the body.

Alpha-Female Triptych was hung below *Hermetic-Female*, three more photographs depicting a figure in a full rubber suit and a mask. The doll-like creature is relaxing and smoking a cigarette in a distinctly domestic setting: behind them is a small metal bed with white sheets, a sheer curtain and a white wall with an outsized shadow. At the time, Westwood lived with other artists, describing their lives as 'one big playground' of experimentation and exploration, which ranged between creative and sexual expression. The work is radical in and of itself, but especially so given the intimate, domestic setting: behind closed doors – in the 1980s and today, femininity is supposed to assume regulated, inoffensive, palatable roles. Instead, it stares back as an idle, pensive, self-possessed gimp.

These two examples – of the sinister suburban gimp men and the gimp as a feminist symbol in a major art gallery – expose perfectly how the figure can exist in many contexts at once. The gimp is real, but it is also a cultural container for fears and anxieties of all kinds. It has therefore been taken up by a range of countercultural contexts, which extend beyond the fetish world. Queer performance artist Leigh Bowery favoured face masks for many of his outrageous and camp characters. In fashion, Jean Paul Gautier, Vivienne Westwood, Olivier Theyskens, Richard Quinn and Maison Margiela played with full-face coverings – stretching, modifying and embellishing the gimp trope. But it was more recently that Demna Gvasalia's Balenciaga went full throttle on its uncanny and menacing yet seductive appeal.

For their spring 2023 season, Balenciaga staged its show on the trading floor of the New York Stock Exchange. In the dark glow of the monitors, all flickering with the logos of major global corporations, models emerged anonymised by latex suits and masks. It was a vision of sinister elegance – a black, immaculately tailored coat, a silky oversized neck bow, thin rim glasses – combined with a rubber mask and rubber-covered hands. The mouth of the rubber hood was almost absent, only a small dot of an opening, which gave the rubber faces an almost alien-like appearance. The collection zeroed in, however, on distinctly human perversions: capitalism, twisted corporate luxury, and the shark pool that is a modern office environment. The gimps wore suits and silk trench coats, bodycon gowns and reconstructed tuxedos, leather pencil skirts and rave-y Adidas sportswear. Held while a financial crisis drained individual and collective resources worldwide, the show was a metaphor for a strange, omnipresent power exchange, hijacking the system as much as bowing down to it. It reached beyond the desire of individuals and into the social circumstances which shape them. Culturally, the gimp becomes a tool to speak about all kinds of perversions – the private, the sexual and the public. Here, it speaks to those lurking in plain sight: the dehumanising force of capitalism. The gimp becomes a conduit for the darker side of the imagination, a shadow to project onto.

In French, there is no real translation for the word 'gimp', but I am one when I wear latex from head to toe. Latex is a kink and is a huge part of my identity. I love the shine, the smell, the look. When I wear my latex suit, I feel safe, I feel like being hugged, I feel fierce, self-assured, I feel cute and sexy. When I put on my hood and appreciate the tight and cold latex on my face, I am finally complete.

GIMP 4

But if the gimp's public persona is that of a perverse anti-hero, what is its erotic essence when out of the limelight? There's no doubt that among the old-school fetishists, the definition for gimping is strict: it involves full body coverage and an interest in heavy bondage. But in the contemporary fetish scene, I have heard this word thrown around freely, sometimes ironically and with a laugh. Gimp or gimping would sometimes refer to getting into full rubber, but could also simply mean wearing a latex hood to a party. While traditionally a gimp is supposed to be fully covered, restrained, stationary, it has since acquired a more active and playful role. But beyond the hood or full bodysuit, what defines a gimp? And how is the gimp different from any other anonymous player?

In many ways, gimping is a process, rather than a static identity. It is about letting go of one's humanity to achieve a different state, or even a kind of transcendence. Objectification is key – not only by others but of oneself. 'Being a gimp, at its core, is about separating oneself from humanity and individualism, about embracing being an object and a toy for your Dominant's use,' wrote user GimpSkinFag for the blog of the gay fetish dating app Recon. 'When I'm in "gimp mode" I want to be treated as an object, as a thing; just something to be used and stored away when not needed. Additionally, I want to leave all trappings of my own individuality and humanity behind; I even leave human pronouns behind, and when I'm permitted to speak, I refer to myself as "it" or "gimp".'

A gimp, the writer continues, spends the majority of its time waiting to be used, 'stored away' in a cage or a closet, or standing in the corner. The waiting, therefore, acquires meaning, gravity; it is much more than a passive state. Waiting not only enhances what follows, but it becomes a reward itself.

Artist Bart Seng Wen Long has long been exploring how mindfulness is linked to fetish practices. He is especially interested in self-fetishisation: what happens when people turn themselves into a fetish object and how they see themselves in this role. In his practice, the gimp emerges as a Zen-like figure, devoted to the dissolving of the self. He sees powerlessness as freedom.

'Our world hinges on power. On a personal level, you need so much power to control your life. You need to control what's going to happen in the next minute, the next interaction, the next meeting you have. And on a macro level, governments use their power to control the population. In a world like this, it's insane to imagine someone giving up their power,' Bart tells me. 'But I have a soft spot for things that lack power and capital. When someone gives it up, that's just very confusing. It's romantic. I'm very drawn to this kind of powerlessness.'

Gimps crop up in Bart's practice often and in a variety of guises and shapes: as a trickster in a digital landscape, as a figure assuming the pose of Rodin's thinker, as a refugee from the moon trapped in a latex vacuum bed. There is sensuality and vulnerability to these visuals, alongside the slightly unhinged, hysterical, oddly sexual and cartoonish quality of contemporary internet culture. For Bart, gimping becomes an escape hatch into transcendence, an act of rebellion and a quest for inner peace. A rubber suit is just a vehicle with which the very meaning of erotic gratification changes – it's not plainly sexual, but sensory, mindful, escapist, perhaps even political.

This blessed state of passivity is worlds away from the image of the gimp as a sinister figure appearing in the night, chasing gratification at the expense of others.

> *Owning a small range of latex accessories also makes it possible for me to be customised, like a real doll. Depending on how my partner wishes to play with me, they can choose between the black gimp, the bondage gimp, the full-enclosure gimp, the dildo gimp, and so on. I am always looking for new ways to express my gimp identity with new latex clothes and accessories, new circumstances, new games, new partners.*
>
> GIMP 4

Just before I meet Bloodshrimp for the first time, I suddenly realise that I have no idea what they look like. I only know them, like most people, through their anonymous online alias, which is always hooded.

I wait on an unusually quiet small street in central London, outside the place Bloodshrimp is staying while they shower and rinse their latex. They'd been at a shoot during the day, which had taken place at the top of a multistorey car park. I later see the images; they're posed in a shiny black catsuit, black rubber motorcycle jacket, black rubber boots and a hood, against the grain of tarmac, which is covered in black rubber tracks.

When they step outside, the only thing I vaguely recognise is the shape of their grey-blue eyes. Their energy is warm and generous. They radiate something which feels like possibility. Bloodshrimp has a relatively big following in the fetish community, most of it through Instagram: a digital tableau where they try on various guises, but most frequently sport a black latex catsuit and hood by the German brand Latex Nemesis (the almond eye-shape and buckles on the side of the head are distinct to the brand). Their whole world is built around a heavy rubber obsession. Sometimes they appear in all-red or in the big horned mask of a demon, sometimes they only wear rubber waders and a hood. They're framed against snowy landscapes mid-blizzard, crowded streets in Berlin, a corridor of raw concrete, a minimal bathroom. In one of the photos, taken by the artist nonothing, Bloodshrimp and a group of other rubber gimps arrange themselves by the altar of an incredibly ornate Catholic chapel – the image is so camp, so strange, so unique. In another, a black rubber figure emerges from a glowing blue swimming pool on a summer's day, and it's hard to think of anything so aesthetically misplaced. And it's this ability to shape-shift which pulls me irresistibly into the Bloodshrimp universe. The photos and videos are not just about the surface, the look, the gear, but a physical and mental performance which endlessly transgresses contexts, power dynamics and genders.

At first, the gimp alias was a way to evade identification for Bloodshrimp – mostly to anonymously post some photos on social media. Yet they soon got immersed into playing the role of the hooded figure, which acquired a personality of its own. 'The first time I looked at myself when I was in full gear (hood, gloves, catsuit, socks, boots), I felt like an object, in all the best ways,' they remember. 'When you can't recognise yourself, all of a sudden you feel free to do things you normally wouldn't do.'

A former competitive swimmer, Bloodshrimp enjoys both the physical performance when they're in character and the collaborative nature of working with different photographers. Through different outfits and different poses, immersed in different settings, they get to tell a story. In general, performance to them is something incredibly human – we perform at work, with our families, for our friends, in romantic settings – we perform the selves which are expected of us, even though quite often we're not entirely aware of it. Latex allows them to take that performance to a different, more experimental, level. They find playing with gender especially liberating while masked, altering the shape of their body to try out an androgynous way of being. 'People still message me asking whether I'm a man or a woman,' they laugh. 'I just try to joke about it.'

At some point in 2023, one of Bloodshrimp's photos went viral as a meme. Taken by nonothing, the photo depicted them wrapped in a heavy rubber bondage bag and seated on (or propped against) a yellow sofa in an excessive nineteenth-century-style domestic interior. The text on top, in a classic white meme font, read: 'I'm healing'. Clearly, the figure of a tightly packaged gimp resonated with the frustrations of the online audience. There was a promise of liberation in the anonymous confinement.

I remember that when we first met, they told me that Lab.oratory, Berlin's usually men-only gay fetish club, is open to everyone twice a year, and how they go wearing only a hood, a pair of boots and a belt. I felt, again, that electric sense of possibility, and the image has stuck with me since.

'Maybe the gimp is the expression of the shadow self, you know, as defined by Jung,' they say. 'An unconscious part of ourselves that wants to do things that our normal, standard persona wouldn't allow. I think everybody should explore that in a healthy, responsible way.'

Much more complex than the thrills of an anonymous lurker, gimping is the search for mindfulness and peace through the erotic, a quest for opacity in a society where nothing is hidden.

THE CHASER

A few years ago, I had a conversation with Vex Ashley, director and creator of the porn company Four Chambers, which sits at the intersection of adult video, art and experimental film-making. We sat down to talk about *Maman*, a two-part film exploring mommy kinks, lactation fetish and 'body parts and their symbolism and power'; as Vex put it: 'How a MILF is an object but a mommy is a subject, how a breast can feel more like a dick but also how a dick can be a proxy for the breast and what happens when it's Mommy's dick.' *Maman* was, in part, a biohacking experiment Vex conducted with her close friend Valerie as they artificially induced lactation over their mutual love of mothering in an erotic context. The film is tender and vulnerable: drops of breast milk on skin; a large sofa covered with latex, which is the shade of pink used in a 1970s Formica bathroom; tea dresses worn by Vex and Valerie which fit the motherly archetype; a voiceover musing on care, gender and the softer side of submission.

During our conversation, Vex said something about sex which has stayed with me: 'I think sometimes when we talk about sex positivity or normalising sex, there is this idea that we have to strip it of shame or any of the complexity,' she offered. 'Sex is one of the few places in adult life where there's still an element of play, getting to try on different identities and push boundaries. You're putting yourself in a position where you're being held by somebody, but looking into the darkest heart of things. I think to turn away from the difficult elements of sex is to strip it of some of its power.'

A porn performer as well as a director and producer, Vex often takes on taboo topics. She has made films about erotic humiliation, fetish for Christian iconography, voyeurism, glory holes, wrestling and all the bodily fluids you could possibly imagine. Her film *Blood Milk*, which explored blood play, can no longer be watched anywhere online because payment processors deem this kind of content not fit for distribution. Cutting and piercing to extract and revel in the warm red liquid is no doubt extreme and not for everyone, and yet, just like that, it is removed from the digital sphere, having passed the threshold of what is socially permissible.

I sincerely hope that you feel repulsed at least once or twice while reading this book. That you can tap into that deeply uncomfortable feeling – like being called 'Mommy' for the first time during sex. That you feel the electric current which rushes through your body over something shameful, potentially embarrassing, weird. It is a high, of a kind, to test these desires. But once the boundary is crossed, the sense of transgression usually subsides – the high is fleeting.

The barrier between desire and shame or revulsion is moveable, highly individual and an essential part of erotic discovery. When we are drawn to something which is deemed taboo, our first impulse is to turn away – but one could choose to stay with it, to interrogate it, to bring it into the light. If we push past the fear, it becomes clear that our boundaries are not set in stone. For some, playing with taboo becomes a process which helps them thrive: the path to self-discovery and self-love, getting over the internalised condemnation of others. By moving the boundary, they get to experience intensity, closeness and pleasure.

For others, however, shame comes like a roaring, crushing wave – deafening, terrifying, torturous. Our upbringing, cultures and families, our experiences and our bodies have different capacities for interrogating the edgelands of desire. You might get close and then turn away, and there should be no judgement of that. You might try something once and never revisit it – it might even feel anticlimactic. But whatever the outcome, there is no denying that taboos are a crucial part of our desires, especially as we venture into the sexual hinterlands.

My fetishism is set deep beneath my skin, determined by my personal history, the people I encounter and the world unfolding around me. I think my fetishistic drives rest as deep within me as my anxiety. I've had anxiety for as long as I can remember. It makes me sensitive to my surroundings – light, noise, voices – and occasionally rips through my insides like a blunt knife, leaving me dizzy and covered in the acrid, metallic sweat of a panic attack. One of the key techniques they teach in cognitive behavioural therapy to avoid being rendered completely helpless is to focus on the senses. It could be by touching something cold, or noticing something red, or remaining attentive to the faint scent of rain. For many years before I even knew what anxiety was, sexual experience had been my refuge, a place to retreat to when everywhere else felt hostile. Caress a leather jacket, slide your hand along a smooth latex surface, inhale the cavernous smell of a car park, glimpse the right pair of trainers on a hot stranger. Through this erotic anchoring, the world was suddenly less of an avalanche, and existence was a touch more desirable.

Sometimes I think that fetishism is a reaction to the anxiety of living in a capitalist world. There are so many objects to desire, so many things to want every day – as soon as you click to pay for one, there is something else, and then another, and then another. And it's infiltrated how we relate with one another, too: we view a gallery of faces on hook-up apps; the promise of momentary ecstasy or of a long, happy life together is also just a click away. It's overwhelming, exhausting. Perhaps to have a fetish is merely to have a focus, a way of calming the noise of the world by knowing exactly what kind of object does it for you.

My fetishism is so inescapably close to who I am, interlinked with my identity, hard to separate from my sense of self. And yet sometimes I have to peel it off and examine it under a light. We rarely do this unless we are hurt or lost or going through a period of change and introspection. We almost never think to question how certain desires have crept under our skin in the first place – be they symptoms of our erotic agency or our society's collective consciousness.

You might want to ask whether fetish can really be something we think of as 'good'. Whether, despite the stigma, it has the potential to enable a more vivid, fulfilled life. Whether perversion must be a negative by default. For most of this book, I look at fetish as a lens with which to look at the world: as an erotic possibility; as a sexual difference which has been, and continues to be, persecuted; as a pleasure which deserves wider acknowledgement and greater understanding. It doesn't have to be straightforwardly 'good' – it can also be disgusting and still be 'good'. It also doesn't have to be 'good' at all. I don't want to sanitise the dark, the weird and the unpleasant. To take away the complexity would be to take away our agency to interrogate boundaries and taboos. To write on fetish is to face the ugliness and the messiness in ourselves.

Sometimes we are attracted to something which people see as wrong and repulsive. Sometimes we see our own turn-ons as gross and inappropriate. There is also the terrifying possibility that we do not recognise that something is disgusting and wrong while desiring it. After all, engaging with something doesn't equate with knowing it. You might enjoy things and practices without giving them much thought. But fetishes and kinks, just like any expression of our sexuality, do not exist in a vacuum. As we reside within heavily guarded frameworks of identities, careers and social relations, unruly desires can swell like floods, crushing the boxes we place ourselves in. But sometimes it's the boxes, frameworks and social roles themselves which are eroticised. Sexuality, in a way, always exists within the parallel worlds of fantasy and reality. And while fantasy allows us to safely explore things which might be dark or dangerous or silly, it is never completely disconnected from our lived experiences. Fetish is never hermetically sealed in the realm of fantasy, but is informed by the complexity of our lives.

As a non-normative erotic practice, fetishism exposes the power of sexuality to both elevate and dehumanise, praise and degrade, connect with someone and erase them. Shadows pool around the boundaries of consent. Kink, BDSM and fetishistic practices rely on consent and communication between adults to negotiate and explore their desires. But the lines around consent can easily be blurred. The adults in question do not arrive at the scene as a clean slate, but are burdened with their own biases and preconceptions, entangled in pre-existing power relations – not of the BDSM kind, but those which already exist in society.

Through the prism of sexual desire, everything twists and distorts, such that sometimes in the eyes of another you are no longer a person but an object. And objects, as we know, cannot consent.

Linguistically, the word 'fetish' exists on somewhat neutral ground, but make it an action, and complications rush to the surface. To fetishise, as per the *Oxford English Dictionary*, is 'to have an excessive or irrational devotion to or admiration for a particular thing', or, according to the *Cambridge Dictionary*, 'to have a sexual interest . . . in a person as if they are an object'. Fetish usually rules our relationship with the inanimate – with things, commodities and cultural ideals. But it also extends to our ability to use the power of our minds to transform other people into these categories – to ultimately dehumanise them for our gratification.

Most of our visual and sexual culture is built upon the structure of a patriarchal power which prioritises white, Western, male heterosexual desire. By default, it is the central subject position and only true mode of desire, while all other kinds of people take on the role of objects of curiosity, arousal or adoration. And while objectification is a common tool used in capitalist seduction, and can be applied to straight white men – think Calvin Klein billboards featuring seductive bodies in branded underwear – 'otherness' often plays a key part in fetishisation. This otherness can take many forms – it could be defined by the concept of race or country of origin, transness, body shape or disability. But in all cases, it is an act of marginalisation: a point of difference which has been magnified and exoticised. As one joke goes: *Are you a straight white man, or a porn category?*

Fetishisation might sound like an act reserved for certain malicious, ill-willed people, but in truth, we all are capable of it. It often crops up in our day-to-day lives, especially in dating and relationships, even in those remote from kink. People often argue whether having a 'type' and having a fetish are significantly different, and whether having a preference for certain traits in a partner is ultimately wrong. In 2020, queer dating and hook-up app Grindr removed the 'ethnicity filter', which allowed people to seek out users solely based on their ethnicity. Other characteristics include age, height, weight and sexual desires, as well as queer-coded types like 'bear' or 'jock'. Examined against these other categories, however, ethnicity is more deeply entangled in histories of inequality and oppression. A number of LGBTQI+ people of colour pointed out that the filter helped them to find each other among the predominantly white users of the app; however, it also enabled a culture of racism. The fetishised category reigns supreme, while the categorised person is interchangeable, another face in the gallery of faces.

Addressing the interplay between race and desire is especially thorny – both within and outside the kink and fetish communities. And this complexity is not only theoretical but embodied. As a white person, I will never be able to fully comprehend how the history and reality of racism affect one's body. To be white is to be what is desirable, by default, in the dominant Western culture – to be white is, in most cases, to be seen not as white but simply as a person, to have the luxury of opacity and safety.

Race is one of the key lines of exotification, objectification and othering. Black people are routinely hypersexualised in culture and the media, and it is often hard to disentangle this tendency from the general fetishisation of Black culture. Jeremy O. Harris's *Slave Play* is one of the few works to have brought the conversation about racialised sexual desire into the mainstream. The play, which premiered in 2018 and was nominated for twelve Tony Awards, interrogates the issues of race, sex, power relations and trauma through the stories of three interracial couples undergoing 'antebellum sexual performance therapy' to resolve their relationship issues. As they engage in sexual role play based on the history of American slavery, the play deals with deep discomfort, shame, embarrassment, horror and arousal – both on stage and in the audience. It recognises how difficult it is to disentangle history from how we see others, especially those we love and desire.

'It's about the impossibility of loving blind of history and also about how to navigate the fact of power in the context of the stories that are written upon us because of things we cannot control,' Harris has said.

The title of the play is a reference to the BDSM practice of race play, in which the racial background of the participants is used to create a power dynamic. It commonly uses slurs, narratives and objects laden with racial history to create a fantasy the participants desire. Some fetish signifiers make an appearance in Harris's play – a long bullwhip hanging from the waist, the kissing of the heavy leather boot – and serve as a reminder that these artefacts, so common in the fetish scene, come loaded with a history which hits much closer to home for some than others. The objects, however, are not the crux of the tension; rather, Harris's play studies the intricacies of its protagonists' struggle to understand one another's drives and the complex racialised lenses they see each other through. It is the Black characters who long to experience racialised erotic play as part of their own private investigations into the entanglement of trauma and desire. Unmistakably, they have agency in their choice to take this path. Consent remains central to their play, though the way they are viewed by their white counterparts (and the audience) is beyond their control.

In this way, the play also pulls at the threads of desire which lie beyond our control. 'It is humbling to recognise that erotic desire visits us against our consent, indifferent to our politics, unconcerned with what's just or right – which is another way of saying that in the domain of the sexual, the gap between politically correct sex and what actually turns us on may be unbridgeable,' writes psychoanalyst Avgi Saketopoulou in the introduction to the play. The audience is invited both to recognise the complexity of our unruly drives and to consider the ethics of how we choose to play with others and how we see their differences and their histories.

Racial fetishisation can, of course, take other forms, too. The long history of orientalism, for example, means that Western perception of East and Southeast Asia is still ridden with inaccurate and problematic ideas and tropes, which are often made manifest in the politics of sex and gender. At the centre of Katherine Min's novel *The Fetishist* is Daniel, a white man with a fetish for Asian women. Through Alma, a Korean American cello prodigy, Min gives voice to a whole classification system for these 'rice kings', as Alma calls Daniel and his kind: the cultural ambassador (a connoisseur of all things Asian), the (pornography-motivated) carnal colonialist and the rational revolutionary (usually a person of colour whose modes of seduction were politically formulated). That Katherine Min is in a position to form a taxonomy of different modes of fetishising East and Southeast Asian people speaks to the ubiquity of these dynamics. These lines of desire go largely unchecked by white Westerners (Daniel, in the novel, is revealed to have never regarded his desires critically) and are built on years of racial stereotypes and caricatures perpetuated by Western media.

In her 2022 video piece *Narratives and Counter-Narratives*, artist and sex worker Chao-Ying Rao created a moving collage of sexualised Asian femme stereotypes from Hollywood films: it featured a medley of cyborgs, assassins and seductresses. A scene from Stanley Kubrick's 1987 Vietnam War epic *Full Metal Jacket* is part of the montage, depicting a sex worker on the streets of Saigon, offering her services in broken English. 'What struck me was how minor a role Papillon Soo played and how little screen time she took up. Less than three minutes, to be exact,' the artist writes. 'Three minutes of screen time that translated into lifetimes of racial mockery for Asian women living in the West. Three minutes of screen time regenerated via pop culture over and over again. "Me love you long time. Me so horny."'

Sex is full of grey areas, but it is important to recognise that exoticisation and racialised sexual stereotypes are a form of violence. And while our desires are complex, it is our responsibility to recognise when they have been nourished by patriarchy and racism.

There is a term, or even an archetype, which comes to mind when trying to interrogate this desire for otherness: *chaser*. A chaser, simply, is someone who pursues something, or someone, driven by an obsession. But it's used most often within the trans communities, specifically to describe a person who sexually and romantically seeks out trans people. The chaser lurks in the shadows at the far end of the bar at the queer club, or on the other side of a blank Grindr profile, primarily attracted to transness itself, as opposed to someone's personality. The chaser archetype is that of a creep, but in reality, there isn't a demeanour or appearance which would give them away. The chaser could be polite and respectful, but their perspective on those they desire is driven by the perceived otherness of transness, which is constantly magnified by the media.

Some suggest that the chaser is the inverse of the transphobe, 'and that in both cases they don't see us as people, as women, but firstly and above all as trans' – as the user suomikim phrased it on one of the trans threads on Reddit. To not date someone just because they're trans and to desire them just because they're trans are the two sides of the same coin. And this is not an abstract concept or a simple question of personal preference: this othering perspective sits at the crux of real-life violence.

The conversation around chasers, however, and whether being desired in a certain way feels, or is, wrong, is splintered both within and outside the community. 'There's a discussion of "chasers", where it's like, "I don't want anybody who wants my body because they're into trans women",' author Torrey Peters has said. 'To me, it's like, why would you do that? All I want is people who want my body. To pathologise people who want my body, to me, misses the mark. But at the same time, what I actually want is a basic level of social awareness and respect in how you find my body hot. It doesn't matter if you're trans or not, if some guy is after a woman and all they can talk about is one of her body parts, it's not respectful. It's not interesting.'

It gets even more complicated if we interrogate the attraction within the context of queer sexuality. To be queer means to search and to reimagine, to constantly strive for new modes of being together. Queer spaces are often driven by sexual communion yet divided along the lines of gender. As trans people become more culturally visible and create communities of their own, queer spaces also shift to accommodate this change. Yet people within the spaces might struggle to reimagine their desire, to choose whether to label or not to label their own attraction a certain way.

'The cis people I know whose lives are most entangled with the trans people they love are the ones most afraid to be accused of being chasers or fetishists,' writes interdisciplinary artist Zach Ozma. 'They worry they or their lover will be [infantilized] or medicalized ... No one wants to be told that their deep, satisfying love is based on objectification. No one wants to be an object all the time. They worry they will be accused of living in a world of fantasy (and in their moments away from the hateful public, are they not in a world of fantasy? Isn't any pair of lovers?).'

This doesn't mean that queer people can't be chasers or fetishists – but there is infinitely more complexity in relationships within the community. Ozma also interrogates another word often thrown around when people are drawn to difference: 'experimenting'. He untangles the complexity of these novel, potentially unfamiliar desires through the fluidity which is an essential part of queerness. It is a kind of re-evaluation of the word 'chaser', holding this term up to light to examine what it does. To 'experiment' doesn't denote

ASMR, Bart Seng Wen Long, 2021.

Simon with Chain,
photograph by Steven Harwick
for *Bound Leather* zine, 2024.

Sir Malice and Rahim,
photograph by Steven Harwick
for *Bound Leather* zine, 2020.

Portrait of Eva Oh, Lanee Bird, 2019.

Web, Maxime Ballesteros, 2022.

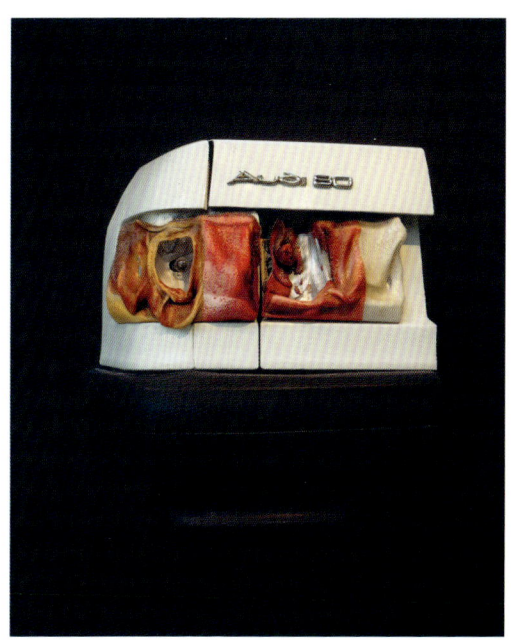

Fondue, sculpture and photograph by Ada Zielińska, 2019.

Klub Verboten, photograph by Heavy Consumption (Gold and Cummings), 2023.

Kim Rub's submissive, Heavy Consumption (Gold and Cummings), 2023.

Klub Verboten, photograph by Heavy Consumption (Gold and Cummings), 2023.

Klub Verboten, photograph by Heavy Consumption
(Gold and Cummings), 2023.

Portrait from the *Mask* series, Heavy Consumption (Gold and Cummings), 2023.

Portrait from the *Mask* series, Heavy Consumption (Gold and Cummings), 2023.

Bloodshrimp and Sweet Severine, Heavy Consumption (Gold and Cummings), 2022.

Pup on red 1, Matt Ford, 2022.

Still from *Surrender*, Jenkin van Zyl, 2022.

Knitted body bag, art and photograph by Lady Hinako, 2023.

the outsider status typically held by 'the chaser', who is an intruder or interloper. Rather, it speaks to the fluidity of our identities, that there is always more becoming to be done.

'In the summer of 2022 on grindr the ftms want to experiment with the cis men, and the cis men want to experiment with the ftms, and the baby ftms want to experiment with the actualized ftms, and some of the non-binaries want to experiment with the ftms because they might be ftms later, and some of the non-binaries want to experiment with the ftms for the usual reasons, and many of the mtfs want to experiment with having a deep and satisfying love with the ftms, and sometimes the people get what they want. On my knees in Fairmount Park there is no difference between me and any other type of man,' Ozma writes. Queer becoming often starts from that desire for difference, away from the heteronormative default. It can start before we come out, or even after – if our sense of self refuses to calcify. 'In experimenting we reach beyond what we are. The experiment reaches forward, seeks to know more, seeks a different condition and so creates it. Whether or not something is proven, we are changed in the act of experimenting. That's queer futurity baby.'

Not only does queer sex draw strength from a yearning for the new and the unknown, and perhaps feeling foreign or alien in that territory, but it's also ripe with symbols and its own material language. Take the staple of lesbian culture, the butch–femme duality: the work boots, white tank tops and biceps of the butch; the sharp long nails and red lipstick of the femme. The fetishised gendered language is taken apart and reframed – still a conduit for desire, but a consensual, collaborative one. In the queer bar, we playfully perform as hunks, himbos and femme fatales. Leaning in to the stereotypes you're often cast as in daily life can also be a source of pleasure, feel liberatory or simply feel hot.

This book interrogates the complicated relationship between people and objects – the fantasies and world-building these objects enable, the erotic dimensions they open, the intimacy and intensity they allow us to experience. But the duality of 'people' and 'objects' isn't actually clear-cut. It is seemingly simple to separate the inanimate from the human, and yet we often neglect or muddle these definitions. At times, it comes from a place of consent – like a gimp who finds happiness in being treated like a piece of furniture. But at times, we succumb to fetishisation and objectification without consent because it can be thrilling or arousing, because it gives us a sense of power, or simply because it is a habit enabled by social hierarchies.

The complexities we navigate when playing with objects and people are not solely about taboos. As Huw Lemmey has said: 'Who amongst us has not been thrilled even to orgasm by a thought or sensation that, in the cold light of day, or printed on paper, seems embarrassing, troubling, humiliating or, worst of all, *problematic?*' We do not get any further in our understanding of sexuality if we deny, ignore or refuse to address taboos.

It does, however, matter how we act on these desires when others are involved. The chaser, as an archetype, is a solitary creature, the fetishising gaze from the outside. But fetish and kink have existed for decades as community practices, where healthy boundaries and consent are prioritised – and where conversations about taboos and grey areas are encouraged. People still get it wrong or hurt others – that is part of human nature. But it is the striving for safety, risk awareness, care, kindness and respect which allows us to navigate the darkest and most intense edges of desire.

FEET

A stream of ruby-red liquid snakes from above, landing on the skin and running down the foot, covering the big toe with a liquid gloss, before dripping from the exquisitely manicured French-tip big toenail and into the crystal wine glass. The foot is pointed gracefully, framed against a pale pink backdrop. The red wine splashes over the silver tray and a silky pale pink tablecloth. Above the ankle, a small smiley face is tattooed: a little wink of joy.

The foot belongs to OnlyFans creator Emilie Rae, and it's positioned carefully next to a bottle of Simp Wine, a limited-edition Cabernet Sauvignon produced by Renegade Urban Winery. The winery is located in London's Walthamstow and makes twelve to fourteen wines a year. The grapes are sourced from Europe as well as England, and all the destemming, fermentation, ageing and bottling happen in London. The crushing is usually done by electrified presses, but for Simp Wine, it is performed by Rae's feet. What could be seen as a nod to traditional winemaking for some here becomes a perfectly hedonistic expression of foot fetish.

With curvy fuchsia-pink letters and a cartoonish drawing of a wine-stained foot on the label, Simp Wine retails for £100. In one photo on the wine's website, Rae is balancing a round silver tray with a bottle of wine and a glass on it on the heels of her feet. In a short video clip, her big toe elegantly squishes a single grape. In another, she has both feet fully immersed in bursting grapes – pale yellow and lustrous brown – as she bursts them, stalks and bits of jelly-like flesh sticking to her skin. The video is on a loop; she is endlessly stepping and crushing the fruit. Big pink letters float over the screen: 'Quench your thirst with the fruit of your desires.'

The word 'simp' is often used as a mildly derogatory term for someone who shows excessive attention towards another person with no reciprocation. It is commonly used in relation to the audience, or admirers, of online sex workers and models, but it can also refer to that one person who pops up in the comments of every thirst trap you post. Rae felt that it could be reframed as a playful identity for her fans. To make the consumption of wine more of an experience, on the website one can watch a POV video of her stomping grapes, captured by GoPros attached to her legs (the views from the right leg and the left leg are uploaded separately).

If a foot fetish involves the commodification of feet as an object of erotic obsession, Simp Wine exposes how foot fetish itself can be commodified as a marketing strategy. Authentic, playful and tongue-in-cheek, it reveals the precarious place this particular desire occupies within contemporary culture. Foot fetish is benign enough to be talked about openly, in non-kink settings, yet it's still perceived as an oddity, and sometimes even a joke. It therefore ends up in a no man's land: too niche for the vanilla world but not niche enough to be considered as taboo as other fetishes. Similarly to the word 'simp', it's non-threatening but still pretty weird.

However, a quick internet search is enough to reveal that foot fetishes are common. A 2018 study of 4,000 Americans conducted by social psychologist Dr Justin Lehmiller found that twenty-one per cent of gay/bisexual men had fantasised about feet. For heterosexual men, the number was similar: eighteen per cent. The figures for women were ten per cent for lesbian/bisexual women and five per cent for heterosexual women. (The researchers do point out, however, that the gender disparity could be partly due to socialisation and that men might be more outspoken about their fetishes). In the 2021 NowPatient survey of the most googled fetishes and kinks in the US, foot fetish landed in eleventh place. According to the data, Americans search for 'foot worship' 40,000 times per month on average.

A foot fetish is broadly defined as a sexual interest in feet. It could be sensory: licking, rubbing, kissing, sucking and massaging any part of the foot, or enjoying giving or receiving foot jobs. It might also be aesthetically driven: simply looking at feet, or being particularly interested in painted toenails and ankle bracelets. Under the BDSM umbrella, feet can be connected to power dynamics, becoming objects of worship for the submissive partner, or a tool for humiliation play, which might involve being stepped on or being told to clean a dirty pair of boots. It can be enjoyed in real life as well as online. In fact, there is no other fetish which exposes sexual diversity quite so well: the horizon is expansive. Any definition of 'foot fetish' quickly becomes elusive: it is futile to try to encompass all the different ways to erotically engage with feet.

There is no such thing as a singular fetishistic perspective when it comes to feet (or any other fetish, for that matter). Looking at feet in visual art, photography and popular culture can be an interesting exercise in gaining a deeper understanding of your own views and desires. No doubt, if you are a foot fetishist you are aware of this. But if you aren't, or aren't exactly sure, it's fun to second-guess the intention behind certain images. A fetishistic depiction radiates an indulgent, daring energy. The curve of a high arch in black stiletto heels. Muscular calves and pristine white Nike socks. Feet are so quotidian that eroticising them (at least for non-fetishists) takes a certain degree of embodied imagination, of expanding the meaning of what is beautiful.

In the cultural iconography of foot fetish, the name of Quentin Tarantino looms large – due to both the depiction of feet in his work and the sensationalised rumours about the director's sexuality. In a famous scene in *From Dusk till Dawn*, a 1996 classic horror directed by Robert Rodriguez, Salma Hayek performs an erotic dance wrapped in a live python – before putting her foot into the mouth of Quentin Tarantino (who co-wrote the film). Her move is forceful, as she proceeds to pour tequila down her leg and into his mouth, alcohol streaming down from her toes. However, as a rule, his fetishistic gaze is reasonably benign, with his films simply featuring prolonged shots of feet – resting on the car dash in both *Death Proof* and *Once Upon a Time in Hollywood*, for instance. They're there if you're looking, hiding in plain sight.

The work of American photographer Elmer Batters is more focused – created with fetishists in mind. After serving in the US Navy in the 1940s, he made artful images with an emphasis on stockings, legs and feet, which were collected in self-published magazines such as *Man's Favorite Pastime* and *Black Silk Stockings* in the 1950s and 1960s. The imagery, in black and white, or the soft hues of the 1950s, often focuses on the soles of the feet in the gentle fabric of sheer stockings. There are particular recurring poses which form a fetishistic visual language not known to the outsider: a particular angle the foot slides out from the high-heeled shoe, a particular way models show off their toes. There's no escaping the sensuality of these images; they still leave much to the imagination, but they're undeniably tactile, suggestive of foot worship. Batters was eventually arrested and dubbed 'dangerously perverse' by the American legal system, but nevertheless stuck to his passion. Towards the end of his life, the work gained critical acclaim beyond the fetish community, with an anthology published by Taschen.

At the other end of the spectrum to Tarantino's innocuous foot content is the fashion photographer Steve Klein. In 2017, he produced ten original works for *Visionaire* magazine, to be sold as its sixty-seventh issue. The issue is simply titled *FETISH*, and the photographs depict extreme scenes featuring ultra-high heels. In one, the heels are crafted from metal and photographed against the scratched hood of a car. In another, the heels are replaced with sharp knives, which mercilessly slice an apple. In the third, a heel is pressed to the chest of a forlorn-looking but muscular victim. The scratches, the cuts, the coldness and the tension channel an almost thriller-like suspense, arousal tinted with fear. It's brash and commanding, aware and unapologetic of the fetishistic gaze, revelling in emotional and sexual extremity.

Even a quick look through the work of these three artists shows how much fetishistic perspectives differ and the extent to which people seek different things in their aesthetic and erotic appreciation of feet.

Foot fetishes are now also largely shaped by online spaces and, to a degree, they mirror the general fragmentation of sexuality on the internet. Everything is out there, however niche, with its own communities and services for passionate appreciators. For example, Rate My Feet! is a Facebook group where people upload pictures to be evaluated by strangers, while wikiFeet is dedicated to the feet of celebrities and public figures. FeetFinder describes itself as the 'safest, easiest and most secure website' for users to view, buy and sell custom foot content. And since its inception in 2016, OnlyFans has also become a destination for custom foot content.

The burgeoning marketplace for those willing to sell or buy pictures of feet online looms large in the public imagination. For some, the idea of being caught up in someone's fetish without their consent or knowledge is rightfully terrifying, while others are potentially keen on the idea of financial gain. In the gig economy, why share something for free if you can charge? The mainstreaming of foot fetish content involves a shift in perspective in how one views one's own body parts: from seeing feet as something mundane and unremarkable to the laser-focused sexualised perspective of others – and especially anonymous others on the internet.

As a result, it's not surprising that Gen Z's controversial relationship with feet has been making headlines in the past couple of years. Zoomers, the headlines tell us, are not only hesitant to post photos of their feet online – they're allegedly hesitant to even bare their feet in public. On TikTok, the hashtag #dogsout, in which dogs stand for toes, is used when posting videos of people 'embarrassingly' having their 'dogs out' in public, while millennial teachers post confused monologues on seeing their students never wearing sandals or flip-flops, even at the height of summer. Gen Z's conflicting feelings around feet might be connected with the benign awkwardness about the body one feels in one's late teens or early twenties, but it's also undoubtedly linked to the mainstream proliferation of foot fetishes online. How we eroticise body parts is incredibly cultural and depends on the time and place. In our extremely online culture, our bodies easily become fragmented, repackaged and transformed. 'No free feet', as they say online, in an attempt to safeguard one's agency over random and anonymous sexualisation. Sometimes it's serious, sometimes tongue-in-cheek, but you can now see the definite influence of fetish discourse in our day-to-day language.

Historically, there have been many attempts to find a scientific or psychological justification for the foot fetish. Sigmund Freud suggested that feet might be appropriately phallic – yet another substitute for the penis. Others favour a scientific justification of the attraction: a foot fetish could result from some cross-wiring in the brain, as the areas which control the genitalia and feet exist in close proximity in the somatosensory cortex, according to V. S. Ramachandran, director of the Center for Brain and Cognition at UC San Diego. Fetishes, however, tend to be learnt social behaviours as opposed to part of our biological or physical make-up, and while the cross-wiring has long been used to normalise the foot fetish, there remains a question about whether we really need to rely on statistical and scientific arguments to expand what we see as 'acceptable'.

In his essay 'My Hole', published in the 2024 *SLUTS* anthology, American writer and actor Gary Indiana writes about a sexual encounter involving feet. The narrator's lover is keen to photograph their foot-fucking but debates whether being depicted with someone's foot in your arse might be embarrassing. Without missing a beat, the narrator responds, 'Why should I find it embarrassing? You're doing it too.'

We could argue whether this particular encounter could be qualified under the foot fetish umbrella. The foot is certainly used sexually, but is it the star of the show, the focus? The foot's appearance is pretty quotidian, another tool in the arsenal (a thankfully appropriately thick tool). But the exchange at the end speaks to how foot fetishes are often discussed: with gimmicky embarrassment as well as genuine confusion around who is to carry the shame – the person with the fetish, the fetishised, onlookers or bystanders, or simply everyone involved?

Perhaps a disclaimer is due: I don't think I can call myself a foot fetishist. I have an appreciation for feet in the erotic context. Feet are sexy, playing with feet is fun, tickling can be a great pastime, and who doesn't appreciate the beauty of extra-high heels (on others – I find them too painful to walk in)? I also suspect that the comfort I get from wearing pristine white Nike sports socks goes a tiny bit further than just a simple pleasure. And yet there seems to be a difference between this and having a fetish. Or is there?

Many people perceive fetishists as an impenetrable black box. Fetish, in their mind, becomes a defining factor of that person's ability to connect with others, but it's one they are absolutely unable to understand. It is true that we can never gain a complete understanding of how another person's desire works – in the same way that we can never truly understand how they see the world in general. Facing sexual difference can be frightening and unnerving, habitually giving rise to moral panic and judgement. Disappointingly, it rarely spurs earnest conversations. How does it actually feel? Is it actually that different? These questions and answers are barricaded with cultural taboos, making them hard to address, especially with people we might be fond of. To understand foot fetishes beyond the stereotypes, I have decided to turn to fetishists themselves – not in search of any clear-cut definition, but to document a raw, imperfect, highly personal snapshot of what kind of role it can play in one's life and definition of sex.

D, a self-identified leatherman, admits that, for him, looking at feet can be as erotically charged as penetration, which makes it a bit of a paradoxical obsession – one which might feel extreme for him but would look very tame to any outsiders. His fetish is more about the visual, rather than about physical contact. Feet can even completely transform his perspective on the attractiveness of an individual: 'It is *the* determining factor of whether or not I can date the person. The feet don't need to be perfect or anything. Like they just have to be good enough,' he says. 'Sometimes I look at some people's feet and think, "They can save my life."'

D speaks of his fetish with cultural curiosity, admitting that while he's not typically fond of Quentin Tarantino's cinematic perspective, he did greatly appreciate a cast crafted in the shape of a high heel for *Inglourious Basterds*. He also highly rates shoes designed by Prada and Miu Miu – 'The shoe is kind of like the extension of the foot; it's hyper-fetishised. They make the sexiest shoes I've seen.' To him, however, there is a difference between the generalised understanding of what pretty feet might look like and a fetishistic perspective. We often think of beautiful feet as tiny, narrow and perfectly manicured, but this is not necessarily the case: 'I like skeletal feet. Large, strong nail beds and toes that look like talons. It's more sexual to me than anything,' he says. While his own preferences are specific, he reiterates that there is a fetishist out there for any and every kind of foot, especially with the wide variety of online content available. But as foot fetish becomes more widely known in the mainstream and more people join the ranks of foot content creators, he sees a lot of imagery as watered down and potentially not truly created with fetishists in mind. The fetishistic quality, to him, is different to just beauty; it is something quite hard to grasp but which is immediately recognisable to those who feel it. He sends me some foot fetish accounts of women who have broad, undying fan bases. 'It's like their feet were made to be fetishised. It's the craziest fucking thing.'

The very term 'foot fetish' can be divisive, even among those who practise it. Not everyone who likes to erotically engage with feet identifies as a foot fetishist, and because a 'fetish' is more commonly used to describe a relationship to an object, some hesitate to apply the word to a body part. But many agree that it is the right word to describe the dynamic at play, especially as it tends to be so laser-focused on the foot, such that it's almost transformed into a separate erotic entity. 'I think for a lot of foot fetishists, it's close to being a kind of paraphilia and it is very specifically about the foot,' says pro-domme Simone Reage, who describes herself as 'a receiver' when it comes to her foot fetish. 'It often has nothing to do with the person attached to the foot. Sometimes you just take your shoes off and they are only looking at your feet, staring, obsessed with the feet. Not every single person who likes feet has a foot fetish; some people might just have a little bit of a thing for it or find it enjoyable ... But my general experience of foot fetishists is that they need to engage with feet to feel sexually complete and satisfied, and that's how I would define a fetish.'

At the same time, the definition of fetish still relies on what is regarded as 'normal' and what is a deviation from that norm. 'We don't think of other body parts as fetishised because they're normalised as part of sex, but the way that people talk about boobs or asses is fetishistic a lot of the time – it's just what people expect,' Simone adds. 'You don't say "I have a boob fetish", even if many guys will be like, "I'm a boob guy", which is kind of another way of saying I have a boob fetish. But it just sounds off.'

Simone enjoys massages, foot worship and looking at her own feet during play. Having grown up in Ireland, she didn't have access to much information about fetishes, 'apart from maybe Tumblr'. Her interest was sparked when one of her boyfriends worshipped her feet during sex, even though they didn't call it a fetish back then. Not labelling the behaviour allowed for more space to explore.

Foot fetish is often stereotyped as something distinctly male. But in reality, there are people of diverse gender identities who call themselves foot fetishists – as well as a broad range of ways to sexually and erotically engage with feet. 'I love everything about feet, but I think it started with my own feet,' says J, who first realised she liked feet about a decade ago. 'It started with somebody licking my feet during sex and then me thinking, "This is not just how it feels like when someone licks your neck or behind your ear, this is a different sensation. This is something that is really turning me on."' Her interest is emotional, as well as physical: playing with feet allows her to truly get to know the other person.

'I think feet are quite a vulnerable place for a lot of people, so they don't expect to get pleasure from them,' J adds. She also points out that this vulnerability, along with certain stereotypes attached to foot fetishes, often holds people back. Social preconceptions are still very common, 'especially in men who strictly call themselves dominant. Because they think that to have a foot on you is something submissive. This position might look quite vulnerable, but I've been in a dominant position and asked a partner to fuck me with his foot on my face. Even though he was the submissive one, I was the one telling him, "I want your foot on my face."' To her, no sexual act is inherently dominant or submissive — it's more about the meaning the participants ascribe to it.

Foot fetish is often perceived as a solitary obsession, in which desire is mediated by online content, photos or videos. This idea is most likely a direct consequence of past stigma. In fact, most people I talked to admit that their fetish evolved while playing and experimenting with others, and that the connection and vulnerability involved in negotiating and exploring fetishes together is the ultimate turn-on. This collaborative approach means that people are able to explore sex beyond culturally prevalent understandings, which typically revolve around penetration. That fetishes are discursive also shines a light on how our desires and fetishes are not fixed; they're fluid and ever evolving, changing shape with our changing partners.

'I think a lot of people have this idea that you have a very defined sexuality from your childhood, and then that's fixed from that point onwards,' says Simone. 'You get your kinks from different things that happen in your childhood, and then there's a cut-off. But you're much more likely to develop new sexual interests when you start having sex and having relationships and meeting different people; it's never going to be a fixed thing.'

Even outside of a sexual context, people tend to have a complex relationship with feet. Any part of our bodies can be a source of self-consciousness, but feet especially are often ridden with shame. They're often seen as unclean due to their contact with the ground, while many people are also insecure about the appearance of their feet: their shape and size, protruding veins or cracked heels. For L, her feet had been a source of discomfort rather than pleasure up until recently. Very tall since the age of twelve, she had detested her long skinny feet, and what she saw as her abnormally long second toes. She had compulsively tried to squeeze into smaller shoes and even considered surgery to make her toes smaller. For years, well into her time working as a professional dominatrix, her feet had been absolutely off limits for her, sexually or otherwise – she couldn't even sit through a pedicure. Until one day, during a session, a client offered to worship her feet. After denying this request for years, she finally agreed. 'It felt like someone was having sex with me, but it was literally just the way they slid their tongue between the toes ... They were kissing my foot like it was the most precious thing in the world.'

This experience not only changed how she felt about her feet but also sparked her curiosity, and so she started attending foot parties. There are a few events in London she tells me about which could perhaps be described as quasi-sexual or erotic-oriented, where women get paid to have their feet worshipped. All the working participants are screened and approved by the party admins and must have a pedicure prior to the session – the rest is down to having a drink, socialising and maybe ending up on the receiving end of a ten-minute worship session.

'As with everything, it's a spectrum,' L explains, speaking of the desires and behaviours she's encountered at the events. 'You get the softer side – one guy just wanted me to put my feet on his chest, and he would softly stroke and look at them, saying that they were beautiful. You get the ones who like foot massages, kissing and licking them, and having your feet on the face or genitals. And then you get those who like you trampling on their face, trampling with heels, and ballbusting, which surprisingly can be all about the feet.'

Shame is a strong emotion which can affect one's relationship to fetish in many ways. D, for example, admits that for years he didn't want anything to do with feet and even disliked looking at them, which was a way to avoid his complicated attraction to them. But for others, like S, who enjoys rubber and leather as much as feet, shame and the idea of fetish being perverse only ignited his interest further: 'I quite enjoy the fact that for some people it's still a taboo thing to enjoy sexually,' he says. 'I think one of my favourite things is when somebody is maybe curious about it, but still kind of thinks it's a bit of a taboo. And they're interested in trying but have never had the opportunity. If you're the first person to indulge in that for them, that's a really big turn-on for me.'

S attributes his obsession with feet partly to discovering Elmer Batters' 1950s photography as a teenager. ('I saw myself as a bit of a hipster so I decided I wasn't gonna watch normal porn, just vintage porn.') And while foot fetish is no longer as stigmatised as it used to be, he believes there is still a lot of prejudice, which manifests differently: people treat it as 'the butt of the joke a lot of the time, or think it is inherently quite funny to have a foot fetish'. Part of it, he suggests, is the fact that the fetish itself is often conflated with the more problematic practices it encompasses. 'Websites like wikiFeet, for instance, enable quite strange behaviour, to have access to an archive of pictures of people's feet there purely for sexual needs, but without any sort of consent attached to it. It's already seen as this gross, perverse thing, but then websites like that only cement that idea with the general public.'

S considers himself lucky for having open-minded people around him with whom he can explore his kinks without judgement. Having a sex-positive environment is something which allows him to playfully embrace being labelled as a pervert. 'I quite enjoy the fact that it's a little bit stigmatised. I like to feel like an old-school pervert. I like the fact that it feels like a classic sort of perversion.'

'So yeah, I'd say it's still stigmatised,' he adds. 'But we're quite resourceful.'

———

In the cultural iconography surrounding the foot fetish, footwear understandably plays an important part. Having a fetish for a particular shoe is, of course, not the same as having a foot fetish, yet these affinities often intermingle and influence one another. The (erotic) semiotics of shoes is expansive. Placed in immediate contact with the foot, a shoe creates distinct physical sensations, but it also turns the foot into a cultural symbol, potentially transforming the wearer. This dynamic exists with regards to the shoe as a commodity – think of how an expensive pair of shoes is able to channel a certain idea of class or desirability – as well as within a sexual context. Boots are an important part of leather culture and its protocols of domination and submission, as well as its ritualistic practices of leather care. High heels are a shortcut to playing with femininity, be it femdom, worship, or even masochistically embracing the discomfort of wearing them. Trainers, in this way, are especially interesting as an example of sexual fantasies becoming muddled with consumerism and brand economy.

Academics and researchers are usually set on creating clear distinctions between the different sides of fetishism – a luxury shopper, a K-pop fan and a leather daddy are each assigned their own demarcated placement with their own anthropologies of desire. But the different facets of fetishism – sexual gratification, consumerism, fandom and aspirational desires – overlap. Neat distinctions are not able to contain our messy, embodied drives. Trainers are a perfect object to soak up the theory of fetish: a commodity, an object of sexual desire, a collectable, a subcultural obsession, a sex toy.

Trainer obsession involves memories of the scent of nylon, of echoey basketball courts, of muscle strain and grainy porn videos. They are also well-known erotic signifiers in the queer and gay communities: from jockstraps to white sports socks and tiny nylon shorts, a sports aesthetic channels a powerful homoeroticism which is popular across genders, while the archetype of the football lesbian can be a vehicle to reinvent queer womanhood. There is a relationship between sports, the body and nostalgia which creates a powerful – and highly customisable – sexual language.

'Gym class was both a nightmare and a fantasy,' writes NikeShoxJock on the blog of the fetish gay app Recon. 'In terms of brands, Nike, Air Jordans, Puma, Adidas, Asics, Under Armour, all get my cock hard, particularly basketball and running footwear. I have always looked out for those brands. Per my handle name, Nike Shox are my absolute favourite.' This piece from 2021 unpacks the hands-on application of the footwear fetish in erotic play: from worshipping, trampling, crushing and kicking to using the shoelaces as bondage gear or swapping kicks during sex. It also details both the author's personal history and the significance trainers have for their erotic inclinations.

'When I engage in "vanilla" sex, the bare minimum for me is to wear my sneaks on my feet during intercourse. If I'm topping, I like to pick out the sneaks my bottom wears. If I'm bottoming, I like my partner to pick out his favourite pair of sneakers that he'd like to see on my feet. I typically have the top grab hold of my sneaks during sex or slap them around, feel them up a bit, adding in some verbal comments about me and my sneakers,' he writes. 'Just hearing a guy, in a sexual situation, say words like, Nikes, sneakers, sneaks, and degrading me with phrases like "sneaker slut" drives me wild. As the sex becomes kinkier, so do the roles of my sneakers and the sneakers of my partner.'

He also writes about how trainers can become a conduit of power and masculinity: 'Sneakers & socks illustrate the masculinity and power of one's feet . . . When I wear them, I am in control. When the dom uses them against me in any way, the power exchange is immensely sexual and erotic.' It's all mixed together in the moment: people's almost semi-conscious, inherent turn-ons, personal memories and cultural symbols. The trainer is more than the sum of its parts; it acquires fresh meanings as it's parsed through different contexts. The image of an unattainable jock or an athlete is absorbed into queer culture to produce a new kind of irresistible erotic archetype, which in turn slips back into the mainstream as a new hybrid ideal.

Trainers also carry a close connection to class and are often called upon to eroticise this other axis of power. The working class has been an object of cultural and sexual fetishisation for a long time, and trainers are often a must-have for the complete picture: most frequently Nike TNs and Air Max 90s and 95s. Writer and cultural critic Joe Bobowicz has written about these models of Nike trainers as, alongside tracksuits and sports socks, integral to the fusion of the erotic and the cultural which drives a 'scally lads' subculture. Having interviewed men who identify with the label about the things they wear and the things which turn them on, Bobowicz defines scally lads as 'a community of British gay men who fetishise the style and affective codes attributed to a working-class subculture. Centring around sportswear and sometimes "rough and ready" behaviour, the community, emerging in the early 2000s, is an appropriation of what's typically seen as heterosexual subculture. Those of the original subculture are known as chavs, or in North West England, scallies, understood as a lumpen proletariat, stereotyped as feckless and tacky, associated with tracksuits and fake designer brands.' Bobowicz's research, in part, looks to unpack the queer potential of a subculture which is most frequently presumed heterosexual, and how it subverts codes of working-class masculinity. For Bobowicz, these trainers become a metonym for a particular vision of 'Britishness'. The hyper-local image of the English working class goes global, somewhat detached from its roots by queer desire.

Looking through the fetish material around trainers, one encounters plenty of examples in which nylon, plastic and leather come into contact with the body and rub against the skin, in which sensation and tactility are central. But the 'scally lads' subculture goes a step further: it becomes central to an erotic imaginary, evoking much broader social realities. There are also examples in which trainers and socks feature in a more elemental transformation: as armour or a part of the body. In an indie porn film I watch on the independent website Frock the World, titled *Shoe Boy*, two people are wearing balaclava-like masks crafted from sports socks, with shiny (PVC? latex?) black sportswear and white Nike high tops. As one of them descends to lick the top of the other's white Nike trainer, his face, obscured by a pattern of Nike-printed cotton, creates a poetic union with the shoe: a moment of wholeness, a communion. In a similar vein, the work of Madrid-based fetish creator Albinohector transforms trainers into something which defines your whole body. He turns trainers into masks and codpieces to be worn with matching harnesses or sportswear: recognisable ribbed fragments of Nike TNs framing the sides of the face, securing the mouth like a muzzle. It is a way to affirm creative agency over a commodity, but also perhaps to transform yourself into something closer to the hot, erotically charged commodity itself. Another example of the never-ending sexual and consumer reinvention of shoes.

'I have seventy-five pairs, and I still think it's not enough. That means that I could go over two months without having to wear the same pair of trainers twice, but still I want more,' artist, dominatrix and trainer collector Miss Gold tells me over an afternoon drink in a sunlit pub. Her aim is to have at least 365; one pair for each day of the year.

While a trainer fetish is often coded as something exclusively masculine, it definitely manifests in diverse ways across genders. At a party, I once watched Miss Gold having her Nike TNs licked by a beautiful woman, before she proceeded to take one of them off to spank her with the plastic sole. But there is more to the obsession than the carnal, physical acts. Miss Gold describes her Nike fetish as a compulsion of sorts, in which she loves the whole process: selecting a pair, purchasing them, their arrival in the mail, the opening of the box, first spying the fresh trainers as she unwraps them. 'I like it more when I haven't paid for them, which I often don't. I've traded trainers for different things, like a photograph of me wearing them,' she adds. Miss Gold's fetishism, in that way, is pretty holistic, merging the straightforward sexual drive with the simple pleasure of a new purchase, as well as elements of power exchange.

The roots of her compulsion towards collecting and admiring trainers probably come from pining for them while growing up, she admits. As children, she and her siblings would get expensive school shoes, but there was no budget for trainers they could wear in their free time. Having multiple trainers beyond the immediate practical needs therefore felt like a luxury. Not just any trainers though, but Nike specifically. 'I used to like the Air Max 90s; now I only wear 95s. I've got some 90s but I like TNs and 95s best; they're the sexiest ones to me. I'm looking for them all the time . . . I fancy a person if they have 95s or TNs on. You see it on my face – my eyes get that

Air Max glow. I've bought trainers for girls I've dated just so I could see them wearing them. I'm more attracted to someone if they are wearing trainers.' ('I'm sorry but you're wearing the wrong kind of trainers,' she adds somewhat sombrely; I immediately feel guilty for wearing my very battered pair of Salomons.)

One of the most interesting things about talking to a fetishist is discovering all the various ways to engage with an object. Having a fetish means unlocking the pleasurable and sometimes gritty playfulness of the object, as well as attracting people who might share your love of it.

'Sexually, it's a very visual thing for me. I like seeing people in them or seeing myself in them. I love having them worshipped. I was once in a disgusting Wetherspoons toilet with dirty floors; I knew I was standing in piss. I couldn't wait to get them licked clean when I got home. I like the journey of the trainer. I made this twelve-minute-long video – you've got to be a complete trainer fetishist to watch it all – I spent two days videoing this one pair of trainers and all the surfaces they'd touched, puddles, dirty streets, and the voiceover explained the specific journey. I would always narrate the journey to whoever cleans them for me,' Miss Gold says, smiling. 'I did once lick a pair when I was drunk – I don't think I could worship the dirty ones, but if they were clean out the box I definitely could.'

I wonder if there is really a difference between a regular sneakerhead and a fetishist. And how substantial? Of course, there is the straightforward answer – a difference between the consumer's aspirational desires and the fetishist's engagement with the erotic. But I wonder if there is also a more intricate element of world-building which applies to both, a personal blueprint of gratification – those memories of high school gyms, the homoerotic iconography, the defining power of particular trainers to completely reshape how someone is perceived.

But for a fetishist, the story doesn't end with the purchase and ownership of a desired model – it keeps evolving as sneakers penetrate the fabric of their day-to-day existence. In a way, a fetishist's trainers merge with the wearer; they become an enhancement, a part of them which facilitates an erotic experience. Foot fetishes and a fetish for trainers and other footwear, in that sense, are similar and different at the same time. With footwear and other fetish objects, we long to collapse the boundaries between our flesh and the material, we want unity and augmentation; while with feet, we have to artificially create a distance from our body parts to enable an erotic perspective: taken together, they form a photograph and its inverted negative.

MEDICAL GLOVES

As the thin material snapped at my wrist, my mind short-circuited. I was at home, in my bedroom, yet I became fixated on a memory: my body sinking into a big, raised chair, blinding light, the scratch of metal, and the faint smell of rubber. The memory wasn't recent, nor was it focused on a particular situation. It took me way back, perhaps to childhood, to a feeling of being small, intimidated, full of fear while receiving necessary care. The memory rushed through my body as raw feeling. A reminder of how history is written on the body.

We are torn between an intimate familiarity with our body and a relative lack of understanding as to how or why it works as it does. This understanding is the preserve, or responsibility, of science and medicine. The knowledge is far too layered, too technical for most of us. And so, we are often in the dark. The inner workings of our physical condition are beyond us.

I've always thought of my formative bodily experiences as unsettling: my body expanding too fast, growing in size and height, stretching within its skin; my joints aching; my body suddenly becoming a sexual object for others and therefore a source of danger and unwanted attention. Puberty as body horror – my body harbouring unknowns, just as any female body does, due to being understudied and overpoliced. But what I was scared of most was sickness. Every autumn, the weather in St Petersburg turned bitterly cold and I was convinced that I was dying of an incurable illness. This undetected fatal illness was my most recurring childhood nightmare. It wasn't an unfounded terror, as I was sick a lot at that time, and I would often end up in hospitals. I remember them as echoey and empty places, very bare and not at all pleasant. Even today, I will sometimes begin to hyperventilate at the idea of 'the unknown' making a home inside me.

Why do I love going to raves, or leaping into the cold sea from a rock? Why do I fuck for hours, or try things which hurt me? For a long time, I did it to forget the possibility of sickness, to take control over my body and my choices, to shirk this lingering fear. Because I remain sick; I live with a chronic health condition. And it has taught me that it's very unlikely that anyone is truly healthy. 'Good health' is a social fiction. I enjoy the sticky sensation when I apply transparent hormone-infused gel to my thigh and say a little prayer to Paul B. Preciado. I have co-authored my body, or at least shifted the way I see it: as a queer body, as the body of a pleasure-seeking pervert. I calm my mind and try to trust it.

So, when I snapped medical gloves on during sex, I didn't know what to do with this baggage – these emotions and memories which rose like a wave. The gloves were a semi-sheer beige; they appeared smooth but were, in fact, grippy, with a stamp on the wrist to indicate the size. As my hands got sweatier, translucent patches started to appear in the material, and I could see a net of small lines as it started to cling more tightly to my palm. The texture was beautiful, like translucent magnolia petals on a footpath.

To someone who's exposed to them through their work, gloves are standard PPE, but I have a soft spot for them, erotically. Gloves not only make you feel powerful, but also encourage you to touch things you otherwise maybe would not dare – for me, that means health and sickness, institutional care, fear of mortality, and pathologised desire.

Medical Gloves

Medical fetishism is one of the most multifaceted fetishes out there, partly due to the vast bank of experience it draws upon. When anyone steps into a doctor's office, or over the threshold of a hospital, they carry with them individual histories and individual pains. But in the doctor's office, we become a 'patient' – a general, unifying category. We sacrifice some of our humanity in order to be treated and saved. We become bodies in the hands of an authority empowered with knowledge.

Medical fetishists derive sexual pleasure from clinical scenarios. These might involve the roles of doctors, nurses, surgeons and patients, or be built around a sexual attraction to medical uniforms, hospital gowns, intimate examinations, injections, dental objects, temperature-taking, medical restraints or even anaesthesia and respiratory therapy. The list is truly endless – and at times poetic. Some people have cardiophilia, or a heartbeat fetish: they get off on the sound of their own or their partner's heartbeat through a stethoscope.

Medical fetish lies on the fringes, linked so inextricably to the uncomfortable, the embarrassing and the terrifying. It so often involves extreme vulnerability – that feeling of being a little bit too cold while sitting atop an examination table, fragile and exposed, on the brink of a loss of bodily autonomy. Given that it's often inspired by real-life clinical scenarios, a medical fetish is ironically often perceived as pathological, as sick. It is also often read as camp: role play performed in a little nurse's outfit, a standard item to be found in a box of erotic thrills retailed at a low price in a local sex shop.

I've met doctors and nurses on the kink scene, and they have mostly been ambivalent about medical fetish. After all, the erotic world was put together from tools and signifiers all too familiar to them in the day-to-day. Online retailers like the UK's MedFet offer all you need for a starter kit: individually packaged sterile needles in small plastic tubes, with different-colour caps for different thicknesses; plastic sheets; catheters; metal dental tools; speculums; and gloves, of course – nitrile, latex, long, short, in any colour, with any desired feel. In fact, the world of medical fetishes sits so closely to the real thing that the equipment is often exactly the same across both contexts. During the COVID-19 pandemic, MedFet was praised for donating all their stock to the NHS amid the shortages. It was a tiny fraction of what was needed, they admitted, as they rarely keep extensive stock – but still, it was a goodwill gesture as the lines between real and imagined care collapsed.

At first, looking at gloves and medical tools can be intimidating, uncomfortable. It takes an effort to stay with it, to not be deterred by one's initial reaction – to deploy imagination and empathy trying to imagine why and how this could be erotic. It takes introspection and attention to detail to learn how one can turn any space into an examination room, how one unpacks the layers of institutional care which is so constant in our lives.

October 2022
A text message, received at 18.48.
I think for me, especially with it being something that I've felt on some level since childhood, probably following a few hospital and dentist visits, there's something in a medical setting that overlaps there. In a (wildly eroticised lol) medical setting you're vulnerable to a doctor, nurse or whoever understands how your body works physically more than you do – if you're a patient that can obviously make for a very vulnerable and nerve-wracking feeling, while the limited verbal feedback you receive from them can feel quite cold and sterile.
There's this feeling that they're in a position of power and have dealt with all kinds of things before – putting people in embarrassing or uncomfortable positions, sedating, maybe even restraining people, etc.

You get the feeling that they are able to do this all so effortlessly and that it doesn't really faze them, even when it's uncomfortable to the person on the other end. So there's a huge amount of power in their position, and this possible vibe that you're kind of at their mercy and you better hope they're nice to you.

Received at 19.00
So I guess as sexual fantasy it's a lot to do with the invincibility complex or whatever, being humbled in a very particular and possibly dehumanising, objectifying or humiliating way.

There's this fantasy in my mind that the person doing all these things to my body (pleasurable, painful or just uncomfortable) knows exactly what they're doing, it's kind of an effortless thing for them and I'm just vulnerably along for the ride, whether I'm enjoying it or not.

Received at 19.10
I think the surgical mask fetish kind of came about as a result of all that, particularly the way they hide facial expressions so that the other person can be hard to read. It can make you feel slightly uncomfortable or intimidated (well, until the pandemic normalised seeing masks everywhere lol).

When I received these texts from someone I was in love with, the height of the COVID-19 pandemic was still fresh in our memory, and elements of the altered routines were still present in our lives – fragments of news reports, and small day-to-day rituals and their unique material culture. A thin white plastic swab at the back of the throat. The faint smell of hand sanitiser. Buildings which had been repurposed as testing centres – and later, vaccination centres. The small choreography of hand washing, affixing a mask to one's face, wiping down surfaces. I found it fascinating how the pandemic temporarily unkinked face masks, as they had become so commonplace. The dread of sickness became quotidian too, as well as the idea of the institutional management (or mismanagement) of contagion. If I'm honest, the question of whether it was wrong to fetishise something like this in a time of crisis never came up – we were too thrilled to be alive.

Still, I had my doubts about medical fetish. It's hard to tell what put me off more: the fear of stirring up memories of hospital settings or the seemingly trite dress-up element of it. Initially, I felt revulsion towards the idea of dressing as a nurse, but the aftertaste lingered as curiosity, which drew me towards traversing the distance between you and someone with radically different erotic sensibilities. Later in our lengthy text exchanges, my love interest once described medical play as 'cold, sterile power exchange', and something clicked in me. I bought a latex dress: short-sleeved, with a front zip, in a deep red – sharp manicure-red, blood-red – with a small white cross above the right breast. I enjoyed seeing myself in it; the dress was a gateway into the fantasy space. I imagined how fun and how empowering it would feel to step into the room as this completely new persona. I loved the idea of giving them a gift – giving them pleasure, a future memory, a hot moment we'd craft together. I experimented with different kinds of touch – authoritative, assertive, comforting but firm. I thought of different tones of voice, the timbre of those who care for us, and how they command power.

I inhaled the rubbery scent of the latex gloves, and I felt something like an itch at the base of my skull, as though the deep repository of my memories, those which I will never reach, were sparking. My body, a spring of energy. Soft skin and hard metal. The inappropriateness of it all: a mocking reinterpretation of a real-life interaction, transformed into obscene role play. Inside me, arousal chipped away at the traces of my hospital memories until I let them go. The memories had been dislodged. I smiled, my red lipstick the same shade as the dress; it felt wild.

The connection between fetish and trauma is a widely debated topic — in psychology, in sex-positive communities, as well as on an individual level. While unpacking personal histories, it is natural to wonder if I have always been like this or if there was a foundational event which imprinted my desires on a subconscious level.

Much of this links back to the Freudian interpretation of fetish, as well as the field of psychoanalysis at large: the formation of sexuality in our early years, the concrete memories which fade into the background, leaving us with yearnings and inclinations, holes we are desperate to fill. But this school of thought has led to the pathologisation of kink — a practice of deeming certain sexual desires as unhealthy or abnormal, which has historically encompassed queer sexualities and contributed to the suppression of women's pleasure, among other things. Kink, as a manifestation of trauma in one's formative years, has historically been weaponised, used against individuals. Medical fetishes, however, expose how complex the link between our sexuality and our lived experiences can be. It often draws from memories which are challenging, painful and uneasy, and experiences of trying to fit our tender bodies into hierarchies of power.

While many approach medical fetish purely from a fantasy perspective, Berlin-based dominatrix Deva Venera has experience working in a dental office. She recalls the job with fondness. Having worked as a dominatrix since 2016, she offers a variety of sessions, but has also utilised her previous work experience to offer dental play which is as close to reality as it can be. She even works from a space which has an actual dentist's chair identical to the ones in ordinary dental practices. The aesthetic is a sliding scale: in some photos on her website she is wearing a black latex apron and bright red lipstick, and the room is dim, but in some she could be indistinguishable from an actual health professional, dressed in crisp white, in a brightly lit room, leaning over a fantasy 'patient'.

Deva admits that she appreciates the playful character of medical sessions. Being a dominatrix for her is not a persona she steps into just for work, but an authentic part of her sexuality. But when transformed into a fictional doctor, she feels free to indulge in role play. 'I very quickly step into the kind of behaviour I was very used to from working in a dental office. Friendly, very professional, distant but caring, and I use all the phrases that are typical of that environment. I enjoy it very much. And at the same time, it's not exactly the same because I combine it with kink, a bit of a bizarre character,' she tells me on a video call from Berlin.

When it comes to the link between fetishes and personal history, Deva admits that it varies. Some people might have had a traumatic experience, while others did not. And those who did might have already partially reframed it for themselves through eroticising it as a fetish. But a lot of the time dental fetish makes for a powerful experience because living out this fantasy is not easy compared to other kinks one might be able to try at home. 'People are coming to me who are carrying this fantasy or this need maybe for decades. It can definitely make it even more intense.'

Deva loves the psychological complexity of medical fetish: 'In general, everything which has to do with the clinical settings has a lot to do with care, and this nurturing aspect is very important because these scenarios are doing something with your emotions and your nervous system. You feel like you are cared for and someone is not only controlling you, but doing something for you, and you are getting a lot of attention. So it can even bring you higher levels of relaxation.'

Deva practices what she calls 'holistic fetish', which is an approach which emphasises that having a fetish is not just about straightforward sexual gratification, but a more complex drive. Working with fetish can encompass not only the body, but also emotions and memories. It is, of course, different to therapy, but people sometimes turn to fetish to satisfy an exploratory urge to delve into a part of themselves which desperately needs attention, or to experience care and validation in the erotic setting. More generally, BDSM can be a tool for working with complex emotions, and the care aspect inherent to medical role play lends itself especially well to this exploration. 'I also have a background in trauma-sensitive work and body work,' Deva adds. 'Having knowledge about the nervous system and how someone is reacting in different situations is very helpful, so that you can better read the body language and understand what is going on and to support the person.'

Among those who engage in medical play, as well as other aspects of BDSM and kink, not everyone is interested in excavating trauma or deep-rooted personal experiences. It is, in fact, an ongoing debate within the kink communities whether the filthy and potentially deviant sex you're having has to be healing or if it can simply be fun. Domina Dia Dynasty specialises in creating similarly trauma-informed experiences and what she calls Wholistic Femdom. Apart from the specialised skill set for BDSM play, she has trained in reiki, hypnotherapy and yoga, and prioritises cultivating bodily awareness and mindful breathing. Breathing, she emphasises, is especially crucial for navigating experiences which are emotionally or physically painful or challenging.

'My sessions always start with the client removing all their clothing before getting into the child's [yoga] pose on a clean towel. And then they remain still and breathe in that space. And it's almost like they are in a darkened cocoon of the body. And I have them take some very deep and cleansing breaths with me.'

According to Dia, 'This trauma-informed BDSM, with the intention of holding space for re-enacting or rewriting a traumatic experience, is its own thing. It's not all BDSM, which is a spectrum. There are people who practise it solely for sexual pleasure. But there are people who practise it for the ability to reconnect with their bodies so they can enjoy sexual pleasure.' This process is not always (if ever) linear. The healing journey rarely takes someone from point A to point B in a direct line – instead, it can be unpredictable, volatile and hard to grasp. 'Some people don't realise that they have been traumatised and are kind of functioning on this belief that they're normal. And so I get to understand them a little better in observation and in play. And then I have people who are not the least bit traumatised and can get pretty heavy into the immersion of whatever we're doing without too many check-ins. And so that's another thing that I have to learn myself: not many people can articulate these things.'

Dia's professional interest in medical play is as a space which is incredibly impactful mentally, physically, psychologically, sexually and even spiritually for the client. For her, however, it is completely detached from personal history. 'It's a playground,' she tells me. 'I love the aesthetic . . . It's a little absurd and playful. I think that that's why it's play for me, because it has to be fun.'

Medical fetish, in a way, emphasises the complexity of fetish more broadly, and how there are multiple facets to the play: it can be healing, transformative or fun; it can be all at once and can fluctuate between them. Only the players in the moment truly know.

Medical fetishism is often perceived as especially visually driven – a highly textured fantasy which draws on certain realistic settings, as well as a broader pool of references from art, horror films and erotica. And while the objects are crucial, it is also interesting to see how the play at times transcends its material boundaries – both sexually and politically.

Jean Cleverley is a visual artist and a leatherdyke. They have a mullet in a deep hue of plum red and always wear the best vintage leathers. A lot of their work archives and documents leather and queer communities, but a lot of it is also shot in and from their bed. Jean lives with a disability and chronic fatigue, which significantly limits their capacity for both work and socialising. I visit Jean in their cosy flat, and we chat about how being ill inevitably changes how you are able to function in society, with its overbearing expectations of beauty, productivity and energy levels. Disabled people make up around one-fifth of the UK population but are under-represented in politics and are usually among the first to be deprived of social support during budget cuts. For Jean, sexual politics are always linked to politics of other kinds, and medical fetish has been a way to explore both on a deeper level.

'I feel like I first got into it because I was often in a dynamic where I would get fully head-to-toe inspected. And I found it so relaxing, and I would just feel extremely cared for,' they recall. 'When I got sick, I would go to the doctor a lot. And I started fantasising about situations, so I could find going to the doctor hot. I guess I was trying to turn a bad situation into something exciting.'

The delicate balance of care and vulnerability is what interests Jean the most – taking the vulnerability which is usually felt in medical environments and carrying it into sexual contexts to safely play with the uneasiness and fear. They also love the ritual of medical scenarios and have gone to the length of getting their play partner to write up prescriptions for them as a patient in need of care. Jean's enjoyment of this realistic element comes partly from having to deal with the uncomfortable reality of sickness far too often: 'As the NHS deteriorates, I need a space where I can really be looked after. And I know that's so depressing. But I've had so many bad situations in medical settings that I want to keep something for myself. I want to have good experiences. I want to rewrite it, basically.'

They add, 'In a weird way, that has made me have a different perspective on medical appointments. When someone's like, "OK, we're just going to inject this into you," I think, "Whoa, this isn't consensual, I haven't agreed to that." It's made me question consent within the medical system, because someone does just decide what is best for you — but another medical professional might think another thing is best for you. So, like, in a weird way, I now feel safer in my kinky medical life rather than the actual medical situation.'

Medical play, in a way, creates a possibility to rethink care — care as a given, care as someone else's responsibility — and cultivate a more proactive approach to it. Through sex, care becomes less institutional and more embodied, personal, generously shared.

'Accessibility, especially in kink spaces, is caring. Whether you're neurodiverse, disabled or not disabled, everyone has access needs. Understanding what everyone's individual needs are, and what everyone's limits are — that is care,' Jean says. 'I really like the term "access intimacy", which is a level of intimacy you can only get by understanding everyone's individual access needs. It is a beautiful way of looking at things within friendships, romantic relationships and kink — how much we can give and take.'

CARS

I've walked through the Barbican car park twice. Once for an art exhibition located in an emerald-green metal storage unit, and this time for a hook-up with someone who lives in the Barbican Estate. The building complex, located near London's financial district, is one of the finest examples of British brutalist architecture, with its combination of lakes and lush greenery with raw concrete and tower blocks. Its Grade II-listed status means it's a much-coveted residence, which explains the cars: they are expensive, vintage, rare. Many are covered with dust sheets. I leave my fingerprints in the layer of dust covering a red BMW convertible which has been left uncovered. I touch it lightly, tenderly almost, just to leave a small trace of my presence.

There is the faint hum of the heating systems, ventilation, boilers and pipes – of infrastructure. The near silence is ruptured by the sound of tyres against tarmac, the click of an indicator, a door opening and the flash of a melody, before the door closes again. There's the high-pitched full-stop beep of a locked car and someone shuffles away, voices in the distance. A sequence of sounds so familiar we hardly register it. The fluorescent lighting leaves pockets of darkness which are only illuminated by the headlights, the red of backlights, and flashes of amber. Then there is the smell: damp concrete, rubber, dust, oil and a whiff of petrol. The smell is unique to these spaces; it's why I've always loved underground car parks the most. Multistorey and open-air car parks lack the strange cavernous warmth. Underground, the density of stale air creates a tension which hangs above the idle cars.

I walk through the car park together with my hook-up. I wonder whether my fascination is obvious. The walk is a brief precursor to arriving at their apartment to have sex. But truly, for me, the sex has already begun. I want time to slow down, so I can savour the moment. The space is vast and impeccably lit, and the way it extends underground makes me feel that I could get lost in it. I am still making conversation, but I walk slowly. I'm enjoying my body in this space. I try to take it in as much as I can.

Looking back, most of the hook-up has gone from my memory, but the car park remains. I think that in another life, I could have been someone who writes sexually charged reviews for car parks on Google.

Certain kinds of erotic perception go much deeper than we're used to thinking about. They might be grounded in personal history so foundational that they grow with us, embedded in our emerging bodies, leaving their blueprint in our nerve endings. These inclinations are different from straightforward sexual preferences or desires and so they're harder to decode, explain, make sense of – they're beyond words. It's a feeling of embodiment, the desire to drink something up, which extends beyond any immediate sexual gratification. Which leaves a question – how should we engage with this more subtle kind of desire? How do we frame erotic energy which exceeds the sexual act?

I have collected car spaces my whole life. A tyre shop in central Athens, where the smell of rubber and exhaust fumes mixed with dirt and orange blossom from a garden across the road. A cavernous workshop in the arches under Hackney Downs station in East London. A frigid, metallic gas station high up in the French Alps. A maze-like multistorey car park in LA. I never take photos; I just file them away neatly in my mind so I can revisit them later. Everything before and after fades, just the snapshots remain.

They all link back, perhaps, to a row of tin garages which were a short walk from an apartment block where I grew up in the mid-1990s. In my mind, they were a secret space, because they were so far from the routine of school and home: little metal constructions filled with DIY tools and junk. Rows and rows of brown tin huts which held cars, instruments, and various objects rejected from domestic spaces. Or perhaps it all began with the car markets my dad used to take me to, the asphalt cracked and full of potholes, the ground soaked in oil. There were boxy radios laid out for sale, along with assorted car parts: doors, bonnets, semi-transparent plastic oil canisters filled with yellowish viscous liquids. The markets were full of men. The sounds of engines starting. I felt so small. I looked for the most fascinating and relatable objects: car emblems laid out on fabric – BMW, Mercedes, Toyota. In my mind, they were the best part of the car. I wished desperately that I could have them – that I could carry them from this harsh world back to mine.

Cars were a big part of the environment where I grew up. It would be wrong to say that car culture arrived in Russia in the 1990s (in the Soviet Union, having a car had been synonymous with status, especially when it came to the Volga or Chaika), but the decade following the dissolution of the USSR brought foreign cars, entrepreneurial opportunities to make fast money and a sense that reinvention was possible. Everyone wanted a BMW. Car customisation was on the rise, from elaborate aerography to pieces of cheap plastic which transformed your car into something which looked like the models later immortalised in the *Fast & Furious* franchise. DIY glass tints were applied on top of the glass in one sleek motion, the windows so black you could see nothing through them. They were made illegal before long, and the police would make you peel them off with your own fingers — but the boys still went for them.

In my childhood world, the car encompassed desire and control — but also destruction. Reckless driving and distorted risk assessments (on the part of individual drivers, authorities and car companies) meant that the freeways were punctuated with metal carcasses: squashed, torn apart, their insides pouring over metal frames. These husks, which were sometimes of ridiculously expensive cars, were a manifestation of the surrounding political and social chaos. Car imports soared, with minimal regulations in place, and the rapidly emerging class of new-money entrepreneurs wanted to show off their extravagant new purchases. An insatiable hunger raged for the next sexy, shiny thing, and the last thing they cared about was driving safely. Traffic cameras were far off in the future, and bribing traffic police was commonplace. Shards of glass from smashed windscreens seemed to be everywhere. Fascinated, I scraped them up and collected them in a little box.

As a child, I spent a lot of time in cars during the school run, but ten-hour road trips were pretty normal, too (Russia is a big country, after all). In the hands of some, cars were violent, unpredictable. But with my family, they were peaceful places. They were also an exercise in trust: each time I climbed in, I was trusting my life and safety to someone. They were in charge of navigating the tumultuous road. Even if they were speeding or driving recklessly, I promised myself not to fear. That feeling of an intimate connection shaped around safety still manifests today. I re-enter this calm state whenever I am in a car with someone I'm close to. I got my driving licence at eighteen but I haven't driven since, partly, I suspect, because I like to chase that feeling; I love to be a passenger.

My obsession with car culture, however, goes beyond this sense of tranquillity. Now, whenever I'm in these spaces, something sexual happens. I don't know when it entered the picture, or why, but the intimacy and trust of being in a car morphed into an erotic response. The smell of oil and petrol is now linked to a sense of thrill and excitement. I find myself attracted to chrome and metallic colours and mesmerised by car design. I have saved a few vintage catalogues listing all the colours and types of leather used in 1990s BMW cars. Personal history is layered over material culture, infusing it with erotic possibility.

Watch any YouTube video of supercar-spotting and it's clear that the car is an incredibly common, culturally accepted fetish. The sleek shapes of a Bugatti Chiron, LaFerrari Aperta or McLaren 600LT whizzing past, their vibrant colours like lightning ripping through the street on an ordinary day. The videos are usually filmed on a smartphone in a casual manner. We follow as car enthusiasts wander the streets. At times, the lens briefly captures a car driving past. Sometimes, the camera dips as the person filming crouches to check out a custom exhaust on a Ferrari in a manicured West London street. They gasp with satisfaction and joy. It's easy to see how a sought-after model which commands a six-figure price tag signifies status, wealth and power. But there is more to it than status and aspiration: our ideas of gender, pleasure, technology, change, conformity, nostalgia and connection are all filtered through the car. Our sexuality, in some sense, is linked to something we often do not even perceive as straightforwardly sexual.

Cars have always generated devoted communities: from those who enthuse over the hot rods of the 1950s or the muscle cars of the 1960s to the growing fandoms around Japanese and Italian automakers in the 1970s and 1980s. Car subcultures are diverse, from aficionados of lowriders – cars with the distinctive customised dropped chassis, which originated in LA's Latino communities – to adepts of spinning, who perform stunts while the car does 'doughnuts', spinning around in circles at high speed. In the 2000s, franchises like *Fast & Furious* and *Need for Speed* romanticised illegal street racing and an associated masculine archetype – the handsome risk-taker of few words who is devoted to their car and their racing crew above all else.

The emergence of contemporary car culture is intertwined with the evolution of what sociologists call 'technical masculinity' – an identity which relies on niche, detailed knowledge and skills. As masculinity became less contingent on physical strength, the theory goes, it started to rely more on other capabilities. Namely, technical know-how, appropriating technology – including the car – as a signifier of masculinity, be it driving well, being able to parallel park or fix the car, or being clued in on the latest models and their technical characteristics. More recently, 'petro-masculinity' has evolved as a new category describing a performance of gender which is reinforced by denying climate change and having a preference for oil and gas over renewable energy.

But while car culture is usually linked to an over-the-top macho performance, there is sometimes an emotional, sensitive, nostalgic undercurrent to it. It shines through in a rare emotional scene in the UK show *Top Gear*. 'I know Hammond and May think my 928 Porsche is a bit dull, but for one very good reason, it isn't dull to me,' Jeremy Clarkson revealed during *Top Gear* season 22's 'Patagonia Special'. He proceeds to tell the story of how in 1994, he received a phone call from his mother with news that his dad was in hospital in Sheffield. He had the 928 on test drive that week, so he jumped in, with a cooked chicken he had taken out of the oven for his mum, and set off immediately. Clarkson arrived in town just in time, with the car playing a crucial role: 'The truth is, if I hadn't been driving a car which could sit quite happily at 170 miles an hour, I wouldn't have had the opportunity to say goodbye to my dad. So as far as I'm concerned, the 928 is all right.'

The austere 'all right' at the end of the story signals a deep emotional bond from someone usually restrained with feelings: an attachment to the undervalued Porsche. The short clip of Clarkson – wearing a navy polo shirt and a camel-coloured blazer, shot from the passenger seat – would often go viral on TikTok and YouTube in the early 2020s, with thousands of car enthusiasts – some self-described grown men – in the comments admitting to unrestrained tears.

With their direct link to masculinity, cars are often eroticised. The handbrake, steering wheel, gearstick, pedals become sensual objects. The car also provides a space for intimate play, facilitates experiences – it's both private and public, under control and moderately risky. To be in a car means to arrange your body in a certain way, to surrender to how the seats shape it. Occasionally, this cultural fascination finds its sexual embodiments. Dogging, the practice of engaging in sexual acts in a public or semi-public place, often involves cars and has its own symbolic language emerging around it (blink the headlights twice to see whether there might be others seeking connection around), while the term 'carplay' is used on gay hook-up apps for those who specifically prefer sex in cars.

Among the car-related fetishes, pedal-pumping, also referred to as revving and cranking, stands out due to the direct physical interaction with the vehicle. Pedal-pumping videos show pedicured feet (whether bare, in sandals or in heels) pumping the gas pedal. Some describe it as a kind of foot fetish, though it extends further to incorporate multiple scenarios: a damsel in distress unable to take control of the vehicle, a dominant, imposing woman who can start a car better than a man ... But these videos get truly interesting when the subject of arousal is the mechanics of the car itself; the repeated attempts to kick-start it, the repeated failure, especially if the car is bulky and old. The main focus shifts from the person struggling to get the vehicle running to the car itself – the edging of the release, the desperate hope that it will start eventually – exposing an even tighter bond with the car.

Sex in the car is hot, but arguably it is less interesting than the car's status as an endearing cultural obsession, a fetish which underscores a contemporary worldview. In this chapter, I turn to things which are in plain view, just like daily traffic – films, books, advertising – to trace how cars seep into our memories, bodies, genders and sexualities. Especially for those of us who are on the sidelines of motor culture – women, queers – this vision offers a radical possibility.

The moment I tell people that I have a car fetish, they always come back with the same response: *Crash*.

J. G. Ballard's 1973 novel and David Cronenberg's 1996 adaptation rule supreme in the imagination when it comes to getting a sexual kick out of a vehicle. The story starts with the protagonist, James Ballard, getting injured in a car accident, which then leads to him getting entangled with a group of car crash fetishists. Led by Dr Robert Vaughan, a former TV scientist turned 'nightmare angel of the highways', they are sexually aroused by staging and participating in car accidents. *Crash* could be simply interpreted as a meditation on the death drive – the tendency in all living things towards destruction and obliteration, as outlined by Freudian psychoanalysis – and the nature of adrenaline-fuelled arousal. But it also covers much more complicated ground: fetishism, objectification, technology, pornography and the urban landscape, and their tight grip on our lives.

When *Crash* was published, it prompted widespread revulsion from critics and readers alike. Fucking in cars might have been palatable, but the text is generous on all kinds of human fluids – sperm, blood, piss, spit – and all the ways they could be extorted from the disfigured, horny bodies. (Penis entering the leg wound of a female driver, anyone?) The book is a cocktail of arousal and disgust, narrated in a pared-back, detached voice. It pushes back against various social taboos, too: loveless casual sex practised by women, bisexuality, fucking in public spaces, desire and disability. Ballard described it as 'the first pornographic novel based on technology'. The idea of the pornographic as political was crucial to him: 'In a sense, pornography is the most political form of fiction, dealing with how we use and exploit each other in the most urgent and ruthless way. Needless to say, the ultimate role of *Crash* is cautionary, a warning against that brutal, erotic and overlit realm that beckons more and more persuasively to us from the margins of the technological landscape.' It is not an accident that he has inserted himself, through his eponymous protagonist, into the heart of this pornographic nightmare – as if to remind us that pornography is not something which happens to other people, but is baked into how we all engage with one another.

The celebrated British novelist Zadie Smith admitted to having been disturbed by the novel initially but eventually concluded that it was one of Ballard's most radical and poignant creations: 'The real shock of *Crash* is not that people have sex in or near cars, but that technology has entered into even our most intimate human relations. Not man-as-technology-forming but technology-as-man-forming,' she has written. She points out the 'flatness, repetition [and] circularity' of the pornographic narration and continues that in the novel, 'the distinction between humans and things has become too small to be meaningful. In effect, things are using things.' Could there be a more fetishistic point of view?

When directing his 1996 adaptation of *Crash*, David Cronenberg amplified these fetishistic undertones. In the opening scene, we see Deborah Kara Unger taking her perfect breast out of an immaculate white bra and placing her skin carefully on cold metal. It is only the beginning of a long trail of fetish signifiers littered throughout the film. High heels, stockings, lingerie, leather gloves, leather coats and a diamond bracelet all signal both transgression and consumer ennui. The costumes, designed by the late Denise Cronenberg, follow the colour scheme of a bruise. Even the protagonist's wife's Mazda Miata was upholstered in purple to match the aesthetic. The model of the car is also an apt choice: Miatas were well known for flipping and killing their owners.

Having pushed countless boundaries around how we think about desire and consumerism, *Crash* remains an iconic work – albeit caught up in a somewhat phallocentric perspective. The 2021 Palme d'Or-winning *Titane*, in turn, takes cars and sex in radically different directions: different bodies, different sex. The film follows the protagonist Alexia, who's had titanium implanted in her skull as the result of a childhood car accident. In the opening scene, she walks through an unconventional workplace: a hybrid of a car show and a strip club, an erotic performance space where body parts and metal curves are equally seductive. The camera zooms in on Alexia's ride, and the sound drops a little, enough to let in an inviting engine groan. It is a flame-embellished Cadillac. Alexia, clad in a bronze metallic bikini and Day-Glo yellow fishnets, has a fanbase which responds eagerly to her sexual connection with the car. The scene plays on existing cultural stereotypes of women at car fairs and street races and how they are expected to perform desirability when in the proximity of desired objects – but it quickly turns surreal and slightly disturbing. The film provides us with no answers as to why, but we watch Alexia perform an actual sexual act with the car which results in the conception of her baby.

The director, Julia Ducournau, has stated many times that *Crash* was not an influence – indeed, the film is very different in its tone, perspective and storytelling and veers far from the car show of the opening, towards a killing spree and a story of identity theft. Instead, *Titane* speaks to the brutality of objectification, the pervasive gender regime and the violence lurking within it, as well as our boundless lust for objects – or what we deem as objects. At least, this is what I saw, from my cinema seat and from where I sit on the gender spectrum.

The 2022 short film *Alex's Machine* explores the bond between woman and machine even further. In its mildly speculative world, Alex is the only girl in her automotive biomechanics class. For her degree, she has chosen to build an engine made of artificial flesh. The engine is constructed from metal and organic matter: pink, rubbery, wet, bony, reminiscent of what's concealed under our own skin. One night, Alex's roommate Chloé discovers that the pleasure of working on a living machine is of a very close and personal kind. Straddling the motor between her thighs, she is able to synch with it – for its enhanced performance and her own orgasm.

When she's discovered, Alex is offered a choice: to quit her experiments and keep her place on the course or be expelled. With conviction, she responds, 'I will never give up.' Here, perversion pertains to embodied, untraditional methods of discovery. The film traces how, while it might be OK to be eroticised in relation to an object, it's definitely not OK to fuck it for pleasure. From *Crash* to *Titane* to *Alex's Machine*, as the female or gender-nonconforming body draws closer to the machine, it transitions from a pin-up model to a source of horror. But while indicative of perversion for some, machines, gears and metal become a tool for a new body politics for others.

I first connected with the artist Romeo Roxman Gatt in London in around 2018. We already somewhat knew each other, but suddenly we were in the corner of a back garden at a friend's house, intensely discussing the BMW E30 for around half an hour.

I am a car fetishist but I'm by no means a car nerd – in fact, I usually find my Uber using the number plate alone, as all urban cars tend to merge into a nondescript sludge of metal, noise and light. Usually, I am simply attracted to the abstract *essence* of a car. The E30, however, is different.

The BMW E30 is the second generation of the BMW 3 Series and was produced from 1982 to 1994. Its appearance is a classic example of 1980s automotive design, with its boxy, angular lines. The E30 features a distinctive twin-kidney grille and round taillights. You might recognise it without realising: an orange E30 featured on the cover of Frank Ocean's *Nostalgia* mixtape; a lowered E30 featured in Tyler, the Creator's music video for 'Bimmer'; and the car has featured in numerous Hollywood films. It's a car steeped in nostalgia for certain kids of the 1990s. Every time I look at one, or even a picture of one, I feel a pang of unexplainable melancholy. I think of the E30 driving over the potholes of the road I grew up on, swishing by the scenery of a barren pine forest under grey skies. Where I was from, people loved the E30, and I still feel a sentimental attachment to it.

On the palm of his right hand, Romeo has a tattoo of a crudely drawn BMW logo, and below it an inscription: 'Be My Woman'. He also has a tattoo of the whole car – an outline in his own signature style, as if scribbled in a notebook with a pen – with wings and 'ANGEL' spelt on the number plate. Like me, Romeo is queer, but he grew up in Malta. Yet despite being from different corners of the world, we have a similar fascination with car culture and the masculine spaces which define it.

Fragments of the BMW E30 have made their way into Romeo's practice: sculptures configured from car doors, mirrors and gearsticks, as well as a BMW logo debossed on a large slice of polyurethane foam, imposing but strangely fragile. In a video called *It's a Passion*, the artist carries the back bumper of an E30 like a cross, merging Christian iconography with car culture. His *Imħabba bl-addoċċ* (*Hardcore Love*) performance from 2018 featured a real-time interaction with the car, which by turns could be described as a dance, a caress and Romeo sizing up against it, turning rituals around car maintenance into erotic gestures. He remembers fondly how the performance came to be: he had met a couple who were both deeply devoted to this particular BMW and had bought and refurbished several – they would even gift each other car parts for their birthdays and other significant dates. For the choreographed dance with Romeo captured in the film, the woman drove her own E30.

Over the last few years, Romeo has been spending more time in Malta, working on his practice as well as setting up Rosa Kwir, an archive revolving around alternative notions of masculinity and bringing together stories of trans men and non-binary and masculine-of-centre people in Malta. The idea for the archive was brought on by his own transitioning and coming into his identity as a trans man. Cars feature less straightforwardly in his work now but remain a handy tool for thinking about society and gender.

'In Malta, men are very macho, they wanna show their masculinity, but then when they're connected with their car, they often refer to it as their wife or baby, or "my angel". The way they polish the car, the way you close the door, like you really need to be gentle. There's this sensitivity and tenderness in contrast with this kind of really hard physique,' Romeo recalls, before speaking of how cars form a focal point for masculine community spaces in Malta. He notes the garages and car washes, but also those more ethereal and transient spaces: a car park next to a McDonald's drive-through where boys drive around, leaving black rubber marks on the pavement, or simply just hang out next to their cars. There is safety and intimacy in this pastime, which is arranged carefully along gender lines and can be seen in many locations around the world.

Having embarked on the journey of crossing these lines, Romeo's work captures the complexity of his shifting perspective. From reclaiming automotive iconography through the language of queer desire, Romeo moved on to contemplating the construction of the masculine body through several tonnes of metal hardware. He remembers the gearstick sculptures from his 2018 show *Perfiction* and how phallic they look in retrospect. They are not, however, phallic in a way our culture often aspires to: neither long nor hard; the three gearsticks are leathery, their material and folds reminiscent of skin, gentle and timid almost. Looking back, they are an expression of curiosity, questioning biological determinism.

It was Romeo who first introduced me to the work of Helsinki-based artist Teo Ala-Ruona, who works in the extended field of performance. He too looks at cars through the lens of trans embodiment, though his work substantially differs from Romeo's. Ala-Ruona rejects petrol nostalgia by reaching into the futures born from our societal addiction to oil and petrol. In Ala-Ruona's work, car culture – including all the mundane and intimate things we do in and around cars – becomes the birthplace of techno-genders and techno-sexualities. *Slow-sex-death-drive*, performed in 2022 in Copenhagen, sees the artist surrounded by car parts, meticulously polishing a car bonnet with a splash of Monster energy drink, before caressing and kissing it. A voiceover narrates Ala-Ruona's desire for the object while the artist's gestures are carefully choreographed: they begin with the smallest of movements and culminate in the artist gulping from a white canister and gargling black liquid (motor oil?) for a painfully long time, before spitting it onto the white bonnet and then licking it up again. It gets close and personal, visceral, straddling the line of disgust and the erotic, between arousal and embodied revulsion.

In his meticulously researched essay 'Car and I', written in collaboration with Remi Vesala, the artist offers a complex take on cars, unsettling their relationship to masculinity through a consideration of how they alter our biochemistry. Ala-Ruona explores the dissolution of the barrier between the human body and the machine: car exhausts enter our lungs and the bloodstream; we breathe them in and sweat them out while the microplastics of the dashboard rub into our skin. It's a collision which is much slower and more subtle than that shown in *Crash*, but Ala-Ruona charts how we're gradually merging into one entity, our bodily presence and sexuality altered, the process irreversible. The technological advancement, however, also offers a possibility of change, self-creation and control previously unknown. 'Sustanon, the synthetic testosterone I inject monthly, is tied to the same petrochemical production structures,' the artist writes, linking automotive technologies with body chemistry during transition. Ala-Ruona also points to theories of how pollutants might act as hormone disruptors, suggesting that the air we breathe and the water we drink might make us trans or queer. 'Driving a car creates a sense of capacity and agency, similar to self-administered hormone medication.' This reading of the car and the automotive industry goes radically against the heteronormative notions we automatically prescribe to them.

Ala-Ruona's take on the car is also tender at times, as he recalls his late father, 'who lived actively through driving' and how this connection with the vehicle impacted the artist's vision of masculinity. But he wants to move past the 'masculinizing effects of car culture', and past the idea of the technologically untouched body, which is linked to gender essentialism, and towards new modes of freedom and pleasure which do not ignore environmental harms: 'I attempt to think towards worlds where the relationship with cars is different than now,' the artist writes. 'Where the relationship with technology is something other than exhilarating and patriarchal, and where the relationship with pollutants is complex – not longing for purity, imagined neutrality, and naturalness.'

In the last couple of years, self-driving cars have become a reality and are on track to change how we interact with vehicles. This near future is currently unevenly distributed, but it is present in a few corners of the world, most prominently in San Francisco. In a promotional image for the Cruise Origin car revealed in October 2023, we see four people facing each other in a spacious cabin, its interior designed in softly futuristic, glowy shades of grey and navy, with a luminous landscape caught in motion behind the glass.

'The Cruise Origin is a self-driving vehicle with no driver's seat or steering wheel,' reads the joint press release from GM, Honda and Cruise, a robotaxi provider, as the three companies plan to launch the driverless ride-hail service in central Tokyo in early 2026. 'It features a vast cabin space that can be as private as a personally owned vehicle and that allows 6 people to ride simultaneously, face-to-face.' The Cruise Origin itself looks like a boxy minibus, but is sparkly white, eerily symmetrical and topped with an orange roof. It's entertaining to imagine how the gestures we use in relation to cars and take for granted now – steering, moving the gearstick, slamming the door – and the very position of the body in the driver's seat will be forgotten. The very interpersonal dynamic between people in car seats positioned in two rows facing the same way: the leaning over, the glances, the sincerity or emotional openness allowed by sitting side-by-side, all might be a thing of the past soon enough as new physical and emotional responses to this new kind of vehicle begin to emerge.

In San Francisco, robotaxis operated by General Motors-backed Cruise and Google-run Waymo have been a reality since 2022. Predictably, people soon found a way to have sex in them, despite the strict rules, which don't even allow alcohol to be consumed inside the car, and the constant video surveillance inside the vehicle. In August 2023, the *San Francisco Standard* published an article titled 'San Franciscans are having sex in robotaxis, and nobody is talking about it', in which they interviewed a couple, Alex and Megan, about their experience of having sex inside one of the Cruise cars. 'Was it the most comfortable? Was it the most ideal? Probably not,' Megan said. 'But the fact that we were out and about in public, the whole taboo of it being kind of wrong made it more fun and exciting.'

The ubiquity of fully autonomous vehicles might remain far in the future, but the car is also being reshaped today, mostly via the arrival of electric vehicles. Our relationship with cars is intimate on an individual but also collective level, as their presence dictates sensory aspects of our environments. I love to try to make out the sound of an electric car in London, which is still largely dominated by petrol or hybrid vehicles. It often registers like an aftertaste when the car has already rolled past you, the sound still too novel to act as an alert signal. Engineers in the Audi sound lab made the lower frequencies of the Audi e-tron GT quattro's pedestrian alert by algorithmically mixing different tones produced by recording an electric fan through a long metal pipe, as well as references to soundscapes of the film *Tron* and its sequel. Danni Venne, the head designer behind the Nissan LEAF Canto sound palette mixed wind instruments, like flutes, oboes and clarinets. There is, however, still a prevalent sense of nostalgia in the understanding of how a car should sound and feel. 'You can rev it ... and it even vibrates as well,' says Tim Rodgers, product development manager at Hyundai Australia to the *Guardian*. 'It feels like an internal combustion engine, for lack of a better term, but it's an EV.'

A few years back, I interviewed artist Ada Zielińska, who spent several years photographing burning cars. The cars would not have been burning if she hadn't set them on fire. The artist's father was an unlikely collaborator for the project: a former firefighter, he was always keen to help his daughter organise destruction in the name of art. Collected together in Zielińska's book, *Pyromaniac's Manual*, the images are a mesmerising meditation on fire as it consumes a precious object. But it also raises the question of whether it's actually possible to control or contain destruction. In the images, we see the fire delicately licking the steering wheel, flames filling the whole interior of the car, clouds of black smoke enveloping the frame, as well as a stream of the artist's selfies with the burning vehicles. In the end, it's never clear what our human nature is more drawn to: our ability to control chaos or our will to submit to it.

'There came a point when I knew exactly what would happen to the car,' Zielińska told me. 'I knew when the airbag was going to blow, when the windows were going to break, and when the tyres were going to explode. I knew when the right time was to put it out so it would look beautiful, with dark smoke changing into white smoke. As I arrived at this point, it actually stopped being so exciting for me.'

Her subsequent project, *Post-Tourism*, explored 'the human drive toward the dark', or disaster tourism – the urge to visit sites of natural or human-made disasters – in a world increasingly shaped by climate change and extreme weather events. She has shot floods, earthquakes and forest fires, manifestations of truly uncontrollable chaos. The photos are free of human presence, almost serene in the aftermath of devastation. A radiant pink glow above burning hills;

a flooded horizon; a collapsed road, squashed carcasses of cars looking small and insignificant. Speaking with me, she said that when a fire broke out, she would drive towards it – into the blazing heat, alone – as most people were driving the other way. The car is a piece of technology which exemplifies our consumptive logic, it is a cause of our dire environmental present and future: it is both a vehicle and a driver of this world. Zielińska's work exposes our strange yearning to experience destruction, not as a mere witness, but as a driver setting a course for the epicentre of the chaos.

I think briefly of her set of sculptures from 2018, titled *Fondue*: fragments of cars carefully cut off from the body to leave only a cut of a bumper and a single rear light. The rear light was melted, red plastic foaming and sagging before settling into a soft, almost erotic shape.

MONSTERS

I was at WHOLE festival outside of Berlin, and it was maybe the second year that ever happened, so it was very small back then. I went by myself and brought my dog mask, which was a leather mask with zippers. It was very early in my journey around party drugs and the fetish subculture, and I was kind of adopted by a little band of German punks. They really got off on me just being their dog for the whole weekend. I really got off on that as well and I would just have my leash and I'd be led around the forest by different members of this 'Lost Boys' little German punk gang. There were maybe five of them, and they would just continually feed me mephedrone and ecstasy and acid all weekend long, and I was just really fucked out of my mind, and it was so hot that we'd just fuck in the woods, constantly just humping each other.

That was such a powerful experience for me, just being in this totally submissive object state for almost three days on end and cuddling with them at night and wearing the mask for hours at a time sometimes, with no one really talking to me.

Jordan Tannahill tells me this story at the end of our video call. We've talked about writing, raves, abjection, the dissolution of the self, but in the final moments he brings the conversation back to the fact that it is always, inevitably and gloriously, about fucking. 'It's like a collective fantasy,' he adds. 'It only worked because we were all buying into it; we're all imbuing this mask with this transformative power to make this collective fiction happen.'

Tannahill is a Canadian novelist, playwright and director. His career has spanned a decade, from running independent art spaces and publishing houses and staging plays to getting his second novel, *The Listeners*, adapted into a series by the BBC. The same novel, the story of a strange hum which can be heard by a number of inhabitants in a small town, formed the basis of an opera by composer Missy Mazzoli and librettist Royce Vavrek, which was staged in Oslo's Den Norske Opera & Ballet.

However, I first came across Jordan not through his writing but through a short interview with him featured in *Interview* magazine in 2022. In the accompanying shoot, his face is obscured by a black rubber dog mask, and he is wearing a long leather coat by Alexander McQueen. The mask is shiny and looks perfectly solid, regal and a little ominous, with only his blue eyes visible through its holes. In another photo, he is wearing a tank top in black translucent latex which says 'PUP' in large black capital letters, beneath which you can see the tattooed outlines of anthropomorphic dogs, reclining, playing. I was mesmerised – partly by someone being so open about traversing the boundaries of weird fringe sex while also producing cultural work for the public eye, but partly by something I had no definition for: a strange draw towards the unknowable and non-human, towards transformation.

I bought my dog mask on a whim. I saw it on a friend's Instagram – the designer and artist Sam Jamieson. It was crafted using leather offcuts bonded with denim, and was inspired by the face of a Dobermann, all sleek lines and pointy ears. The mask had its own sharp jawline, which accentuated that of the wearer, and strips of thick denim stitched into elongated pointy dog ears. The leather nose and forehead were slightly boxy, imposing yet elegant. Three versions were on sale: one in light blue leather and blue denim, one in blue denim with ochre-brown leather, and one which was black on black. I remember looking at the images while sitting at my desk at my copywriting job in an office, and the draw was too powerful, so I bought the black one there and then.

I was seduced by it as I unfolded the thick brown paper it came wrapped in: by the contrast of the shiny leather against the black denim with a raw edge, by the almond-shaped eye holes, which were now meant for my eyes. After I picked it up, it sat under my desk at work, wrapped, for the rest of the day. I thought of someone who might have just purchased one of the mass-produced neoprene puppy hoods, and I contemplated whether the craftsmanship of my mask – its striking design, the fact that it had been made by hand – made a difference. Both masks elicited the same sense of possibility, after all. Each of us would be asking ourselves the same questions: how do I relate to this object? Is it offering a kind of escape or a different way to be?

I don't think I had a dog persona before owning the mask, and I don't think I have one now. I have, however, a kind of fetish identity which has emerged around the object. When I first put the dog mask on to go to a fetish club, I paired it with my black latex catsuit, corset and gloves. I felt imposing, and it was in this moment that I felt the inception of what I would end up calling 'Demon Poppers Dog'. It was a joke, at first. And even though we were bent over laughing when we first put these three words together, the joke soon wore off, and it just became a part of me.

Klub Verboten was as overwhelming as ever on the night of the mask's first outing. It was summer, so there was lots of skin on show, contrasting with the latex and leather. But I was wearing the dog mask, and so it was suddenly different. My hair was in two braids behind my ears, the strokes of my eyeliner long and broad. No one recognised me, and yet I did not feel invisible or hidden. I felt like I had made a choice to step into a different dimension.

Demon Poppers Dog doesn't speak, apart from when it needs to order a drink. Demon Poppers Dog doesn't recognise the friends it arrived with. Demon Poppers Dog prowls the dance floor slowly, completely unfazed by the ecstatic press of sweaty bodies all around it.

Demon Poppers Dog is a dog in the same way that a cartoon dog is – its dogness the sum of certain dog-like signifiers. Inhabiting this alias doesn't feel like playing at being a dog – it feels like inhabiting a strange, erotic, occasionally menacing energy.

I have since worn the mask while otherwise naked, and it felt like it transformed my body, leaving my arms more muscly. I've worn it with a short-sleeved catsuit in a lustrous sporty green, with Nike trainers. While wearing it, I've licked and fucked and been horny. I've inhaled poppers and met the eyes of others differently from inside the leather and denim armour, from inside my animalistic self.

Sam Jamieson is well known in the fashion industry for working with denim. They have long been interested in the social history of both denim and leather as materials, but also how they feel on skin, how they bend, move and bulge. There's something intangible which happens when their designs come into contact with the body. 'The things that I make have more to do with eroticism than they have to do with sex. I don't think they have the practicality of an object for sex, but I try to create a sense of sexuality, of wanting to be seen in a certain way,' they explain.

During their Fashion MA at the Royal College of Art, one of the themes Sam was exploring was the body in the cruising grounds. In one of the sites, they came across a discarded pair of underwear:

'It just felt like there was so much potential for a narrative and a story that exists in this quite intimate garment in a public space.'

This tension between intimacy and public spaces, and an eroticism which is so endearing and so inherently queer, shines throughout Sam's work. Take their 'Belted Jock', for instance: black vintage leather belts stitched together to make a jockstrap, with a white triangle of fine knit over the crotch. It is subtle but sensual, juxtaposing resilient, tough leather with more delicate fabric to expand the item's expressive potential, making use of the queer codes of seduction which are not always visible to those on the outside.

Against these more nuanced objects, a dog mask might seem a little too on the nose; it's far closer to what Jamieson referred to as an 'object for sex', after all. But even here, Sam makes clear how this iconography can transcend sexual acts. I ran into them once at Adonis, a queer rave taking place in an industrial neighbourhood in East London. They were wearing a red oversized hoodie, with a dog mask strapped to a leather handbag hanging across their body. The object had clearly found its own way to exist outside of a straightforward fetish context, in the eclectic space of the queer rave. It was an accessory but also a quick way to access an alternative way of expression, a way to dive into a particular headspace while on the dance floor.

Once again, fetish exceeds its bounds, bleeding into day-to-day life. For Jamieson, these objects are linked to the idea of post-humanism or pre-humanism, as well as the process of self-creation. They first started making masks during the COVID-19 pandemic, originally inspired by the liberatory nature of digital spaces: 'Online you can create your own identity or build your own body, and it doesn't necessarily have to be limited by a human form. I was quite fascinated by that, and also I guess I was super horny at the time,' they recall.

Their masks play with animalistic identity, bringing these opportunities to experience transformation into reality and allowing one to 'access mental spaces in your head during sex that kind of take you away from yourself'. This isn't just a change in context, but rather a more radical transformation.

Not long after I had my Demon Poppers Dog experience, I came across a piece of writing by New York-based author Davey Davis on their Substack. It was titled 'Pony Brad' and was part of a series exploring fantasy. The piece describes an encounter with Brad, a dungeon client from 'a thousand years ago', who had a penchant for pony play. It usually started as an incestuous fantasy involving various members of a fictional family, but then the pony would suddenly appear. It was a role assigned randomly to people in the room. Only, the pony could speak and walk on two feet. And often, it was the pony who rode Brad, rather than the other way around. In other words, the pony was not at all pony-like.

The pony's entrance was always sporadic and unexpected, Davis writes. Pony Brad assigned its role like 'a hyperactive kid at recess, tyrannizing the make-believe of his friends with a game that no one else understood'. Even though I do not subscribe to this hectic way of playing, I thought that the Demon Poppers Dog did share something with the imagined pony. Both were pure agents of chaos which ruptured the everyday.

Play which is based around fictional animals does not have to work by the rules of our conventional universe. It might work to creatively disrupt them – to reach outside the boundaries of our (human) routines, into a plane which is ruled by a different, darker, playful and chaotic animalistic energy. The mask, in this sense, is just the beginning.

Similarly, when Jordan Tannahill first put his dog mask on at queer raves in London, surrounded by sweaty bodies and dazed stares scanning through the dark, he was looking for a different way to interact with others, a different way to be sexual: one which cut against the rhythms of his male, human self. He discovered that wearing the mask immediately attracted strange and persistent attention. He found himself depersonalised, with people grabbing and touching him in a way which they wouldn't have if he'd been presenting as his usual, human self. On his outings to clubs and raves, Jordan didn't feel that the persona he inhabited was in any way submissive or cute – on the contrary, he felt like a more powerful version of himself, a dog who takes himself for a walk to the club, holding his own leash.

'These warped social interactions [were] combined with taking party drugs – being on ecstasy or ketamine or acid – and it just felt so *true*. It began to feel transformational whenever I donned a mask and I really did kind of enter this total other frame of mind. A space that was supercharged and sexual. I felt almost like a jaguar moving through a jungle: it was a heightened sensorial space and the mask felt like the appropriate way in which to inhabit that space, as opposed to my usual body,' he remembers.

Earlier in our conversation, Jordan had touched on abjection, a term explored most famously in philosopher Julia Kristeva's *Powers of Horror: An Essay on Abjection*. As we talk about fetish, it seems entirely fitting to delve into the breakdown of the boundary between the body and the object. In critical theory, abjection is the state of being 'cast off', either separated from the body or from norms and rules at the scale of society and morality. Kristeva claims that within the boundaries of what one defines as subject (a part of oneself) and object (something which exists independently of oneself) reside pieces which were once categorised as a part of oneself or one's identity but have since been rejected – the abject. This tension is a constant in fetishism: the (re)negotiation of what is and isn't taboo, what is and isn't you, the modification of the boundaries of self – at times even the loss and re-emergence of the self as something different, something reimagined, something monstrous.

If you separate out a version of yourself, if you become an object, are you still human? Imagine being strapped into a dog mask and looking up at someone from the floor. Imagine inhaling poppers in a dark room full of bodies, being touched and fucked by endless limbs. Imagine surrendering to the desires of others. These feel like the perfect sites for questions inspired by post-structuralist philosophy.

This desire to test the boundaries of one's subject position is what led Tannahill to play with the animalistic: 'I really relate to the idea of a kind of self-obliterating desire or self-obliterating pleasure. The closest that I can think of as a kind of impossible fetish that I possess would be the fetishism of the Symbiote or of Goo, of being totally consumed by and transformed by another being, kind of like Marvel's Venom,' Jordan adds. 'I can't quite even say why it feels so erotic, but it really is to me – this pleasure which alters you permanently, the idea of becoming, of changing bodies. I think maybe [it speaks] to this kind of existential agony: why just this one body, why this one form?'

In 2023, a Redditor posted a photo in r/boston with the comment, 'Which one of you freaks hijacked the South Boston green space photos with your furry photoshoot.' The photo, in fact, did not depict a furry, but a pup. The individual in the photo is wearing a black rubber suit with a grey handkerchief and a turquoise collar around their neck. They are also wearing a puppy mask: black with green and blue inserts and purple ears. They're standing on a pier, which is part of the waterfront in South Boston, also known as South Boston Green Space: you can see the dark grey water and warehouses with light blue roofs in the background. The colours and lighting are a bit barren, and the person's posture is relaxed, slightly aloof. It could have been a regular touristy snap – if not for the full puppy outfit.

The photo was posted to this location in Google Maps, which is how the Redditor came across it: the internet's equivalent of appearing as a pup in a public place. The photo was posted by Nat Werth, who has appeared in the pup guise in a few places in the US, including Boston, Palm Springs and Chicago. It is a bit of a hobby: he's trying to get the Expert Photographer badge on Google Maps while simultaneously raising awareness of the pup community.

Pups first emerged as part of the gay leather scene. The submissive partner would assume the position of the puppy, while the dominant one would be the handler, with their roles having a strict hierarchy. With time, however, the hierarchy increasingly dissolved, and the role of a puppy transitioned from this link to power play, or even humiliation, to a wide array of different dynamics. Pups can be singles or strays, can belong to a handler, a trainer or a Sir, and some pups may even join larger pup packs and adopt puppy roles such as alpha, beta and omega. The pup gear has also evolved: designed in a variety of materials, it's often crafted in bold colours. Some stylistic variations include an intersection with motorcycle or motocross equipment. A neoprene pup hood is almost synonymous with the subculture: with colourful panels on the ears, brows and nose, it's uniformal but playful, a constant at sex parties, raves and Pride marches worldwide.

In fact, pups are also often mentioned in relation to the Kink at Pride controversy. Every Pride, there is always footage of human pups getting friendly with actual dogs or unsuspecting passers-by. The pup play can sometimes be pretty benign, at least on paper, as it can be performed with no nudity or sexual acts involved. Some, however, see the behaviours as something more problematic than innocent role play in a public space, especially as it's performed for sexual gratification and without the consent of the accidental audience. Pups, however, have been part of the LGBTQI+ community for some time, but this contention around how their behaviour is viewed means that finding a place within the community is not always easy.

In 2019, the *New York Times* published the article 'We Live in Packs', which documented the lives of San Francisco-based pups. In it, Blake Montgomery emphasised the role of online platforms for the community: from Tumblr before adult content was banned to Twitter (now X) and Instagram. These online spaces allow the playfulness of the practice to blossom – hedonistic, exhibitionist or community-oriented. All you need is a pup hood and a hashtag (#pupplay, #humanpup, #gaypup) and you can find your people. The puppy headscape, however, remains at the centre of the practice: joyful, non-verbal, different from human. 'You stop using words and start communicating in growls. It's really fun,' Phillip Hammack, forty-two, a University of California Santa Cruz psychology professor who goes by Pup Turbo, told the *New York Times*. 'You're disconnecting from the human side of thinking about every little thing you're doing. You're being instinctual and playful.'

Pups are a part of cultural iconography, yet the Redditor's question channels the mainstream sentiment towards the practice: a sense of wonder and concern, as well as an overall lack of knowledge. The term 'furry' is (mistakenly) dropped as a joke, the usual stand-in for the strange. Pups and furries are distinctly different subcultures, even though they do intersect. The idea of taking an animalistic persona lies at the heart of both, but where pups seek to enter an animal-like headspace, furries push in almost the opposite direction. They have an interest in anthropomorphised animals with human characteristics, such as the ability to walk on two legs or talk. These animals can be related to existing cultural franchises – Sonic the Hedgehog, Pokemon, My Little Pony – or can be the furry's own creation, known as their 'fursona'.

The furry is a fetishist insomuch as they invest psychically in objects and cultural signifiers to channel a desired narrative about the self. However, their thrill lies much more in authorship and the creation of their persona. Only a third of furries surveyed in the US in 2015 admitted to having a full fur suit, and most agreed that having sex in one is absolutely impractical and undesirable. Instead, most furries prefer accessories – tails, ears, fluffy paws. While some furries desire sexual activity with other furries, others maintain a completely non-erotic fetishism that is primarily about cosplay.

Furries largely exist separately from the broader fetish community. I wonder sometimes if this is purely due to the difference in the preferred material: the soft plushy fur suits, masks and paws don't readily sit alongside latex and leather. These lines, however, aren't drawn in the sand: the Hong Kong-based brand FORFUN trades in inflatable animal suits made from latex and rubber, for instance.

Furries are often brought up when people want to make an extreme example of sexual difference. It is something they use to signify the other, to say 'this could never be me'. The practice, however, is no longer as fringe as it's perceived to be. With our sexuality increasingly shaped by the internet, as well as fandoms becoming more prolific and expressive, sexual diversity is on the rise. Animal ears and tails are now a common staple in pornography and erotic content, and playful animalistic undertones have seeped into the broader internet culture: from catboy and catgirl role play, in part stemming from manga and anime, to judging whether your face is bunny pretty or fox pretty on TikTok. Plus, with the rise of AI, furry fan art can now be generated in seconds.

In other words, it's easier than ever for anyone to imagine what it would be like to have animalistic traits, to create an avatar which is more than human.

In any erotic play which draws from the animalistic, there is an element of becoming but never being. You do not become the animal – you carve a space for yourself which is between you and the animal of your imagination. This space becomes a lawless zone, where things are suddenly possible – silly, playful, dark, transformative, disgusting, abhorrent, sentimental, joyful, odd. As such, it's sometimes misleading to think of these erotic identities as 'animals'. Sometimes, one might just slip into *the other*, something non-human, something monstrous.

'I thought it was a chicken,' a friend once said to me, looking at the tattoo on my right thigh. I quickly realised that only the lower half of it was visible under the fabric of my skirt: feathers and a bird leg. It could well have been a chicken, but it's actually Sirin: a half-woman, half-bird creature from Slavic mythology. Sirin sings beautiful songs foretelling future bliss, but the men who hear them forget the world and follow them to their death. Sirin is most likely a reimagining of the sirens from Greek mythology and Homer's *Odyssey*, ancient stories which travelled with Byzantine merchants. I've loved images of Sirin since my early childhood: they were cool and self-possessed and irresistible and beautiful, in a scary way. 'Sirin would not experience dysphoria,' I always thought, 'they would not feel fat or unlovable or gender-confused.' Sirin, to my mind, prides themselves on pure power.

The monstrous sometimes feels unbelievably accurate as a way to grasp what it's like to live in a queer body: to be deemed 'ugly' or 'unpleasant' within dominant cultural discourse. It can also be a source of pride. The queering of the monstrous has been a significant cultural process in recent years: we have seen the Babadook-as-queer-icon go from an internet in-joke to a Pride Month figurehead, and Godzilla has been reclaimed as an expression of queer rage towards corporatisation (#LGodzillaBT); we've seen the recoding of Disney villains (Ursula from *The Little Mermaid*, Scar from *The Lion King*) as queer heroes, as well as the rise of independent queer horror. The monstrous can feel like a refuge, an escape from categories, explanations and institutional hurdles. *What do you mean, what is my gender? Don't you see I have the body of a dinosaur?* In other words, sometimes there's more at stake than simple 'play'. Sometimes the other which one inhabits through one's fetish is an attempt to find space outside the structures of heteronormativity.

Dressed in a red high-neck bodysuit and red stockings, GRACE dances. Her head is covered with an elegant, perfectly fitting bonnet, and long red gloves expose slender shoulders. Her movements are graceful. She is a rat. Her face is a rat face, wrinkly and pale, not in a pretty, cartoonish way, but in what you might imagine a rat would look like if it had to endure the challenges of our contemporary lifestyle. Her eyes, in the middle of that wrinkly face, are so beautiful.

In Jenkin van Zyl's film *Surrender*, GRACE enters the P.E.E.P. hotel to compete with other rats at the hotel's ballroom in an endurance dance tournament. 'Here the dance floor variously becomes a cell, a nightclub, the belly of a whale, a courtroom, a treadmill and a beating heart – a space for negotiating community, desire and risk, but also to seek out victory, exhaustion and The End,' van Zyl's introduction to the artwork reads.

The idea was partly inspired by twentieth-century dance marathons: gruelling endurance competitions where couples danced almost non-stop for hundreds of hours. It also echoes some of the qualities of queer nightlife, Jenkin admits to me. It makes so much sense – not as a direct reference, of course, but as a memory stored somewhere in the lumbar spine. If you've ever desperately looked for closeness in the queue for the bar or for the club toilet while deep on K, if you've felt the 7 a.m. elation at being with the other dancers who just wouldn't go home, then you know.

The film was part of Jenkin's eponymous immersive exhibition at London's Edel Assanti gallery in 2023. One entered the gallery through a giant silver inflatable of a rat's head and proceeded along the dimly lit walkway, pipes of a pneumatic tube system snaking on the sides. The film was screened in a room which evoked an austere love hotel; it was a double of the room we were watching on screen. The back of the installation contained a separate mirror-lined trophy room, where plinths made from towers of energy drink cans glistened, with a smoke chemtrail marked out on the ceiling: *SURRENDER GRACE*. The film was a perfect loop with no ending, and I watched it twice, feeling a strange kinship with the rats on the treadmill of hope, ecstasy and exhaustion.

The artist's interest in monsters is multifaceted. On the one hand, it is an attempt to interrogate the stories we tell about ourselves – using the monstrous to illuminate the oddities of our behaviour and to survey the debris of the human-driven crisis. On the other, Jenkin admits that his original fascination was almost a 'cliche of queer development': the 'experience of so many queer kids attracted to the monstrous, to Halloween' and his own childhood love of dress-up. But above all, the monstrous allows him to explore the existing power structures we live within: 'I'm interested in making the monstrous characters the more sympathetic ones. And the human characters become the antagonists, or the frightening representations of power structures that try and manipulate our desires or prevent us from achieving autonomy. My protagonists, the rats in *Surrender* and the more ghoulish characters in previous projects, are trying to thrive in and against the human, heteronormative society,' Jenkin explains.

For his exhibition *Vore* at London's Rose Easton, Jenkin put an inflatable latex monster into a glass box. It resembled an enormous lizard or a bulbous dinosaur, mouse-brown and rubbery. Upon closer inspection, though, it lacked a head. Instead, it was potentially not one creature, but two, intertwined in a deadly embrace, either caught in the act of consuming one another, or a strange erotic coupling. The vitrine was an infinity mirror on the inside, further defamiliarising various limbs and textures, and evoking zoo enclosures, museum display cases and a surreal erotic peep show. The gallery space had a faint smell of latex.

The installation was partly inspired by vore, a kink Jenkin encountered in fringe online communities, which eroticises the extreme idea of being eaten and digested by someone (or something) alive. 'There [is something] innately queer – and by queer, I, of course, mean monstrous – about a self-obliterating insatiability,' Jordan Tannahill wrote in the text which accompanied the exhibition. 'The grotesque hunger that cannot be filled, not even by two fists taken to the elbow. What is the eros we would rupture ourselves for?'

Vore continued Jenkin's exploration of latex inflatables, which had begun with the film *Looners*, commissioned by the Hayward Gallery for their *Kiss My Genders* exhibition in 2019. It was shot in the Atlas Mountains in a big abandoned complex of Hollywood film sets. In it, latex inflatable characters roam the desert. The process involved collaborators dressed in inflatable latex costumes in forty-degree heat. 'It involves reimagining the body,' van Zyl tells me. 'I liked how it linked to Leigh Bowery's club costumes. A lot of the suits I made were kind of muscular or have this intense bravado, where it makes the body into this big kind of pronouncement of gender, but then at the same time, it's comically vulnerable because if you caught the material on anything, then it would just pop and fizzle away. They're almost pathetic while also hyper-masculine.'

Jenkin's interest in the erotic and the fetishistic emerged from coming of age on the internet, in the chat rooms and webcam spaces which had their own way of elaborate world-building. 'That led to going to places like Kaos raves when I moved to London, and other subcultural events that had this strange and exciting mix of music, desire and community all blended together. And I remain interested in how desire and fetish translate to community. So, not only how it exists behind closed doors, but how it exists as a network.'

In my conversations with both Jenkin van Zyl and Jordan Tannahill, there is a reflection on the forces which drive fetish as a consciousness. Both touch on closeness and community and speak of how fetish offers a lens through which to consider how we connect to other people. They both also speak to a desire for transformation: one which leads us beyond societal constraints, and at times beyond our physical forms. There is a sadness to fetish: of becoming but never being. But then, there is also an enduring sense of purpose. If you can never quite arrive at your destination, you are never fully satisfied, and so the drive lives on forever. This pursuit feels fundamentally human.

'But, more broadly, I am interested in a more critical standpoint,' van Zyl tells me, 'in how fetish can speak to society's anxieties. Desire, for me, is not a pure force, it's not something that's totally innate. It's shaped by all sorts of things like technology, our backgrounds and intersecting histories, and I remain really curious about how those things link together.'

Maybe through the monstrous, we assume our true form. Like a fragile inflatable figure in the desert: horrific, but beautiful, nevertheless.

THE FETISH CLUB

Three words ran through my mind when I entered my first-ever fetish club night: *I am home.*

It took place in Bow, in East London, in a nondescript building surrounded by storage warehouses. Boxy shadows, a car park. The usual experience of attending a fetish club night: being somewhere cold and unfamiliar, your fishnets, rubber, lace hidden under your coat. I would likely never be in this location again; even if I tried to find it now, I probably couldn't, despite living a ten-minute Uber ride away. It occupied a unique time and place: it was the first Klub Verboten party after the COVID-19 pandemic regulations eased in spring 2021. We didn't know whether there would be more restrictions on social gatherings, nor when they might arrive; we didn't know for how long we'd be able to have the thrilling possibility of touching a stranger. The excitement of being near one another was palpable.

Something I've gleaned from several years of writing about kink is just how often the pandemic played a central role in people's origin stories. Having to spend days in a confined space, in isolation, with the fear of death and sickness, pushed a lot of kinksters, fetishists and queer people towards self-exploration, testing their personal preferences and the social taboos they'd inherited. Add some extra disposable income saved up from not going out, and the ability to purchase your first-ever piece of latex, and the fetish community was suddenly within reach.

This was my story too. And so I stood there in fishnet tights, a PVC corset from Etsy and latex gloves. *The world is burning; I may as well come out as a pervert*, I thought.

Inside, the corridor and dance floor were flooded with dim red light. I felt a vague sense of familiarity as I looked around, a déjà vu possibly evoked by the outfits on display: leather trousers, fishnets, PVC pencil skirts, rubbery latex bras. It was as if I'd walked into a depiction of a fetish night in a 1990s film. The aesthetic of these spaces is usually harsh, a little intimidating. You walk into the unfamiliar space like plunging in cold water, pushing yourself past timidity and self-consciousness. But oddly, as I entered, I felt the opposite – a sense of warmth. It wasn't just that the heating system was set to account for the skimpy get-ups, nor the warmth gleaned from the other bodies in close proximity. The mood was warm: people were happy and giddy and shy to be so close to others, to be able to touch and smell one another, to co-exist in a shared sexual space.

Someone was dressed as an other-worldly latex doll in eight-inch heels, their hooded head floating high over everyone else's on the dance floor. Two friends invited me to pour some of my drink into a funnel fitted in the mouth of a third friend, kneeling below. When it got crowded later in the night, someone was cracking their long whip at the ass of someone chained to a St Andrew's cross. I've never, before or after, heard a whip tear through the humid air of the dance floor so loudly. That night, the sex freaks were truly out, and, in that moment, I knew that I was one of them – that I'd always been one. It just took me a while to find the right place.

It was a space to which people brought their complicated sexuality and laid it bare (even if every inch of their skin was covered by rubber). And in some ways, the overwhelming and intoxicating space of the fetish club has inspired the shape of this book. Both are packed with diverse perspectives on sex. Both bring together a multitude of voices and visions. Both create a sense of (sometimes unlikely) communion. Both, hopefully, can be a stepping stone for more exploration.

Klub Verboten became my go-to fetish club for a while. Memories of different nights merge in my mind. Heavy rubber curtains forming paths to explore. Walking through the play area slowly, hoping to steal a few more glances at a tableau unfolding like a Renaissance painting: bodies in the soft red glow, on all manner of surfaces, touching, kissing, fucking, moaning, their movement like waves. Playing with a red light beam with my latex glove: lights streaming from the ceiling, looking almost solid, catching particles of dust, designed to create ethereal accents in the space.

Klub Verboten is hosted in several locations around London and adapts to the different spaces. At Fire Club, they turned one of the smaller rooms into a porn cinema with sofas dotted around the room. They showed the Four Chambers film *Blood Milk*, which was banned from all online platforms for featuring blood play – yet in this small space within a sprawling South London club, it was OK. I kept getting lost between all the rooms, and the floor seemed uneven. They sold poppers at the bar, and the toilet smelt so strongly of piss that it was almost sexy in its disgusting seediness. They've since stopped hosting nights at the venue, but these memories remain. I've come to terms with how ephemeral these moments are. A night at a fetish club is almost overwhelmingly textured, full of sounds, sensations, bodies, possibilities. They are imprinted in the mind like flashes in the darkness, but you can never truly recall them in their full intensity. There are some parts of the experience you have to accept that you'll lose. All the more reason to embrace the moment.

At Fold, another London club, I watched my friend, a professional dominatrix, ashing a cigarette into the mouth of her sub, a performance unfolding in a small separate room – her hair so long and dark, her lips deep red and her expression deeply content. The audience could peer in through a small window. I saw my friends fucking. I never wanted to watch too long, but I sometimes caught a glimpse of this other side to them, which is usually kept private.

Every time, every location, I relished seeing how the architecture of the space accommodated our bodies, how it manipulated the gaze: looking, being looked at, forgetting about being looked at and remembering again, landing in your own body, surrounded by sex.

The smell of Dettol spray on wipe-clean leather furniture. People with whom I locked eyes in the playroom once but never saw again, and yet whose faces linger in my mind. I always enjoy how malleable these memories are: evenings bleed into each other, locations merge and conversations evaporate. These memories aren't recorded anywhere – photography at fetish clubs is strictly forbidden – and they're warped by arousal.

Waiting for an Uber by a petrol station. The beautiful pale morning light. At home, falling asleep on the fresh sheets. You close your eyes, and darkness is not dark enough. You wait for your mind and body to return from the club, a place which it's now hard to believe actually exists.

I still hold on to that sense of warmth from my first time. There was a feeling of relief, too: the club looked like I imagined it would, and I felt like I could belong as my full, sexually deviant self. But as with any community built around the fragile, shifting lines of sexual identity, not everyone gets to belong. Such is the political complexity of the fetish club.

There isn't such a thing as a singular 'fetish club'. Quite often, it is not even a club. There are places which are purposefully designed with sex in mind, but they are rare. More frequently, the fetish club is transient, taking the shape of whichever shell it occupies, and is dependent on the people it brings together and the efforts of those setting it in motion. A leather gay bar set in a small basement, which has been there for decades. An underground space with a dance floor underneath a local gay sauna with no phone signal and a tiled room where patrons can be pissed on. A private leatherdyke play party for a dozen people. A Sunday afternoon in a pay-by-the-hour dungeon. A foot worship gathering in a pub's function room. A cluster of small rooms where rubberists are welcome to cruise each other (men only). A fetish club is a string of many varied, real spaces as much as it is a unifying cultural idea shaped by decades of history, enduring curiosity and a collective experience of sexual fantasy.

Kink, BDSM and fetish clubs are an integral part of cultural and queer history. The memories of them are woven into our cityscapes – Skin Two, Der Putsch, Rubber Cult and SWEAT in London, to name just a few. They have always been spaces of radical freedom and have often attracted active condemnation from conservative powers because of it. In the early 1990s, London's leatherdyke S/M night Chain Reaction (frequented by the Rebel Dykes crew) was stormed by a group of balaclava-clad protesters who deemed sado-masochism anti-feminist. The Catacombs, the cult gay BDSM and fisting club in San Francisco, was shut down in the early 1980s, when the leather community received heavy blame for the onset of the HIV/AIDS epidemic.

London, where I am writing this book, has a broad range of fetish clubs to offer, including ambitious projects which merge nightlife, performance and architecture created specifically for erotic play. Torture Garden has been running since 1990, with an emphasis on performances and theatrical outfits. Klub Verboten started in 2016 as a trendier, darker, more contemporary option which centred around heavier BDSM and fetish, as well as active consent culture. Joyride and Pinky Promise emerged post-pandemic, infused with sensuality, gender experimentation and an abundance of latex and mesh in bold, bright colours. One Night creates a play space for women and non-binary people only, while Hunter London is the latest addition to heavy-play leather gay clubbing. However, this list is merely scratching the surface of the rapidly evolving fetish club culture in the city, which has absorbed the energy of its queer scene, rave underground and ever-changing style. Moreover, there are no longer strict boundaries which keep fetish clubs apart: more and more queer events feature erotic performances, playrooms or a bootblacking stand, where a local incredibly hot dyke can polish your boots in the tradition of the leather community.

In an expensive city, with complicated nightlife licensing policies and relentless forces of redevelopment and gentrification, the landscape is constantly changing. Nights close down, people move on, but the shared desires which drive them remain. Despite the preconceptions, these nights are about more than pure hedonism.

It is a clear, cool night in May as I walk into Torture Garden. It's hosted at Electrowerkz, a venue in Angel, North London. Three or four different rooms are connected via broad staircases, which gives it an expansive, warren-like feeling. There is a burlesque performance in one room, a drag show in another. In the room with the biggest dance floor, there is a catwalk platform at the centre. I stand close by, and as the fashion show is announced, people gradually stop dancing. I've come to see the work of a friend who runs a small independent brand, Primal Leather. The fetish catwalk lands somewhere between a fashion show and a ballroom performance:

high-energy, expressive, placing emphasis on the people as much as the designs. Torture Garden has been hosting these shows for decades, giving the floor to latex and leather makers.

Primal Leather mostly focuses on harnesses, belts and other body-fitting creations crafted from sturdy leather straps. Tonight, it's all equestrian: belts with fitted stirrups, metallic horse bits repurposed as belts – a playful take on a pony show. The designer, Chloé, grew up on a farm, and the local pubs were covered in equestrian memorabilia. She started collecting early on. In one of the leather sets, a belt is adorned with an old browband from a London police horse: a thick brass plate with a star in the middle. The catwalk cuts straight through the dance floor, and the crowd cheers loudly as the models walk down. I don't know many people around me in the audience. The Torture Garden crowd comes in a variety of ages and genders, with a range of career paths and incomes left at the door. There's little uniting us, bar the enjoyment of these creatively designed ways of being a pony for the night.

The word 'community' becomes slippery when interrogated on the dance floor, in darker corners of the club. I once saw a meme floating around online: 'I connect with my community by sharing my ass.' Or another one which goes along the lines of: 'They're not your chosen family, they're just a DJ who puts you on the list.' Queer people have long grappled with community which emerges, woven and interlinked, around nightlife and shared places where sex, alcohol and recreational substances are explored. The gay bars and the queer clubs become the first places where the exploration of who we are and who we want is possible. It also often leaves one feeling empty come morning. Some forge lasting connections in the club; some walk back home alone; some are happy to sneak away as if it never happened.

Some fetish clubs double up as queer spaces, while some remain in an undefined grey area of lusty exploration beyond labels, but most of them bring together people of all political and social stances and backgrounds. People relish being seen: as their true selves, as their alternative personas, as an embodiment of their deepest fantasies. But to what degree does this make us a community? Are we a community if we share some hot group sex? Are we a community if we share a kink? 'I feel like these people wouldn't say hello to me if they saw me in the daytime,' a leatherdyke friend once remarked, nodding towards the rest of the crowd at a fetish party.

In his book *Gay Bar*, Jeremy Atherton Lin traces the history of San Francisco's Castro District, which has become synonymous with the gay community.

> In 1985, a group of sociologists published the book *Habits of the Heart*, arguing that a real community must be a 'community of memory', meaning one that remembers its past, including painful stories of shared suffering. Where history is forgotten, they wrote, community degenerates into lifestyle enclaves. Lifestyle 'celebrates the narcissism of similarity', and elevates private concerns – namely, leisure and consumption – above the common good. The academics announced: 'When we hear phrases such as "the gay community" or "the Japanese-American community", we need to know a great deal before we can decide to which degree they are genuine communities and the degree to which they are lifestyle enclaves.'

I was particularly struck by the term 'lifestyle enclave' on first reading this passage. 'Lifestyle' is a word often thrown around in BDSM or kink contexts: 'lifestyle domme', '24/7 lifestyle', 'been in the lifestyle for twenty years'. 'Lifestyle' might gesture towards personal practice or a commitment, like wearing a subtle necklace which doubles up as a proxy 'collar', or signing a symbolic contract outlining a long-term BDSM dynamic; it might indicate that one's fetish extends into the home, like hosting a party at your private dungeon; or it might be used to emphasise a non-commercial engagement with fetish, drawing a line between a 'lifestyler' and a professional. Lifestyle can sound like a trite word, something which lands between a yoga class and a Sunday brunch, when the human cage fitted in your living room goes on the same list of expenses as car maintenance. But also, it is what it is – we all fit our sexualities, however baroque, into how we spend our days.

On the other hand, leather culture has always been centred around an idea of community – shared visual codes, shared spaces, as well as a shared, painful history and continuous mutual aid. What complicates the community versus lifestyle dichotomy is the fact that everyone who identifies as a kinkster, pervert or rubberist can make their own choice about historical continuity. You can choose to engage politically with others, or you can simply fuck for pleasure. Those who you fuck for pleasure regularly might become friends, or your fetish club crew, but for them to become your community requires one taking a step over a political threshold. No means of engaging with one's fetishes is objectively 'better', but it is an individual choice which you will, at some time or other, have to take responsibility for. It's not dissimilar to thinking about queer people as one expansive, amorphous community – within it, people will have different takes on their unity and how to honour it. We can endlessly argue about how to be queer 'correctly', but everyone will have their own way of being, alone and with others.

I have rooted my personal exploration of fetish in memory, somehow, from the very start: rummaging through boxes in Rambooks porn store, scribbling on lending cards at the UK Leather and Fetish Archive. I didn't find these places myself but usually heard about them from friends, picking up a thread they left me. I am obsessed with memory, partly out of fear, because I know what happens when people get persecuted for their sexuality. I like to hold on to evidence that there is not just 'me' but also an 'us'. Within the fetish club, I have found both a community and a lifestyle enclave. The difference, however, is not always clear-cut. Sometimes, it is more of a feeling. I do not single out, effortlessly, who else is preoccupied with history and the intentionality of play – and I am not always this conscientious. Sometimes we experiment, sometimes it's just for fun – we want something new, beyond our known boundaries – and we aren't thinking beyond the moment. But it makes me think that saying 'I connect with my community by sharing my ass' is more than just a joke. If spending hours in fetish clubs has taught me anything, it is that there are always more ways of connecting with each other.

My hands rest on the desk on either side of a microphone. I am sitting in front of a panel of Tower Hamlets councillors in a large auditorium, and I'm wearing over-the-elbow black latex gloves. This is perhaps the most unlikely result of getting into fetish clubbing I could have imagined.

'You might look at us and find that we are a bit funny in our outfits, but for us this is where we can truly be safe; this is our family.' I don't remember what else I say, because my voice trembles unintentionally at the word 'family'. Perhaps, if I were less nervous, or if I had more time, I would tell them something closer to what I have written here, but I only have five minutes. The auditorium is large, and a few rows of seats behind me are filled with Klub Verboten regulars wearing regular outfits with an occasional leather harness or latex top sprinkled among them. They have come to show support for their favourite fetish night, worrying that it is about to perish due to licensing policies. At the podium, my body is tense, and my gloves have lost their shine. Outside, people cheer while watching the hearing on a big screen provided by Klub Verboten. I thought that councils mostly dealt with noise complaints and rubbish collections; I can't believe that I am here explaining the importance of fucking in public.

The hearing, which took place in August 2022, was in response to a series of events which had happened a few months prior. Klub Verboten events usually consist of a sizeable dance floor with booming techno and a separate playroom where one can safely and consensually practise BDSM and kink: from bondage to impact play to power exchange, as well as what is typically defined as 'sex' in vanilla terms. Sex is a crucial part of these nights, as is the dress code – from latex, fishnet and mesh to being fully naked. But this time, Tower Hamlets Council had taken issue. They had contacted the venue ahead of a planned Klub Verboten event and were seeking to prohibit 'nudity and semi-nudity' and threatening to revoke the venue's licence if these stipulations weren't followed. With the definition of 'nudity and semi-nudity' being both obscure and violently binary (it includes exposed nipples for women but not for men), it created a problem – not only could people not enjoy the kind of fetish clubbing they loved and were used to, it also implied the existence of just two genders.

On the night of the event, my play partner and I both decided to go for full-coverage latex catsuits. Under the thin layer of skin-tight black latex, we hoped that our bodies would not be considered semi-nude – and therefore not a threat to public decency and well-being. We were both perplexed why what we wore inside a private event at a club suddenly mattered so much to the authorities. There wasn't any sex that night; we mostly just stood around chatting in our full-coverage latex outfits, contemplating the nude and the obscene. The venue was expansive, and there was a palpable sense of the void left where sex had usually been – the sound of bodies in movement, the moans, the sexual energy. We felt like kids at the prom, unable to kiss under adult supervision.

The core issue faced by Klub Verboten was around licensing legislation for sexual entertainment venues. On paper, their licensing is intended for sex cinemas, strip clubs and sex shops. It is by no means the right category for a kink and fetish event, but it is the only option available. This is why we attended the council hearing: a group of promoters, lawyers and club-goers trying to convince the councillors that the licensing policy needed updating, and to articulate how meaningful fetish clubs were for our community – for the queers and perverts of all kinds. A few people who spoke came from more conservative backgrounds, like me.

No fetish club is ever perfect, but Klub Verboten felt like a place worth fighting for. Especially so given a wider trend of closures. Around the same time as the hearing, the legendary leather bar The Backstreet shut down – the latest in a long line of queer venues closing their doors. In fact, more than half of London's LGBTQI+ venues closed between 2006 and 2022, with numbers falling from 125 to 50. Venues cited the cost-of-living crisis and rising rents among the key reasons.

Things were looking dire. These closures remind us that, ultimately, fetish clubs are there for a good time, but not for a long time. These spaces are fragile, they rarely last; organisers burn out, venues close down, something terrible slips through the cracks of safeguarding or the authorities step in. Every time we are together in one space, it always feels too good to last.

―――――

Klub Verboten started in 2016. It began as a relatively small seventy-person gathering in Murder Mile dungeon in Walthamstow. It has since considerably outstripped these humble beginnings, with events in London and Berlin attracting up to 1,500 people. For the majority of the event's existence, it has been run by Karl Verboten and Hanny Amin. For Karl, who is originally from Germany and has worked in events since his teenage years, the desire to start a kink night came from a deep interest in human sexuality. Or, as he puts it, 'I just sat there and had to admit to myself that perhaps I am a pervert.'

'Pervert' is a widely embraced, even affectionate term around London's younger kink scene, especially among KV-goers ('a cummunity of caring perverts', the website proclaims). 'To me, pervert is about the state of freedom,' Karl tells me. 'It's someone who allows themselves to be whoever they want to be, regardless of societal views, while not doing anything to harm another, of course. I think a lot of us pride ourselves on being perverts these days, because we're still living in a society that tries to shut down these spaces and communities, whether online or offline, based on moral views or for legal reasons. That's why "pervert" has become almost this protest character.'

Karl is skinny and heavily tattooed, with long dark-blond hair and a 1970s-style moustache. He's surprisingly introverted for an event organiser. During events, he usually runs around fixing various issues, avoiding any kind of small talk. Being widely recognised by KV-goers, he's had to deploy a gimp mask or a puppy hood a couple of times, which has helped him keep a low profile.

Back in 2016, Karl's main motivation to start Klub Verboten was to create a sexual space which would feel contemporary, in line with what London had to offer in terms of music, art and design. They got rid of the soft textures, red velvet and boudoir-style embellishments typically associated with fetish clubs in favour of a minimal, wipe-clean set-up, sleek lighting and a soundtrack of heavy techno. But above everything else, the space had to be safe. Human sexuality is a complicated matter to handle en masse. So they introduced a set of rules for all attendees to follow and started training a safeguarding team which could provide assistance in complicated situations. They didn't want to leave the responsibility of how to behave with attendees; they weren't prepared to accept any 'human collateral damage'. While community care and self-regulation have been staples of the BDSM culture, these standards often got lost when it came to running sexual events – some promoters prioritised profit, some perpetuated sexual harassment, while others simply didn't belong to the community themselves and were unaware of the risks. Before Klub Verboten, there was a certain level of acceptance that uncomfortable situations, harassment and sexual assault were things which 'just happened' at these nights. Karl wanted a safer future for their party and the wider scene.

The oldest set of play party rules I've held in my hands was from a 1989 party by The Society of Janus, a San Francisco-based BDSM education and support group founded in 1974. It was a thin yellowing piece of paper with an intricate black-and-white illustration of someone's cock caught in rose thorns. The rules were pretty standard: don't interrupt scenes, practise safe sex, clean up after yourself, flag if you're worried about someone's wellbeing. KV's rules, displayed on the website, are similarly focused on looking after each other: prioritising consent, not touching anyone without explicit permission, no discriminatory or hateful behaviour, no photos. The team of safeguards at every event are trained to supervise the space and act on any issues. And there is also a membership system – every new member still gets vetted, in person, by the safeguards. So much for the 'anything goes' idea of sexual excess . . .

After discovering Klub Verboten, I stopped going to regular clubs for a while. A year in, I had forgotten how to dress up in anything but fetish wear. (Jeans and a T-shirt – and that's enough to go out in?) But it was also surprisingly easy to adapt to a different way of expressing your sexuality in the club space. I quickly got used to feeling safe regardless of how revealing my outfit was – at Klub Verboten, there was no catcalling, groping or staring, and if there was, the person would be promptly escorted out. It was a new kind of freedom. I could walk through the space wearing a sheer mesh dress or tight latex or even be topless, and feel powerful, sexual and safe. Klub Verboten has worked hard to cultivate a consent-focused environment which prioritises safety and good communication – something which might not be the case at other fetish parties and is far from the norm in wider society.

But how does one create that sense of sexual excess and hedonism within seemingly rigid boundaries?

'It comes down to a tasteful use of shadows, sounds, as well as the right humidity and temperature levels,' Karl says. 'And then there is the act of creating sightlines in the space that allow privacy, but also allow room for expression on display; that allow for action in some places and limit it in others. You want to give people a backdrop and a few possibilities. With the alignment of furniture, every corner, every separation, the room you make, you always want to give people the chance to sit down here. Or maybe there's a little angle through this gap, and they connect with someone at the other end of the room. Maybe there's also another piece of furniture here, a chance to actually bend this way, and make a connection with another entity playing over there.'

As Klub Verboten is hosted in a variety of spaces, it comes down to drawing and redrawing various ways to create the right alignment for play: where BDSM furniture is placed, where a new walkway is created with PVC curtains, where sex toys are placed . . . Apparently, doughnut shapes work well, big squares and triangles not so much, as people don't like being put in corners. The ultimate aim, however, is to 'create a space that shouts sex sex sex in all directions, but makes it a community-shared pleasure'. There is always a tension between the care aspect of the fetish club and the desires these spaces allow to unfold: a balance between each individual's sexual preferences, drives and desires and maintaining an accessible space for all. There's been a shift, Karl adds, in the last ten years: 'We're less transactional with each other, we're thinking a little bit more about responsibility for each other.'

When contemplating erotic spaces, it's easy to forget that the charged atmosphere is not so easy to create. It is not a simple equation, in which certain furniture and music immediately create arousal. In fact, I believe there is always a difference between a sexual space and a sexually charged one. I remember being palpably aware of it when visiting Berlin's Berghain for the first time, in my early twenties. A notorious cathedral-like techno club in Ostbahnhof, Berghain is located in the same building as the gay fetish club Lab.oratory, so there are always guys in full gear around – in leather harnesses and rubber vests. I'm unsure whether it was because of Lab.oratory, or the sound system designed to penetrate your bones and organs, or the substances people indulged in, but there was always a sense of sex that extended beyond the act of fucking. It was there in the ecstatic movements of clubbers, in their sweat-soaked gym shorts and pearl jewellery.

Other times, a place in which people are fucking can feel the opposite of sexy. On paper, it should be, and yet you just stand there, bored, not sure what went wrong and why you feel nothing. Desire needs to be teased out; it needs potentiality and the modulation of (sexual) tension; it also needs a certain amount of spontaneity. Once, I spent the hottest time making out with someone in the toilet, trying to hide from the poorly curated lighting and music of a private kink event. It's down to finding whatever shape that erotic charge takes in the moment, wherever you are. Orchestrating hot moments for people is an intricate job.

I wonder if, after eight years of organising fetish nights, it still feels as new for Karl. Does it still feel as boundary-breaking?

'Sometimes people form a close connection, and there are these moments when you end up doing something you'll probably never do again in your life. But between those two consenting adults in that moment, based on how this moment evolves, it's just the absolute right thing to do,' Karl says. 'And sometimes you see this on a larger scale, where it's not two but ten people creating an image unfolding right in front of you, and you stand there, like: wow, this is beautiful.'

The boundaries of the fetish club are under constant negotiation, with questions around who is allowed in and who isn't. These spaces are already precarious and are often under pressure from authorities. But inside, the power dynamics and inequalities remain just as complex.

Ajamu X, British artist, curator and activist, is best known for photographic work celebrating Black queer desire, joy, pleasure and the body. His work plays with many fetish signifiers – high heels, lingerie, leather – but also creates a complex portrayal of the Black queer experience, beyond the cultural context where Blackness and masculinity have both long been fetishised. From 1996 to 2000 Ajamu also ran Black Perverts Network, a sex club for Black and Asian men into leather, rubber, PVC and nudity, from his apartment in Brixton.

He remembers going to gay clubs in the 1990s, and at the end of the night he would always see Black men in a certain area of the club having sex with each other. It was a spontaneous, ephemeral, erotic space Black men had created just for themselves. This, alongside US-based sex parties like Black Jack, was the main inspiration. Black Perverts Network was meant to help Black gay men into

BDSM feel less isolated, but also to push back on the exclusionary politics – no fats, no femmes – that some Black spaces upheld.

'My theory is that within Black queer politics, there are still certain kinds of sexual practices that get excluded. So, while a lot of us might be out around our sexual identity, we might still be marginalised for our sexual practice,' Ajamu tells me. 'Kinksters, sex workers and other unruly Black bodies get pushed to one side. I always try to create a conversation about what's been excluded.'

Flyers for the Black Perverts Network, printed on coloured paper, invited potential attendees to 'leave all your inhibitions behind' and featured playful illustrations by artist James Belasco: figures engaged in unapologetically joyful gay sex. They were handed out to friends and fuck buddies at saunas and cruising grounds. Much in the spirit of its name, the sex party created a network which lasted beyond the events themselves and is still widely talked about.

Ajamu laughs that the entry back in the day was £3 with a bottle and £5 without, as the parties were run completely not for profit. He is still drawn to the intimacy of private parties, but mostly attends those inclusive of trans and non-binary people rather than those which are exclusively male. The Black Perverts Network, he admits, could still be running today, though he suspects that some of the original attendees might not be as open-minded to the shifting boundaries of gender – the continuous negotiation of what kind of Black bodies are worthy of desire even within these community spaces.

The experience of running sex parties and being in these spaces, however, remains central to his life and his art: 'The pleasure and the erotic inform the work. It has to have a particular kind of energy that I feel when I'm in the sex club, or the dark room or the backroom.'

The kink, BDSM and fetish scenes remain overwhelmingly white, even though organisers strive for diversity. Today, at the intersection of queer clubbing and erotic spaces is WET, a lesbian night run by people of colour in South London; Sex and Rage, a sex-worker-run party with a regular lesbian strip club; and the now-defunct Pxssy Palace, which used to put up kink-themed nights 'celebrating Black [and] Indigenous [people] and people of colour' from time to time. It's not just that erotic spaces which centre the Black experience are rare, they also often slip through the net of historical records. In 2019, artist and researcher Monique Todd (then part of the Pleasure Principles collective) created a map titled 'Black Sex in the Archive'. The fold-out A3 map locates sites and projects which centre around Black desire, intimacy, sexual health and connection. The Thames snakes through the light grey paper with thin white veins of streets. Above and below the river are marked community spaces: Black gay nights like Silk, Funky Feel and Pressure Zone; Black lesbian meet-ups and club nights like Shugs; Black sexual education initiatives like Big Up and London Black Mesmac. Black Perverts Network is marked in the Brixton area. A glance at the map leaves one with a new perspective on a city which has largely eradicated both Black community spaces and erotic possibilities from its landscapes – a bitter revelation, with a pang of sadness for all the places which have been forgotten.

'"Black Sex in the Archive" is as much about the loves, orgasms, kisses, exchanges, nights, affairs, and embraces that have escaped the archive, as it is about the recovered ephemera that survived the ecstasy,' the project statement reads. 'It's a testimony to a social memory that lingers amongst current spaces and the ghosts of others, held together by an urgent ambition for community centres and erotic sites. This city is nothing without Black Desire and its movement, complexity, expression, codes, sincerity.'

Gender is another facet which can divide fetish spaces. One Night Parties, founded by Miss Gold, are exclusively for women and non-binary people to explore their femininity. 'One Night was born out of a love for sexual spaces, but a disdain for entitled men,' the description reads. 'Mainstream clubs and bars have shown us how predatory and intrusive male-centric spaces can be, with even mixed-gender sex parties often feeling intimidating, cautionary or tailored to the desires of cisgender men.'

Miss Gold, who is a photographer, artist and dominatrix (as well as a trainer fetishist), first had the idea for a women-only fetish and kink space in 2016. She ran a couple of small events in 2019, and it has been growing exponentially since 2021. I've been a couple of times. Undeniably, it was a carefully curated queer venue, with BDSM furniture, a dance floor, performances – and it was filled to the brim with women in lingerie. But there was also more to it than just sex-positive entertainment; there was a clear desire for an erotic space which was free from the male gaze, for experimentation beyond labels. One Night emphasises the importance of talking to one another and fostering connections by providing quiet spaces, soft surfaces and educational events.

'We deserve this space and we are allowed to exclude. There are so many spaces that marginalise us and fetishise us, and it's just so nice to have a space that's ours, without the physical presence of men,' Miss Gold says. 'I think we're getting braver about speaking up about our sexuality and our wants, needs and desires. And having a community of people who think the same way is really important – all the friendships born in this space. I feel like kink is one of the few worlds that women run. I feel like we are the power: we're the ones who are desired and we can control that desire.'

Gay leather bars – mostly male-only – occupy a prominent space in the history of fetish clubbing. The Backstreet, a leather and gay bar located in East London's Mile End, was open for thirty-seven years before closing in July 2022. The owner, John Edwards, opened the club in 1985 and worked the door and cloakroom until 2013, but remained the owner until closure. The dress code was leather and rubber, and the bar was strictly male-only. It continued the tradition of spaces which have defined the cultural significance of the leather bar: Mineshaft in New York (which closed just months after The Backstreet opened, its poster gracing the London bar's walls for decades), The Catacombs (which also allowed kinky leather lesbians) and other South of Market San Francisco bars, as well as fictional venues which appear in cult gay erotica. Leather bars were places of excess and sexual nonconformity, as well as belonging, especially in the era of the AIDS crisis. Not many of them lasted, yet The Backstreet remained well into the years of the mass adoption of PrEP and the changed landscape of gay bars, reshaped by both gentrification and the advent of Grindr.

After the closure of The Backstreet, twenty-eight items from its archive were donated to the Museum of London, including the club's Pride banner; items of rubber and leather clothing from The Box (a box containing a mixture of donated clothes and lost property for those who turned up not in accordance with the dress code); prints of Tom of Finland's leathermen and rubbermen drawn especially for the club; and ephemera, including posters, flyers, a taxi card, beer tokens and beer mats. Many items are now stored at the UK Leather and Fetish Archive, from leather boots to the notorious human cages.

The historicisation of the leather bar is vital for collective queer memory and for preserving a vision of cities as sites of desire. It also transforms the nature of the spaces – usually tucked out of sight of outsiders, with no photography or visual record of what goes on inside – it brings them into the light, allowing for a wider awareness. In 2024, *The Backstreet* premiered at Sheffield DocFest: a twenty-eight-minute documentary which combined footage from the last night at the bar with interviews with the regulars, owner John Edwards, and barman and manager Mark Allnutt. It also captured a process of transformation. Watching the Museum of London archivists carefully wrapping posters, leather harnesses and rubber shorts in pristine white tissue paper, it was clear that The Backstreet was transitioning: the grit of the site itself would fade into a memory; 'The Backstreet' was becoming a story, an idea, a phrase which would encapsulate a particular sexual space in queer memory.

My gender means I would never have been able to witness The Backstreet in the flesh, so it was enticing to see footage of the inside: its leather bar posters, red and purple lighting, leather boots hanging on chains above the bar. The documentary is tender, elegiac, community-focused. Its treatment of the patrons, their stories and their memories is touching, gentle and attentive. However, under the gaze of the camera, the nature of the space shifts. Something evaporates in the daylight; its actual essence is only really alive in the no-camera basement space for a certain kind of people, bound together.

One Wednesday evening, I sit in the basement of The Nelson's pub in East London, at a casual leatherdyke gathering. The basement's walls are covered with astroturf and sprinkled with fairy lights. I pick a seat next to Astrid, who has brought a case of her bootblacking gear and is shining someone's New Rocks. I like to sit close because I enjoy what happens between people during bootblacking – that intimate connection, the choice of making it more or less erotic. Also, the scent of leather grease. It smells amazing.

London can feel harsh sometimes – vast, impersonal, demanding, expensive. It is a city with a wild commodifying force, where, sooner or later, every shopfront becomes a high-street coffee chain. Yet underneath it all, it's still alive with these different modes of connection. They form sporadically, spontaneously, maybe only for a few nights a year. These spaces are not bound by property or branding, they're facilitated by word of mouth. I sit there, attuned to how it feels to be part of something – that subtle, small feeling of comfort and contentment that you're around people who are not exactly close friends but are no longer strangers.

Later that night, an image pops up on WhatsApp: a flyer invitation. It's a DIY party flyer, only it advertises a particular day to meet for cruising at Hampstead Heath by the well-known tree in the cruising area. The dykes have renamed it 'The Fisting Tree'.

Fetish clubs are often bricks and mortar, but truly, there is nothing more impermanent, fluid, changing. There are many ways to find home.

EPILOGUE

Sorry to the man I bought these waders from who wished me many happy fishing trips in them x

This line, spotted on a friend's Instagram, has been a bit of a light-hearted mantra to me while writing this book – but also something which has informed my thinking about my own involvement with fetish, as a culture, as a pastime, as a passion and as a turn-on.

It was used as a caption under a photograph which showed the friend wearing nothing but thigh-high waders of thick rubber in a muted dark green, shiny burgundy-coloured latex briefs and glasses. Waders, normally used as purely utilitarian heavy-duty fishing boots, are a staple of fetish culture in the UK. They were worn by those original mackintosh fanatics in the 1960s who went hiking in the countryside wrapped in multiple layers of rubber. I had first seen waders not in their original guise but as an echo, a recreation in high fashion: as rubber Prada boots from the Fall 2009 collection. I was obsessed with their rough appearance, how the loose fit exposed the leg, and the contrast of soft skin and thick rubber. Looking at my friend's waders, I loved the intersection of these histories, the multiple layers of the known and the unknown: the fact that the previous owner might not have known about the fetishistic history of waders, and that he almost certainly didn't know about the present life of the boots. I love how the item's utilitarian use dissolves. How each of us treads the line between what's offensive and what's respectable, and how fetishes are so often funny, awkward, strange and, to the people outside of the community, perhaps still a touch shocking.

With time and exposure, most things can become normal to us; however strange something is at first, we get used to it. Our nervous systems adjust, and the unusual becomes usual. It is true about sex as much as anything else. There is a joy, however, in holding on to an outside perspective, in remembering the strangeness.

I inhale the smell of rubber flooring, which I've grown to love in the last couple of years. It is laid down in large sheets with a non-slip pattern of little embossed diamonds. It smells stronger when it's warm, and it gleams when it's wet. I'm in my friend's dungeon, a lovingly, beautifully equipped two-level space in East London. There are four of us, and the air is filled with the smell of latex. We inhale and we share touch.

We take some instant photos while having sex – small, credit-card-sized slices of photo paper emerging from my battered lavender-coloured Fuji Instax. Instant photos are the preferred choice because there is no need to take them to the shop for development and they leave no digital footprint. The camera eliminates the red glow with its bright flash and accentuates the shine of the latex, while the skin against it looks pale and glowing.

In one of the photos, taken from below, the oculars of the FM12 gas mask shine ominously. We can't stop laughing. These are *cursed photos* – the sort to be found in someone's attic after they've died, and everyone is petrified of what an old pervert they were. It dawns on me that we are not *like* these people – we *are* these people. Yet again, the layering of contexts, the demands and possibilities of the public and private, a converging temporal plane, a glimpse of the future folded into the present of my strange sexuality and of my gentle, fragile, human life.

In April 2024, I travelled to Japan. It was the first time I'd been so far away from where I lived in some time, and yet the culture shock was deeply familiar. The sudden sense of difference was as powerful as I felt when I moved to the UK in my early twenties, almost fifteen years ago. A crucial part of the experience was being an outsider – when you're oblivious to the wider context and history, your mind frantically scratches at the surface of what you're seeing, or you just passively drift through the overwhelmingly new experience. Being an outsider comes with immense anxiety as well as immense freedom. But as I was in Japan for only two weeks, I revelled in this suspended state.

When we experience a radically different culture, we usually fixate on what's strange to us, what's different. But I thought to myself, *it is as weird as you make it*. Let go of your fixed viewpoint and your biases, and *different*, for a brief moment, loses its meaning. Suddenly, things are less frightening or concerning; they're simply unknown from a sensory perspective. I believe that queerness and alternative, or *extended sexuality* as Jordan Tannahill called it, means that sometimes you can access this plasticity of judgement more easily. Or so I tell myself when I am in the darkness, when I don't understand.

It is a warm evening at the end of April, balmy and humid. It's Golden Week, one of Japan's largest holiday periods of the year, and Tokyo is especially crowded with people shopping, drinking and celebrating. But on a quiet street in a respectable neighbourhood, the city is completely tranquil, with pockets of deep shadow undisturbed. As I walk through a carefully arranged jigsaw of buildings of different styles, I think it is surprising that Tokyo is able to contain this darkness, despite the light pollution. A fluorescent tower block is visible above the rooftops, against the flat indigo skies, and yet the shadows drip from the blossoms and deep green leaves.

Lady Hinako's house is a three-storey rectangular building. In the room on the ground floor, I am greeted by open space: it's a room with double-height ceilings, furnished sparsely and, well, not exactly conventionally. There is a medical examination chair on the right, upholstered with yellowish, eggshell-coloured leatherette. Next to it, a metal bed with white canvas restraints. It all clearly speaks to a medical fetish – this is not a real hospital, but a fantasy one. The whole wall on the right is lined with cabinets: there are hoods and masks on display in dim blue light, along with gas masks and a faint silhouette with a bright pink pig's snout.

Lady Hinako gives me a tour. She is wearing a simple black vest, her arms are covered in tattoos, her long black hair is parted and clipped back, and she wears glasses with classic round frames. We walk down to the basement, which is better stocked than most fetish stores. On one wall, there are around a thousand whips of different colours and lengths. On the other, bondage cuffs, restraints and collars of all varieties and colours: strict metal, spiked black leather, fuchsia-pink collars and belts, and chains. But most impressive is the rail which spans the entire length of the wall, perhaps six metres, with outfits catering to any fetish: leather, latex, PVC, medical gowns – there are dozens of options dedicated to each. Hinako points out some items on the shelf above the row of hangers: a red and yellow German hazmat suit (if you were fully zipped in, you wouldn't be able to breathe), a motorcycle bodysuit in padded red leather (custom-made for a client to include a crotch zip) and a mass of black neoprene which turns out to be a dolphin costume. 'Why not?' I think to myself. How strangely sensual and perverted would it be to be a dolphin, with its soft, slippery skin, its stealthy movements and its uncanny intelligence?

Lady Hinako has collected fetish garments since she started working as a dominatrix in 2018, purchasing the first items of her collection on a trip to Europe, during which she spent approximately €30,000 on gear, mostly in Germany. She remembers visiting Studio Avalon, a large riverside BDSM dungeon in a remote area of Berlin, now closed, which boasted an array of rooms for different fetishes. She's still hoping to one day open an equivalent in Japan. Since then, her collection has grown exponentially. A lot of items have been gifted to her by clients and friends. It is truly a one-of-a-kind space; it feels less like a collector's space or an archive, and more like a living, breathing community temple of fetish.

There is a curious collaborative nature to the space too: on the second floor, a dedicated rope bondage space was crafted by a carpenter friend, who received the privilege of being tied up here first. An under-the-stairs cupboard has been transformed into a small white PVC-coated isolation cell by a friend of Lady Hinako's, who is also our interpreter for the night.

Hinako admits that she has always had a bondage fetish, as well as an interest in BDSM, but that it remained unfulfilled for a long time, due to being in a controlling marriage for eight years. She started attending BDSM clubs when the marriage ended and soon got into sex work too, first as a sub and then as a pro-domme. Since the pandemic, her main source of income has been making fetish videos. One of her websites, *Hinako Bondage Clinic*, is an expansive tableau of fetish practices, which involve a variety of full-body bondage in rubber, leather and transparent film, as well as vacuum beds, shiny zentai suits, ropes and straitjackets. There is even a *Rubber Inflatable Pool Party!* video, which documents a get-together with Hinako's wetsuit fetish friends hanging out in the pool in their scuba suits, with one of them floating around in a heavy rubber inflatable sack.

At the top of the building, Hinako opens a big plastic storage box which sits opposite a bookshelf and pulls out layers and layers of hand-knitted material. It's beige with pink roses and knitted with perfect precision. The flowers are three-dimensional, with actual petals and leaves. It is, in fact, a body bag: a human-sized gimp doily able to cover one's whole body. Another body bag she shows us is sewn together from small fragments of upcycled children's kimonos in red, white and pink – here and there are buttons with cartoon characters on them, as well as signs for protection. They are both art pieces which Hinako has created this year through months of meticulous craftsmanship. Her usual, more overtly fetishistic work, featuring bodies fully covered in leather, latex or nylon, is frequently removed from both social media and subscription-only adult sites. So using these more traditional crafts is a way to challenge and question censorship. After all, who decides what kind of material is harmless and what kind is too perverse?

'Previously I was anti-fetish art,' Hinako tells me. 'My fetish is very important in my life, and I don't like the idea of people who do not have a fetish using it to make fake fetish art. But nowadays many of my photos and videos get suspended, and my social media is shadow-banned. It's hard to appear as a spokesperson for the fetish industry without a credible record, so it motivated me to make art.'

Art brings things usually kept in the shadows into the light, as well as creating a safe distance – the viewer is able to detach it slightly from their skin, to regard it as a notion abstract enough for it to become less threatening. The self-published book *Hinako Art Club* treads the boundaries of this territory. It is a deliciously strange collection of archival imagery from bondage fantasy land: human dolls tucked into satin princess beds; a leather figure enjoying a Tokyo evening under a transparent umbrella; a rubber gimp donning a kimono, their head wrapped in a towel; Hinako in full sheer nylon, transfixed. The images are playful and visually striking –

but most importantly, they are odd, defying the typical concept of 'sexy', either in or out of kink.

It is a running thread in our conversation: the tension between uniformity and erotic self-expression which deviates from it. Most pro-dommes in Japan, Hinako explains, work through BDSM clubs rather than independently – and most conform to a uniformal image, with the same outfits, and the same photos being taken from the same angles. She feels that despite fetish being a big part of the culture, a nuanced understanding of fetish might still be lacking, even in the BDSM community.

In Tokyo, a lot of erotic experiences are delivered in small venues: BDSM bars, some with dominatrixes; *shibari* bars dedicated to rope bondage; latex bars; more upscale hostess bars. 'You have staff working there who are guiding it,' our interpreter chimes in. 'Japanese people don't dance much and they are also shy, so there are more small events and bars. The staff are trained to interact with shy people and coax them out a little bit.' Fundamentally, these places are not dissimilar to the cosplay-themed maid cafes, which are common in the city, where staff dressed up as kawaii maids serve and interact with customers. All these experiences are based on a transaction which buys one time, space and a fragment of fantasy within the dense fabric of the city of fourteen million people.

I think about the uniformity of erotic experience as I enter a love hotel in the entertainment district of Kabukichō, one of dozens which line the streets: Hotel Pasha Resort, Balian, Hotel La France Paris. The room is outlined with a strip of LED lighting to give it a purple glow; its effect is surprisingly soft. Above the bed is a neon outline of a cartoon nurse holding a cartoon aubergine, and the words *sicko sicko* are illuminated in red, reflected in the glass case of the bathroom to the right. I'm in the purple room of a colour-themed hotel. There is a violet leatherette sofa against a black curtain, which hides a blacked-out window. I immediately feel an intimate sense of being cocooned, of a soft separation from reality outside. It is exactly how I imagined it, save for the lingering cigarette stench and the small packets of skincare and hair products and body oil one can buy from the counter downstairs.

There is a big TV with a range of adult (as well as regular) films and a vast catalogue of amenities one could order to the room. I flick through a range of outfits available to rent for 500 yen: aeroplane pilot, schoolgirl, cheerleader. The bed is big and soft, and the whole room has the quality of being simultaneously private and public. There's a ghostly sense of other bodies and other fantasies having filled this room, thousands of them, stretching out both before and after me. The thought could be equally arousing or deterring, but I somehow find it calming. One could also simply order a Nintendo Switch to the room; it is a site of escape, indulgence and safety, whatever form that takes.

As I flick through outfits, it strikes me that this room encapsulates what the mainstream understanding of fetish is: a disposable thrill. But I regard the love hotel room with tenderness and respect, as part of the fabric of this city and this society. It might look strange to the outsider, but it has its place and its purpose. I think about what it means to live a fetishist's life. I reflect on the encounters which have shaped this book and conclude that it means to operate with care and curiosity; to be incredibly nerdy; to confront head-on the seemingly unruly, dark drive; to question whether the drive is, in fact, even that dark. Fetish is a language, rooted in the embodied understanding of signs. I hope to have contributed to that understanding.

I'm reminded of a passage on language learning from *Fifty Sounds* by Polly Barton: 'Language is something we learn with our bodies, and through our body of experiences; where semantics are umbilically tied to somatics, where our experiences and our feelings form a memory palace; where words are linked to particular occasions, particular senses, which gradually fade the more practised we become but remain there nonetheless in memory, forming a personal genealogy of the tongues we speak.' In response to this passage, Klub Verboten's tagline, 'Let Your Body Learn', flashes through my mind.

As I recount the experiences in this book to different people, they inevitably shapeshift. Brought up among friends who share a similar sexual culture, they seem completely mundane, tame even, but when I am asked about my book at work, they become strange, fringe, shocking again. Writing this book has been akin to learning a new language. It is never just about the words – rather, with new words comes a different understanding of the world we thought we knew so well and the knowledge that there is always more to learn. The biggest challenge in writing this book has been this sense of openness – the more I wrote, the more I read, and the more conversations I had, the more I felt that there was more to discover. I hope this book becomes an invitation, an open door, an encouragement – even if briefly – to trust your desires. After all, we reach for language to connect with each other, to get a glimpse of vulnerability and joy, of mutual recognition. I hope you felt the warmth of it within these pages.

When I'm back in London, I come across a video made by Department H, a fetish club in Tokyo. The crowd is eclectic. In the club lobby, against the grey-brown textured walls, the camera skims past a human-sized bunny and a yellow Power Ranger. On stage, a drag show is happening: a figure in a black-and-white star-patterned latex catsuit, a black latex hood and a fuchsia-pink inflatable latex wig. In the spotlight, they move through the dark, self-possessed and graceful.

Truly, I think to myself, it is as weird as you make it.

ACKNOWLEDGEMENTS

This book wouldn't have been written without my agent, Jess Lee, and I am forever grateful. Thank you for encouraging me to revel in the darkest, the strangest and the queerest dimensions of this idea. Thank you to Dan Bird at Granta for being my editor, for his sensitive and thoughtful perspective and for pushing me to interrogate the uncomfortable and celebrate the joyful. Thank you to copy-editor Jack Alexander, managing editor Christine Lo and all the Granta team who worked on bringing this book to life.

My deepest gratitude to everyone who talked to me for this book – your thoughts, vulnerability and fearlessness are my biggest inspiration in writing and in life.

I am indebted to every leather archive in the world, but especially to the UK Leather and Fetish Archive at Bishopsgate Institute. My biggest thank you to everyone who works there and personally to Stef Dickers, the Special Collections and Archives Manager. Thank you, Stef, for indulging my never-ending research requests and being the tireless champion of the community.

My time dancing, playing and connecting with fellow perverts at Klub Verboten has been instrumental to this book and my creative life, so thank you Karl Verboten and Hanny Amin for creating this space. Thank you to the perverts and the leatherdykes, the fetishists, and everyone I shared a moment with in the playroom or on the dancefloor – traces of these encounters electrify this book.

Acknowledgements

Thank you to the Society of Authors for awarding me an Authors' Foundation grant for a work in progress, which gave me peace of mind and allowed me to focus on researching and crafting this book.

Thank you to my fellow artists and writers who are working on reimagining sexuality: Lanee Bird, Monique Todd, Jean Cleverley, Jenkin van Zyl, Jordan Tannahill, Sam Jamieson, Steven Harwick, Gold, Cummings and Heavy Consumption, Reba Maybury, Ajamu X, Vex Ashley, Ottilie Landmark, Sinéad O'Dwyer, Ella Boucht, Jade Sweeting, Janina Sabaliauskaitė, Phyllis Christopher, Anna Sampson, Eva Gold, Jonny Kaye, Layla Kosima, Wolf, Maria Gorodeckaya, Ekaterina Bazhenova-Yamasaki and Fleet Ilya. I am especially grateful to those who, over the years, have involved me in their projects and conversations; it is always an honour. A separate thank you to Astrid for the smell of leather grease and the leather bloc at the 2024 London Dyke March.

Thank you, my dear friends: Eva Oh, Miss May, Miss Sloane, Miss Avery, Mistress Bea, Aitor, Shireen, Romeo, Filip, Anya, Jay, Matt, Bart, Kaisa, Ievgenii and Sergii. Thank you, Rahel, for a life-changing introduction to Jess.

My perspective on fetish and leather has been shaped by several books which will be forever dear to my heart: *Public Sex* by Patrick Califia, the *Leatherfolk* anthology edited by Mark Thompson and *Bound Together* by Andy Campbell. Thank you to Jeremy Atherton Lin for the first line of his book *Gay Bar: Why We Went Out*, which made me believe there is a space to be bolder and sexier – and still get published. And to my mum for encouraging my love of art and writing and always letting me read whatever I wanted.

There are people I can't name here for privacy reasons, and this somehow makes it even more special or even (in a classic taboo sense) hotter. Thank you for the intense, quiet and filthy moments we shared – especially the moments I haven't quite managed to put into words. On every page of this book, there is a bit of you.

NOTES

Introduction

p. 15   '*harmless but fascinating eroticism*': 'Capturing fetishes you've never heard of', *Dazed Digital* (18 September 2015) https://www.dazeddigital.com/artsandculture/article/26490/1/capturing-fetishes-you-never-heard-of

p. 15   '*Uses of the Erotic*': Audre Lorde, *The Erotic as Power* (Crossing Press, 1981)

Leather

p. 24   '*both a temple and a cemetery*': Andy Campbell, *Bound Together: Leather, Sex, Archives, and Contemporary Art* (Manchester University Press, 2020)

p. 28   '*doesn't seem like a gay and lesbian issue*': Mark Thompson (ed.), *Leatherfolk: Radical Sex, People, Politics, and Practice* (Daedalus Publishing, 1991)

p. 32   '*a series of bizarre backdrops for a photoshoot*': Patrick Califia, 'Damned in the USA', *Skin Two*, Issue 13, 1993

p. 37   '*Her very existence was disrespectable.*': Daemonum X, '"Bloodsisters": A Timeless Exploration of Leatherdyke Culture', *Autostraddle* (21 October 2020). https://www.autostraddle.com/bloodsisters-a-timeless-exploration-of-leatherdyke-culture/

p. 40   '*irresistible jackboots*': 'About Tom of Finland: The Life of the Artist', Tom of Finland Foundation. https://www.tomoffinland.org/about-tom-of-finland/

p. 41   '*His arousal was entirely interconnected with his mastery.*': *Talk Art* podcast with Durk Dehner (26 September 2023). https://shows.acast.com/talkart/episodes/tom-of-finland

p. 43	'*what it meant to have a fetish*': Stephen Harwick, *By the Skin of My Teeth* (self-published, 2022)

Latex

p. 59	*The Mackintosh Society was founded by Leon Chead in 1967*: *The Mackintosh Society Magazine*, Autumn 1998
p. 62	'*rather pudgy pair of people getting dressed in a middle-class bedroom*': Patrick Califia, 'Beyond Leather: Expanding the Realm of Senses to Rubber', *Skin Two*, Issue 11, 1991
p. 62	*a spongy material sourced from the Pentonville Rubber Company*: Laura Hawkins, 'The Many Lives of Vivienne Westwood's Worlds End Shop', *Another Magazine* (30 December 2022). https://www.anothermag.com/fashion-beauty/8672/clothes-for-heroes-story-of-vivienne-westwoods-worlds-end-shop-sex-kings-road
p. 63	'*a number of rubber lovers are rather lonely people*': John Samson and Mike Wallington (dirs.), *Dressing for Pleasure*, documentary, 1977
p. 68	*It took 300 hours and 300 seams to construct the monumental dress*: 'HARRI Chapter Four', HARRI. https://harri.store/pages/harri-x-nemo?srsltid=AfmBOooF8fidXYe_YelU1be8yVoUlAO8wGAQCNvcfzyudcnkBRh5JcUR

The Dominatrix

p. 76	*in an unglamorous American-style diner in a shopping centre in London's Islington*: Reba Maybury, *Dining with Humpty Dumpty* (Arcadia Missa, 2017)
p. 78	'*pathetically hilarious in its predictability*': Reba Maybury, *Faster Than an Erection* (Wet Satin Press, 2024)
p. 81	'*I am formlessly alive.*': Ibid.
p. 85	'*recurred again and again?*': Lorraine Gamman and Merja Makinen, *Female Fetishism: A New Look* (Lawrence & Wishart Ltd, 1994)

The Gimp

p. 93	'*It's not you who attends the event, but a character*': Amalia Zatari and Anastasia Golubeva, '"They came to look for sex": what's behind the raids on erotic parties in Russia', *BBC News Russian Service* (8 March 2024). https://www.bbc.com/russian/articles/c724d5mgedpo
p. 100	'*who was crawling and writhing on the ground*': Heather Pickstock,

          'Latex-clad gimp returns to Somerset and is seen "writhing and crawling" on ground', *SomersetLive* (9 May 2023). https://www.somersetlive.co.uk/news/somerset-news/latex-clad-gimp-returns-somerset-8426004

p. 106   *'I'm very drawn to this kind of powerlessness.'*: GimpSkinFag, 'Member Article: What is a Gimp?', *Recon News* (18 January 2019). https://www.recon.com/en/Blog/Article/member-article-what-is-a-gimp/2756

The Chaser

p. 110   *'what happens when it's Mommy's dick'*: Vex Ashley (dir.), *Maman*, 2022. https://afourchamberedheart.com/cinema/maman

p. 117   *'because of things we cannot control'*: JN Benjamin, 'Jeremy O Harris on Slave Play: "It's about the impossibility of loving blind of history"', *Financial Times* (22 June 2024). https://www.ft.com/content/392eabd0-0f41-482e-87cb-43baf17c045a

p. 117   *'what actually turns us on may be unbridgeable'*: Avgi Saketopoulou, 'Reckoning with Race', Noël Coward Theatre Programme, 2024

p. 118   *modes of seduction were politically formulated*: Katherine Min, *The Fetishist* (Fleet, 2024)

p. 118   *'Me so horny.'*: Chao-Ying Rao, Narratives and Counter-Narratives', *LACA*. https://lacarchive.com/item/photographs-narratives-and-counter-narratives

p. 119   *'but firstly and above all as trans'*: suomikin, comment on reddit.com. https://www.reddit.com/r/asktransgender/comments/ofispy/psa_whats_a_chaser

p. 120   *'It's not interesting.'*: Liam Konemann, 'Torrey Peters' *Detransition, Baby* skewers the detransition taboo', *Dazed Digital* (5 February 2021). https://www.dazeddigital.com/life-culture/article/51840/1/torrey-peters-detransition-baby-skewers-the-detransition-taboo

p. 121   *'That's queer futurity baby.'*: Zach Ozma, 'Summer of the Chaser: A Review of *Chasers* by Stephen Ira', Newsletter #269, *The Poetry Project*. https://www.poetryproject.org/publications/newsletter/269-summer-2022/summer-of-the-chaser-a-review-of-chasers-by-stephen-ira

p. 122   *'humiliating or, worst of all, problematic?'*: Huw Lemmey, 'Bad Sex Part I', Substack (8 April 2021). https://huw.substack.com/p/bad-sex-part-i

Feet

p. 129   '*You're doing it too.*': Gary Indiana, in Michelle Tea (ed.), *SLUTS* (Cipher Press, 2024)

p. 138   '*the sneakers of my partner*': NikeShoxJock, 'Member Article: FootWear Fetish', *Recon News* (3 March 2021). https://www.recon.com/en/Blog/Article/member-article-footwear-fetish/3065

p. 139   '*fake designer brands*': Joseph Bobowicz, 'Scally lads: An investigation into the queer appropriation of working-class subculture', MA dissertation, Goldsmith's University, August 2021

Cars

p. 163   '*the technological landscape*': J. G. Ballard, introduction, *Crash* (Harper Perennial, 2008)

p. 163   '*In effect, things are using things.*': Zadie Smith, 'Sex and wheels: Zadie Smith on JG Ballard's Crash', *Guardian* (4 July 2014). https://www.theguardian.com/books/2014/jul/04/zadie-smith-jg-ballard-crash

p. 170   '*not longing for purity, imagined neutrality, and naturalness*': Teo Ala-Ruona and Remi Vesala, 'Car and I', https://teoalaruona.net/car-and-i

p. 170   '*a personally owned vehicle . . . that allows 6 people to ride simultaneously, face-to-face*': 'Honda, GM and Cruise Plan to Begin Driverless Ridehail Service in Early 2026', Honda Motor Co. https://global.honda/en/newsroom/news/2023/c231019aeng.html

p. 171   '*being kind of wrong made it more fun and exciting*': Liz Lindqwister, 'San Franciscans are having sex in robotaxis, and nobody is talking about it', *The San Francisco Standard* (11 August 2023). https://sfstandard.com/2023/08/11/san-francisco-robotaxi-cruise-debauchery

p. 172   '*for lack of a better term, but it's an EV*': Jordyn Beazley, 'Flutes, synths, a human voice – how should electric vehicles sound?', *Guardian* (4 January 2023). https://www.theguardian.com/environment/2023/jan/05/flutes-synths-a-human-voice-how-should-electric-vehicles-sound

p. 172   '*the human drive toward the dark*': Ada Zielińska, 'Post Tourism', 2023. https://adazielinska.com/post-tourism

Monsters

p. 175   Interview *magazine in 2022*: 'Author Jordan Tannahill Is Making Latex Dreams Come True', *Interview Magazine* (19 April 2022). https://www.interviewmagazine.com/culture/author-jordan-tannahill-is-making-latex-dreams-come-true

p. 179   '*tyrannizing the make-believe of his friends with a game that no one else understood*': Davey Davis, 'David Davis 42, part 2: on Pony Brad', Substack. https://itsdavid.substack.com/p/david-davis-42-part-2

p. 181   '*green space photos with your furry photoshoot*': 'Pup Play: Finding freedom in a dog mask', *Endless Thread*. https://www.wbur.org/endlessthread/2023/06/30/pup-play

p. 183   '*You're being instinctual and playful.*': Blake Montgomery, 'We Live in Packs', *The New York Times* (26 April 2019). https://www.nytimes.com/2019/04/26/style/pup-play.html

p. 186   '*but also to seek out victory, exhaustion and The End*': Jenkin van Zyl, *Surrender* (Edel Assanti, 2023). https://edelassanti.com/exhibitions/113-jenkin-van-zyl-surrender

p. 188   '*What is the eros we would rupture ourselves for?*': Jordan Tannahill, *Vore* (Rose Easton, 2022). https://www.roseeaston.com/exhibitions/vore

The Fetish Club

p. 197   '*the degree to which they are lifestyle enclaves*': Jeremy Atherton Lin, *Gay Bar: Why We Went Out* (Granta, 2021)

p. 208   '*and people of colour*': Pxssy Palace, https://www.pxssypalace.com

p. 208   '*complexity, expression, codes, sincerity*': *Black Sex in the Archive* (Pleasure Principles, 2019)

p. 210   The Backstreet *premiered at Sheffield DocFest*: Romain Beck (dir.), *The Backstreet*, 2024

Epilogue

p. 221   '*forming a personal genealogy of the tongues we speak*': Polly Barton, *Fifty Sounds* (Fitzcarraldo Editions, 2021). Copyright © Polly Barton, 2021.

FURTHER READING

Leather

Ajamu X, *Ajamu: Archive* (self-published, 2021)
Califia, Patrick, *Macho Sluts* (Alyson Publications, 1988)
Califia, Patrick, *Public Sex: Culture of Radical Sex* (Cleis Press, 1995)
Califia, Patrick, *Speaking Sex to Power: The Politics of Queer Sex* (Cleis Press, 2002)
Califia, Patrick and Robin Sweeney (eds.), *The Second Coming: A Leatherdyke Reader* (Alyson Publications, 1996)
Campbell, Andy, *Bound Together: Leather, Sex, Archives, and Contemporary Art* (Manchester University Press, 2020)
Christopher, Phyllis, *Dark Room* (Book Works, 2022)
Daemonum X, 'Dead but Delicious', Substack
Handelman, Michelle (dir.), *BloodSisters: Leather, Dykes and Sadomasochism*, documentary, 1995
Harwick, Stephen, *By the Skin of My Teeth* (self-published, 2022)
Lyne, Charlie (dir.), *Lasting Marks*, documentary about Operation Spanner, 2018
Madonna and Stephen Meisel, *Sex* (Martin Secker & Warburg, 1992)
Preston, John, *Mr. Benson* (Cleis Press, 2004)
Samois (ed.), *Coming to Power: Writings and Graphics on Lesbian S/M* (Alyson Publications, 1981)

Thompson, Mark (ed.), *Leatherfolk: Radical Sex, People, Politics, and Practice* (Daedalus Publishing, 1991)
Tom of Finland, *The Complete Kake Comics* (Taschen, 2023)
Williams, Siân A. and Harri Shanahan, *Rebel Dykes*, documentary, 2021

Latex

Henley, Helen, *Enter with Trumpets* (Shiny Books, 1989)
Samson, John and Mike Wallington (dirs), *Dressing for Pleasure*, documentary, 1977
Trunk, Jonny, *Dressing for Pleasure in Rubber, Vinyl & Leather: The Best of AtomAge 1972–1980* (FUEL, 2010)

The Dominatrix

Broomfield, Nick (dir.), *Fetishes*, documentary, 1996
de Berg, Jeanne, a pseudonym of Catherine Rob-Grillet, *Women's Rites: Scenes from the Erotic Imagination* (Grove Press, 1987)
Easton, Dossie and Janet Hardy, *The New Topping Book* (Greenery Press, 2011)
Gamman, Lorraine and Merja Makinen, *Female Fetishism: A New Look* (Lawrence & Wishart, 1994)
Knoll, Eric and Eric Stanton, *The Art of Eric Stanton: For the Man Who Knows His Place* (Taschen, 2012)
Maybury, Reba, *Dining with Humpty Dumpty* (Arcadia Missa, 2017)
Maybury, Reba, *Faster Than an Erection* (Wet Satin Press, 2024)
Harukawa, Namio, *Namio Harukawa* (Baron Books, 2021)
Oh, Eva, *#teakink* podcast, 2023–present
Valkeapää, J.-P. (dir.), *Dogs Don't Wear Pants*, feature film, 2019

The Gimp

Hill, Kashmir, *Your Face Belongs to Us: The Secretive Startup Dismantling Your Privacy* (Simon & Schuster UK, 2023)

The Chaser

Four Chambers, an ongoing collaboration exploring the aesthetic and conceptual potential of pornography. afourchamberedheart.com

Harris, Jeremy O., *Slave Play* (Nick Hern Books, 2024)

Ira, Stephen, *Chasers* (New Michigan Press, 2022)

Lemmey, Huw, 'Utopian Drivel', Substack

Nash, Jennifer C., *The Black Body in Ecstasy: Reading Race, Reading Pornography* (Duke University Press, 2014)

Rumit, Alison and Frankie Miren, *Morbid Obsessions* (Cipher Press, 2022)

Feet

Batters, Elmer, *Elmer Batters* (Taschen, 1996)

Klein, Steven, *VISIONAIRE 67 FETISH* (Visionaire Publishing, 2017)

Tea, Michelle (ed.), *SLUTS* (Cipher Press, 2024)

Cars

Ala-Ruona, Teo and Remi Vesala, *Car and I*. https://teoalaruona.net/car-and-i

Ballard, J. G., *Crash* (Jonathan Cape, 1973)

Cronenberg, David (dir.), *Crash*, feature film, 2004

Ducournau, Julia (dir.), *Titane*, feature film, 2021

Gatt, Romeo Roxman, *Perfiction* (self-published, 2018)

le Mée, Mael (dir.), *Alex's Machine*, short film, 2022

Seabrook, John, 'What Should a Nine-Thousand-Pound Electric Vehicle Sound Like?' *The New Yorker*, 1 August 2022

Zielińska, Ada, *Pyromaniac's Manual* (Propaganda, 2020)

Monsters

Furscience, the public face of the International Anthropomorphic Research Project (IARP), a team of scientists educating the public and media on the furry fandom. furscience.com

Kristeva, Julia, *Powers of Horror: An Essay on Abjection* (Columbia University Press, 1984)
Tannahill, Jordan, *The Listeners* (Fourth Estate, 2021)
Vallese, Joe (ed.), *It Came from the Closet: Queer Reflections on Horror* (Saraband, 2023)

The Fetish Club

Atherton Lin, Jeremy, *Gay Bar: Why We Went Out* (Granta, 2021)
Beck, Romain (dir.), *The Backstreet,* documentary, 2024
Black Sex in the Archive (Pleasure Principles, 2019)

Epilogue

Barton, Polly, *Fifty Sounds* (Fitzcarraldo Editions, 2021)